A New Era
for Wolves and People

ENERGY, ECOLOGY, AND THE ENVIRONMENT SERIES

ISSN 1919-7144

This new series will explore how we live and work with each other on the planet, how we use its resources, and the issues and events that shape our thinking on energy, ecology and the environment. The Alberta experience in a global arena will be showcased.

A New Era
for Wolves and People

WOLF RECOVERY, HUMAN ATTITUDES, AND POLICY

Edited by
MARCO MUSIANI,
LUIGI BOITANI,
AND PAUL C. PAQUET

UNIVERSITY OF
CALGARY
PRESS

ENERGY, ECOLOGY, AND THE ENVIRONMENT SERIES
ISSN 1919-7144

University of Calgary Press
2500 University Drive NW
Calgary, Alberta
Canada T2N 1N4
www.uofcpress.com

LIBRARY AND ARCHIVES CANADA CATALOGUING IN PUBLICATION

A new era for wolves and people : wolf recovery, human attitudes and policy / edited by Marco Musiani, Luigi Boitani, and Paul C. Paquet.

(Energy, ecology, and the environment series, 1919-7144 ; 2)
Includes bibliographical references and index.
ISBN 978-1-55238-270-7

1. Wolves—Reintroduction–Case studies. 2. Wolves–Conservation–Case studies. 3. Wolves–Public opinion. 4. Human-wolf encounters. 5. Wildlife management–Case studies.
I. Boitani, Luigi II. Paquet, Paul C. (Paul Charles), 1948- III. Musiani, Marco, 1970- IV. Series: Energy, ecology, and the environment series 2

QL737.C22N49 2009   333.95'9773   C2009-904654-7

The University of Calgary Press acknowledges the support of the Alberta Foundation for the Arts for our publications. We acknowledge the financial support of the Government of Canada through the Book Publishing Industry Development Program (BPIDP) for our publishing activities. We acknowledge the financial support of the Canada Council for the Arts for our publishing program.

Printed and bound in Canada by Marquis Printing
This book is printed on FSC Silva Edition & Starbrite Dull paper

Cover design by Melina Cusano
Page design and typesetting by Melina Cusano

CONTENTS

Section II – Human Cultures and Ethics Influencing Recovering Wolves

LIST OF TABLES

A New Era for Wolves and People

LIST OF FIGURES

**MARCO
MUSIANI**

**LUIGI
BOITANI**

**PAUL C.
PAQUET**

Biographies for Editors, Contributing Authors, and Artists
(drawings and photos of wild wolves only)

BOOK EDITORS

LUIGI BOITANI, Dept. Animal and Human Biology, University of Rome "La Sapienza," Viale Università 32, 00185–Roma, Italy

Professor Boitani is the Head of the Department of Animal and Human Biology at the University of Rome. He is President Elect of the Society for Conservation Biology. He is also prominent in the Species Survival Commission and in the Wolf Specialist Group of IUCN-World Conservation Union. Professor Boitani conducted an extended series of research and conservation projects on the Italian wolf population, which in the last thirty years recovered from a dramatic bottleneck. Professor Boitani has written more than two hundred peer-reviewed scientific publications and eight books. He is a leading authority on wolves.

MARCO MUSIANI, Faculty of Environmental Design, University of Calgary, Calgary, Alberta, T2N 1N4, Canada

Marco Musiani, PhD, is an Assistant Professor of Landscape Ecology at the University of Calgary and is also affiliated with the University of Montana. He was born in Rome, the city of the famous she-wolf. Marco conducted research and published several papers on wolf management in Italy with "La Sapienza" University, the University of Siena, and the National Research Council, in Poland with the Polish Academy of Sciences, and internationally with the Food and Agriculture Organisation of the United Nations. (Wolves kill livestock and this impacts food available to people.) Currently, his research focuses on genetics and movements of wolves and other large mammals in Canada and the United States.

PAUL C. PAQUET, Box 150, Meacham, Saskatchewan, S0K 2V0, Canada

Paul Paquet, PhD, is an Adjunct Professor with the faculties of Biology and Environmental Design at the University of Calgary. He is also affiliated with other universities in North America. Dr. Paquet has studied wolves for more than thirty-five years and is considered an authority on carnivore ecology in general, with research experience in a number of regions of the world. He has published more than a hundred peer-reviewed articles. Dr. Paquet serves on various international government and NGO advisory committees and was the founder and director of the Central Rockies Wolf Project, Canmore, Canada.

CONTRIBUTING AUTHORS

EDWARD E. BANGS, U.S. Fish and Wildlife Service, 585 Shepard Way, Helena, Montana, 59601, U.S.A.

Edward E. Bangs is the U.S. Fish and Wildlife Service's Wolf Recovery Coordinator for the northwestern United States. He has worked on wildlife programs on wolf, lynx, brown and black bear, and wolverine. He has been involved with the recovery and management of wolves in Montana, Idaho, and Wyoming since 1988 and led the program to reintroduce wolves to Yellowstone National Park and central Idaho. He has published articles on various wildlife management issues. His professional interests focus on human values in wildlife management, conflict resolution, and restoration of ecological processes.

ALISTAIR J. BATH, Department of Geography, Memorial University of Newfoundland, St. John's, Newfoundland, A1B 3X9, Canada

Alistair Bath, PhD, is an Associate Professor within the University in Newfoundland, where he teaches natural resources management issues, conflict resolution, and public involvement. Dr. Bath is a member of the IUCN Large Carnivore Initiative for Europe and has conducted numerous projects throughout Europe focused on human dimensions in wolf, brown bear, and lynx management. He also worked in North America on the reintroduction of wolves into the northwestern United States and on carnivore conservation areas in Canada. Dr. Bath is considered a leading authority in the human dimensions of wolf management.

MARC BEKOFF, University of Colorado Boulder, Colorado 80309, U.S.A.

Marc Bekoff is a Professor Emeritus of Ecology and Evolutionary Biology at the University of Colorado. In 2000, he was awarded the Exemplar Award from the Animal Behavior Society for major long-term contributions to the field of animal behaviour. He is also the regional coordinator for Jane Goodall's Roots & Shoots program. Professor Bekoff's main areas of research include animal behaviour, cognitive ethology (the study of animal minds), and behavioural ecology. During his career, he has published more than two hundred papers and eighteen books.

JUAN CARLOS BLANCO, Wolf Project–Conservation Biology Consultants, C/ Manuela Malasaña 24, 28004, Madrid, Spain

Juan Carlos Blanco is a biologist with a PhD in Animal Ecology and has been studying wolves in Spain since 1987. He is an advisor to the Ministry of the Environment on wolf conservation in Spain. Dr. Blanco is the Director of the Wolf Project (Projecto Lobo) in Madrid. An important part of his research has focused on wolf adaptation to densely-populated habitats. He authored various books and articles on wolf biology, human attitudes, and conservation of ecosystems inhabited by wolves.

CAMILLA H. FOX, Wildlife Consultant, P.O. Box 5007, Larkspur, California, 94977, U.S.A.

Camilla H. Fox is a wildlife consultant and writer with over fifteen years of experience working on behalf of wildlife and wildlands in the United States and internationally. Camilla holds a master's degree in Environmental Studies and has worked for several nonprofit organizations including the

Fur-Bearer Defenders, the Rainforest Action Network, and the Animal Protection Institute. In 2006, Camilla received the Humanitarian of the Year Award from the Marin Humane Society and the Christine Stevens Wildlife Award from the Animal Welfare Institute.

SUZANNE ASHA STONE, Northern Rockies Representative, Defenders of Wildlife, P.O. Box 773, Boise, Idaho, 83701, U.S.A.

Suzanne Asha Stone has worked since 1988 on wolf conservation in the western United States. She administers Defenders' wolf compensation program in the northern Rockies. Suzanne is one of the founders of the annual North American Wolf Conference (now in its twentieth year). Suzanne holds a master's degree in Wildlife Conservation and Conflict Management from Prescott College in Arizona. She received numerous awards for her work, including the "Alpha Award," presented by her peers at the 2005 North American Wolf Conference.

DENISE TAYLOR, Education 4 Conservation Ltd., Hillcrest, Pailton Fields, Pailton, Rugby, CV23 0QJ, U.K.

Denise Taylor is an environmental educator, entrepreneur, and wildlife conservationist. She is an executive director of the UK Wolf Conservation Trust (UKWCT, www.ukwolf.org) and founder and director of Education 4 Conservation (www.education4conservation.org). Denise was the founding editor of the UKWCT's magazine, *Wolf Print*. She has been instrumental in the completion of a Large Carnivore Education Centre in Bulgaria. Denise is in the final stages of her doctoral thesis on the role of education in wild wolf conservation. She is also a panel member of the Canid Specialist Group, IUCN-World Conservation Union.

ADRIAN P. WYDEVEN, Wisconsin Department of Natural Resources, 875 South 4th Avenue, Park Falls, Wisconsin, 54552, U.S.A.

Adrian P. Wydeven is a Mammalian Ecologist with the state of Wisconsin. He served as leader of the Wolf Program since 1990. Adrian also serves on the Federal Eastern Gray Wolf Recovery Team. He authored

papers on wolf ecology and ecosystem management with a focus on predators, prey, and habitat and also on people, who often influence ecological
relationships. In 2006, Adrian received the Outstanding Alumnus Award
from the College of Natural Resources, University of Wisconsin-Stevens
Point, and in 2007 he was a member of a team that received a Cooperative
Conservation Award from the U.S. Department of the Interior.

ARTISTS (drawings and photos of wild wolves only).

PETER A. DETTLING, Terra Magica – Images of Peter A. Dettling,
Award-winning nature photography & paintings, Canmore, Alberta,
Canada, www.TerraMagica.ca

Peter A. Dettling was born in Sedrun, Switzerland in 1972. He is a multiple award-winning photographer and painter whose passion for the natural world has then taken him all over the globe. His images are regularly
published in various magazines, calendars, books, and gallery shows, such
as the world-renowned American Museum of Natural History in New
York, NY. The artist resides now near Banff National Park in Alberta,
Canada. To learn more about his work, check out his website at www.
TerraMagica.ca.

DAVID C. OLSON, David C. Olson Photography, Rockford, Illinois,
U.S.A. www.davidolsonphoto.com.

David finds that wildlife photography is a perfect marriage of his fascina-
tion with the natural world and his love of the arts. He sees his imagery as
playing a vital role in sharing both the beauty and the plight of the wolf.
His photographic journeys take him to remote and wild areas to witness
wolf behaviour and capture stunning photographs. David continues his
exploration of our vanishing wilderness with his camera, and his images
can be seen in publications worldwide. For this project, he produced several photos, some of which inspired the wolf drawings also included in the
book.

SUSAN SHIMELD, Nature in Fine Art, Larmer Tree Studio, Larmer Tree Gardens, Tollard Royal, Nr. Salisbury, Wiltshire SP5 5PY U.K.

We contacted a number of wildlife artists to work on drawings for this book. Su Shimeld was chosen and she completed one pencil drawing per chapter, included under the chapter's title. Su is an accomplished wildlife artist – also see http://www.natureinart.com. Her work lends itself beautifully to the ethos of the book. Su has studied wolf behaviour and produced this book's illustrations in a captive wolves' facility, UK Wolf Conservation Trust. Each drawing took approximately ten days of work.

ROBERT J. WESELMANN, Raptor's Roost Photography, Northwood, Iowa, U.S.A.

Robert J. Weselmann has been photographing wolves since their re-introduction into the Northern Rocky Mountains of the U.S.A.. He is the co-author of Wild About Yellowstone, a book featuring wolves of Yellowstone National Park. He is also the photographer of Wolfs of Northern Yellowstone, a wolf identification chart for the packs living in the northern range of the park. You can find more of Bob's work at www.robertweselmann.com.

ACKNOWLEDGMENTS

This book would not be possible without Education 4 Conservation (www. education4conservation.org), the UK Wolf Conservation Trust (www.uk-wolf.org) and its director, Denise Taylor.

Special thanks go to Mimosa Arienzo, loved wife, who greatly supported the editors of this book, even while fighting terminal cancer.

The book took shape also during endless brainstorming with Tyler Muhly and Byron Weckworth as well as with the other treasured graduate students: Allan Mcdevitt, Astrid Vik Stronen, Carly Sponarski, Elisabetta Tosoni, Hugh Robinson, Isabelle Laporte, James Rogala, Jenny Coleshill, Joann Skilnick, Nick DeCesare, and Sk. Morshed Anwar.

We wish to acknowledge some key individuals and friends, who contributed crucial information or assistance to the book project: Carolyn Callaghan in particular, as well as Carita Bergman, Charles Mamo, Elisabetta Visalberghi, Gary Sargent, Jesse Whittington, Joel Berger, Layla Neufeld, Luigi Morgantini, Mark Bradley, Mark Hebblewhite, Mark Sherrington, Nina Fascione, Piero Musiani, Roberta Mulders, Roger Creasey, Stefano Mariani, Toni Shelbourne, the hunters of Alberta, the Northwest Territories and Nunavut, the ranchers of Alberta, Idaho, Montana, and Wyoming, and the wildlife officers working with various Canadian provinces and territories, in particular Alberta, the Northwest Territories, and Nunavut.

Various organizations supported some key aspects of this book project: the Alberta Beef Producers, Alberta Conservation Association, Alberta Ecotrust, Alberta Fish and Wildlife Division, Alberta Sustainable Resource Development and Community Development, Bailey Wildlife Foundation Compensation Trust, BC Ministry of Forests, Biodiversity Challenge Grants, Calgary Foundation, Calgary Zoological Society, Canadian Association of Petroleum Producers, Circumpolar/Boreal Alberta Research, Consiglio Nazionale delle Ricerche, Italy, Defenders of Wildlife, Department of Indian and Northern Affairs Canada, Government of Canada Award, Government of the Northwest Territories (Department of Environment and Natural Resources), Humane Society United States, Izaak Walton Killam Memorial, Kendall Foundation, Mountain Equipment

Coop, The National Science Foundation (USA), National Sciences and Engineering Research Council of Canada (NSERC), Northern Scientific Training Program Grant, Parks Canada, Shell, TD Canada Trust, TD Friends of the Environment, United States Department of Agriculture-Wildlife Services, United States Fish and Wildlife Service, University of Rome, West Kitikmeot/Slave Study Society, Weyerhaueser Company, Wilburforce Foundation, and World Wildlife Fund Canada.

Two anonymous reviewers provided valuable comments and ideas that were incorporated in all chapters of this volume.

Introduction –
Newly Recovering Wolf Populations Produce New Trends in Human Attitudes and Policy

Marco Musiani, Luigi Boitani, and Paul C. Paquet

In Europe and in the conterminous United States, wolf populations have been recovering since their protection in the 1970s. As part of the recovery, wolves have recolonized regions from which they were absent for decades and, in a few instances, centuries. Concomitant with this resurgence, considerable efforts are ongoing to understand how humans and wolves might coexist without excessive competition or conflict. Addressing these difficulties has always been an essential but problematic part of wolf conservation efforts. Undoubtedly, the lessons now being learned are directly applicable to conservation and management of wolves throughout the world, particularly because the practical resolution of conflicts can foster tolerance toward wolves. More broadly, however, these lessons are helpful for resolving the widespread tension and antagonism that exists between wildlife in general and the expanding social and economic aspirations of humans.

Because of the wolf's remarkable ability to adapt to an extensive array of environments, enhancing our comprehension of wolf/human relationships can serve to advance the conservation status of wolves, even in densely populated regions of Europe and North America. Although wolves in these areas continue to be affected by biological and physical factors, the primary influences are now the diverse socio-economic, political, and ethical perspectives and ambitions of humans (i.e., "human dimensions").

The importance of these factors can be dramatic, has played a role historically, and will continue to affect a range of outcomes for wolf populations, including persistence, recovery, and re-establishment.

This book comprises a set of case studies on how human attitudes influence management for recovering wolf populations. It is not an exhaustive review of attitudes or of wolf-management practices. However, its in-depth examinations of single cases provide much to contemplate concerning the scientific and socio-political realm of living with wolves by illuminating the contemporary relationships between human attitudes, public policy, and wolf ecology. The novel insights and fresh perspective presented herein have the potential for reforming the way society in the twenty-first century evaluates and responds to the inevitable conflicts between wolves and humans, particularly as the number of humans increases and wolf populations recover.

Wolves are one of the most admired, reviled, and controversial carnivores the world over. Public perceptions and attitudes toward wolves vary depending on the temporal and spatial context. Differences in opinions are extreme, from outright hatred and opposition, to deep respect and reverence. Moreover, these attitudes vary when compared across regional, national, and international groups, as well as temporally. Consequently, elucidating general trends in social attitudes toward wolves is a complicated endeavour and a worthwhile research area (Bruskotter et al. 2007; Karlsson and Sjöström 2007; Stronen et al. 2007).

Human attitudes toward wolves continue to be studied across the wolf's vast geographic range, which covers a diverse socio-political and public assemblage. Understanding attitudes is important for evaluating and measuring early changes and trends in wildlife management and conservation in general. For example, the controversial reintroduction of wolves to the northwestern United States in 1995–96, and the subsequent recovery of wolf populations described by Bangs et al. and Stone in this volume, catalyzed a global discussion about management of wolves and a new awareness concerning coexisting with wolves. A dozen years later, the debate and public awareness has not subsided. Accordingly, many people are now well versed in wolf-management issues and the distinctive problems that wolves can create for humans engaged in activities such as production of livestock.

POLITICAL CONTEXTS CONTRIBUTING TO WOLF RECOVERY AND PUBLIC OPINION SWINGS

Since the latter part of the twentieth century, ecologists and most of the public have recognized that wolves are important components of vigorous biological systems. However, it has taken until now for governments and interest groups to promote the recovery and reintroduction of wolves back to areas where they were previously endangered or extirpated. Section I of this book is centred entirely on coexistence of humans with wolves in this modern context of wolf protection, recolonization, and reintroduction. Across most of Europe and the conterminous United States, wolf populations are rebounding from human persecution with their numbers and ranges increasing. Several factors have been identified as causes of these positive trends, including increased tolerance of wolves by humans, restored wolf habitat, and increasing wild prey populations. Notwithstanding these successes, wolves in some regions are still vulnerable to extirpation owing to isolation and small population sizes. Accordingly, recovering wolves often live in highly fragmented landscapes that are typically occupied and used by humans, where a stable pattern of coexistence has yet to be realized.

Chapters by Boitani and Ciucci, Blanco and Cortés, and Bangs et al. highlight the difficulties of managing one of the most contentious conflicts between wolves and humans, the depredation of livestock. Although many government programs allow for compensation of the market value of losses due to wolf attacks on livestock, illegal killing of wolves remains a problem. Wherever wolves and livestock exist together, there is an increased likelihood of wolves being killed, either legally or illegally. Wolf control is applied with mixed results in Europe and North America (this volume; Harper et al. 2008).

In Europe and North America, wolves occupy some areas with good quality habitat. They are, however, naturally compelled to move great distances through inhospitable areas, where conflict is increased and survival decreased due to human-caused mortality (Blanco and Cortés, this volume). Consequently, limited landscape connectivity and lack of genetic exchange among scattered populations adversely affect population viability. European countries in particular are geographically small and cannot support wolf populations of sufficient size to ensure persistence. Rather, wolf populations require unrestricted movement throughout multiple countries to endure the imposing threats of ever-expanding human enterprise. According to Boitani and Ciucci, coordinating wolf management across national boundaries might be the solution to sustain wolf populations across all of Europe. Such an approach could address concerns about connectivity and the maintenance of genetic diversity by establishing a broader spatial context for conservation management.

This book describes in detail the recovery plans for wolf population in two different regions of North America (Wydeven et al. and Bangs et al., respectively). Wydeven et al. demonstrate the success of a multi-jurisdictional management plan coordinated across a number of states in the Great Lakes region of the United States. Wolf recovery in the region was assisted and made possible by the participation and highly coordinated efforts of governments, NGOs, private interest groups, and businesses potentially affected by the presence of wolves. These efforts resulted in the formulation of management rules harmonized across a large region, effectively dissolving the geo-political borders that are meaningless to wolves. This process of coordination lasted three decades and was characterized by varying levels of agreement among interest groups and decision makers. Consequently, wolf populations in the region are now quite robust and unlikely to become endangered in the near future. However, the authors also identify unsettled public opinion as a major challenge for the future.

Nowhere are the problems posed by divided public opinion better demonstrated than in the contentious wolf issues described by Bangs et al. in the northwestern United States. This is a region where wolves were once extirpated and following reintroductions are now considered "endangered" under federal legislation. Although their legal status remains litigious, regional wolf populations are now widely considered out of imminent peril. Whether these wolves are recovered and should now be legally designated as "threatened" rather than "endangered," from a biological or legal perspective, is a point of ongoing and unresolved debate (Bangs et al.; Morell 2008). This potential legal transition is primarily motivated by the federal government's determination that stated recovery goals for healthy wolf populations have been achieved. A 'threatened' status clears the way for greater flexibility in killing wolves for management and recreation, activities strongly advocated by affected states and interest groups. Accordingly, wolves could be killed to protect livestock and wolf hunting and trapping is being proposed in state government management plans. However, advocacy for protecting wolves is equally strong, with various environmental groups contesting the government's recovery goals as insufficient to ensure the continued persistence of wolf populations. These different views could result in policy decisions driven by incongruent socio-political influences and thus disparate and inconsistent multi-jurisdictional management strategies. Such an outcome would be a stark contrast to the coherent wolf-management policies in the Great Lakes region of the United States, but perhaps a hint of difficulties to be faced by those eager to coordinate recovery efforts across Europe.

Boitani and Ciucci identify and outline common patterns of wolf conservation, which, if recognized and incorporated into management, could lead to developing and informing long-term plans, thus heading off and preventing the debacle of inconsistencies between the short-term and local strategies mentioned above. They maintain that wolf conservation goals are scale-dependent and at least five types should be recognized; spatial, temporal, demographic, taxonomic, and ethical. Indeed, wolf conservation actions can be very different depending on the scale we choose to work (e.g., local, short-term plans vs. regional, long-term approaches). The authors further emphasize that successful wolf conservation will require broad-scale spatial consideration, as well as a wide temporal and demographic approach to address the diversity of public views that change over time.

Boitani and Ciucci's emphasis on biological populations rather than divisions based on ecologically irrelevant national boundaries is particularly applicable to the European wolf meta-population. The framework applies similarly to emerging meta-populations of wolves in the contiguous United States, as well as other regions of the globe where there is a need to plan for management of recovering populations – a new scenario deserving new approaches. The strength of a meta-population approach to wolf conservation and management is that it engages land use planning and policy at the highest levels. In Europe, for example, decisions must be agreed upon and made through continent-wide directives approved by and enacted by the European Commission. Wolves are also affected by administrative policies seemingly unrelated to wolves, adding an additional level of pragmatic complexity to wolf management. Among the policies important for wolf conservation are those relating to human health and veterinary care, agriculture, and protected areas. Many of these policies are radically changing the way millions of farmers affect the land, resulting in extensive and biologically relevant changes to an already highly modified landscape. Although the consequence of these policies to wolf management may be obvious, conservation programs often operate blindly, focusing on small geographic areas, short time spans, and narrow policy perspectives (e.g., a protected area or an anti-hunting campaign). To surmount this problem, managers and conservationists must be willing to acknowledge and strive to understand the complexities of biosocial systems. Clearly, this is a difficult task, particularly in the unprecedented circumstances of wolf recovery where populations have been reduced or eradicated.

CULTURES AND ETHICS FAVOURING WOLF RECOVERY, AND CONFLICTS WITH HUMAN INTERESTS

Predators, particularly wolves, are often considered to be 'keystone species'; that is, a species that influences an ecosystem at a greater magnitude than its proportion of biomass or numerical representation within that environment. In most parts of the world, however, humans trump wolves as the most important keystone species. Moreover, people have the capacity, deliberately and selectively, to cause specific changes. Thus, humans must be considered as a dominant factor in the functioning and coevolution of interspecific relationships within different environments. In Section II of the book, we describe how humans choose to influence ecosystems through wolf-management initiatives and conservation plans. In addition, we explore the common and emerging trends that now characterize the complex interactions of diverse human cultures, environmental ethics, and management decisions. Thus, we consider how different human communities affect wolves and the ecosystems that support them, as well as the influence wolves exert on human culture.

The scale of cultures and economies associated with recovering wolf populations has a striking geographic and political range, varying from densely populated rural and urban areas of Europe (Boitani and Ciucci; Blanco and Cortés) to low density ranching and farming communities in North America (Bangs et al.; Wydeven et al.). The current array of wolf-management and conservation strategies is equally expansive, ranging from full protection (in theory) to indiscriminate killing of wolves deemed as threats to livestock. Somewhere in between is the management of wolf populations for commercial and recreational hunting and trapping. The ways in which various societies have responded to wolves reflect millennia of cultural and emotional responses that in some cases have manifested from deeply rooted beliefs that wolves are harbingers of ill will and evil. In others, well-established and evolving cultural traditions promote the importance of wolves in the innate balance of wild nature. At the modern cultural extremes, wolves are now considered as indispensable predators that are integral to robust ecosystems or dangerous 'pests' that should be permanently cleansed from the earth. Consequently, the range of management and conservation initiatives can be extreme over time and space. For example, wolves are protected throughout most of the EU. Yet, when these animals leave the political boundaries of the EU, their protection vanishes and they are often killed by hunters or agents of non-EU governments. Likewise, wolves that are fully protected by federal legislation in the northwestern United States are afforded little or no protection once they cross into Canada. Even within the same geographic location, difference in management from one political regime to the next can affect wolves differently. For example, before the establishment of the EU in Eastern Europe, hunting of wolves was liberal, but afterwards wolves were fully protected.

In this volume, Fox and Bekoff examine the philosophical foundations of various wolf-management decisions and the ethical implications of different approaches to conservation and management. This chapter and those by Taylor and Bath reconsider the seminal work of Aldo Leopold and all agree that the connection between people and wolves is illustrative of a much broader relationship between people and nature. Accordingly, many people worldwide now view wolves as an essential part of the natural environment, the iconic embodiment of wild and untamed lands. Most people are supportive of wolf presence in remote wilderness areas and are convinced of the importance of having wolves as part of the natural food web.

Assuming that the contemporary goal of conservation is to maintain free-ranging and self-sustaining populations of wildlife amidst human-dominated landscapes, then conservation efforts must focus on sustaining the natural environment while meeting human needs. Because of the ever-increasing burden of human demands, coexistence is a difficult objective to achieve, yet essential for self-sustaining wolf populations. When wolves live close to human settlements, human–wolf cultural relationships profoundly influence wolf management. As noted previously, and explained in detail in this volume by Stone, some people disdain or fear wolves because wolves affect, or are perceived to affect, their special interests. Ironically, the species regarded by many as a threat and menace to our survival, has turned out to be a test of how likely we are to achieve a sustainable relationship with the natural world that supports our own continued existence.

Compensation programs are widely used to address conflicts by reimbursing livestock owners for their depredation losses. However, these programs are met with concern and scepticism on both sides of the issue. Wolf supporters maintain that these programs do little to reduce effectively the primary causes of conflict and do not enhance wolf conservation goals. Livestock producers are cautious of these initiatives, as the programs typically necessitate clear evidence that wolves are responsible for the depredation, a requirement that is often difficult to realize. Stone analyzes a compensation program administered by Defenders of Wildlife, an American wildlife conservation organization that reimburses livestock owners for their losses to wolves in the western United States. The author designed a survey that was sent to all livestock owners who received wolf compensation payments for documented losses. Although respondents still objected to wolf presence in their area, most reported that their tolerance to wolves would be even less if they did not receive compensation. Furthermore, how compensation programs affect the attitudes of ranchers and farmers who have not received compensation remains to be seen. Regardless, attitudes toward wolves within this interest group are generally against wolf recovery programs and the challenge remains to find a compromise that ensures viable, self-sustaining wolf populations.

Worldwide, wildlife management is typically the responsibility and jurisdiction of various government bodies. However, as new and effective conservation strategies emerge concurrently with research conducted by non-governmental individuals and organizations, these groups are providing increased knowledge and understanding, and adding valued contributions to government agencies. In this regard, the adaptation and application of participatory wildlife management, which began about forty years ago, is rapidly becoming the norm for the twenty-first century. This book describes how scientists, government agencies, conservation groups, ranchers, shepherds, hunters, trappers, and others in the public now collectively contribute to wolf management and conservation. The collaboration of these disparate groups necessitates a diversified approach to conservation and management. This book describes the consequent complexities and variations in wolf-management practices as a direct result of reconciling the diverse involvement of such heterogeneous collaboration. Accordingly, various chapters present somewhat different languages and styles; the product of the many disciplinary approaches that now contribute directly and indirectly to the management of wolves. Topically, chapters by Boitani and Ciucci, by Stone, and by Fox and Bekoff, analyze the shift toward collective wolf management from policy, public opinion, and ethical perspectives, respectively.

As demonstrated by Naughton-Treves et al. (2003) and explained by Fox and Bekoff (this volume), the strongest predictor of tolerance for wolves is the social group to which one belongs. Hunters, livestock producers, and other interest groups have a unique culture and set of values that influences their lack of tolerance for wolf presence. However, another very important indicator closely linked with wolf tolerance is level of education. Thus, a priority for wolf recovery efforts must include fostering educational programs to inform the public (see Taylor, this volume).

In 1944, Adolph Murie published *The Wolves of Mount McKinley* (University of Washington Press, Seattle), which many consider the first modern synthesis of wolf ecology and behaviour. That same year, Stanley Young and Edward Goldman published *The Wolves of Mount McKinley* (Dover Publications, New York), which was a scientific landmark for wolf biology, ecology, taxonomy, and management. Since these first two contemporary literary and scientific works, a vast assortment of informative books and hundreds of journal articles have been published. Although primarily focused on North America, these publications have been distributed internationally. In addition, 'wolf specialists' typically attend conferences each year to disseminate and share knowledge gained through scientific inquiry to a broader audience. Various large-sized conferences have also been organized that have focused specifically on wolf-related issues. More recently, wolf-related websites have proliferated on the internet and numerous wolf magazines are now distributed throughout the world, providing a layperson's venue for wolf literature and information. In addition, numerous film documentaries have been produced about wolves and wolves have been featured in documentaries about other species or broader natural history topics. Because of the proliferation of these various media, the opportunities for educational resources for the public are raised substantially. In this volume, Taylor shows how wolves are being used in education programs as a 'conservation strategy.' A practical discussion of wolf issues enlightens participants not only on wolf-specific issues but also to broader problems relating to ecosystem functioning and the importance of conserving ecosystems and maintaining biodiversity across trophic levels.

At the local level, wolf recovery can be influenced by people motivated by a complicated blend of economic, social, and cultural factors (Bath, this volume). Because the viability of most wolf populations is now determined by dynamic ecological factors mediated by human aspirations, the authors of this volume conclude that successful management strategies must embrace a wide range of expertise and perspectives. This is most reliably accomplished by combining the diverse skills of conservation specialists with the traditional knowledge of individuals and local communities.

In his chapter, Bath discusses a comprehensive approach to wolf management. The approach is explained with practical examples, mainly from Europe, where recovery of wolf populations is considered a priority. Bath discusses how "human dimensions" comprise a field of research that can help identify public attitudes and beliefs toward wolf-management issues, thus providing valuable insights to decision makers and managers. In addition, he describes human dimensions as a facilitated workshop strategy that can resolve issues, moving the public closer to coexistence with wolves.

Social research is revealing affirmative outlooks toward wolves from people in many parts of the world, whether in examining hunter's attitudes in Croatia or Poland or the attitudes of teenagers in Spain. Bath also takes the reader across Europe and parts of North America, where wolves are also recovering, sharing results of human dimensions research focused on public attitudes of various interest groups toward the species. He compares interest groups across space, illustrating regional differences, showing how attitudes are changing in some countries and illustrating that attitudes can often vary within an interest group, as well as across interest groups. This chapter also offers a real-world example of how to turn research into conservation, by bringing groups together and developing a wolf-management plan in Croatia. In the Croatian model, wolf management and human dimensions are integrated with a facilitated workshop approach. This is the first time that scholarly research on the social aspects of human and wolf relationships has coalesced and that the field of human dimensions in wolf conservation and recovery has been so explicitly described.

Our book confirms that difficulties associated with wolf recovery and conservation reflect fundamental problems facing contemporary society's struggle to coexist with wild nature. This volume is illustrated with original drawings that artistically convey the strong ecological and emotional values inherent in this struggle. For wolves, the pending social question is what probability of species persistence and environmental quality is acceptable to society while maintaining compatibility with economic necessities. The answer unsatisfactorily varies, depending on which sector of the public is queried. Yet this pattern, with minor local variations, is fundamentally similar throughout the world where wolves or other large predators are present. Because of the ubiquity of this pattern, we believe that our book will be of value and interest to those concerned primarily with wolf management and conservation, as well as readers who seek to understand and appreciate the problems facing conservation in the twenty-first century.

SECTION I –
Art and Science in Management Plans for Recovering, Recolonizing, and Reintroduced Wolves

1.1 Wolf Management across Europe: Species Conservation without Boundaries

Luigi Boitani and Paolo Ciucci

INTRODUCTION

The wolf has been and continues to be Europe's most charismatic large predator. The image of the wolf, either symbolic or realistic, can be found in any European culture and may be framed into a complex of both positive and negative attitudes (cf. Boitani 1995). In many early European cultures (especially Greek and Roman cultures), humans shared an overall positive view of the wolf. Throughout history, the original positive attitudes intermixed with negative values, mostly due to the advent of new cultural and ecological human types (e.g., nomadic shepherds from central Europe). This blend of different human ecologies and cultures produced the mixed and ambiguous attitudes toward wolves we find today across Europe (Boitani 1995). Not only are these mixed attitudes stratified among clearly distinct interest groups (conservationists, shepherds, hunters, the public, etc.), but they are at the core of a fundamental ambiguity which has characterized (and still does) wolf management and conservation across European countries. Hated or beloved to the limit, wolves in Europe have been subject to very different management regimes through time and across countries, and this is clearly apparent today in terms of the occurrence, density, and population dynamics of the species, all highly diversified across Europe.

No ecological system in Europe has escaped the profound influence humans have exerted on the land throughout history. Wolves were once distributed across the entire European continent. Destruction of forests and wild prey populations as well as intensive and persistent hunting and poisoning of wolves were the main causes of wolf extinction in many European countries. Exterminated as early as the sixteenth century in England, and later in most of central and northern Europe, by the middle of last century wolves were still surviving in the northwest of the Iberian Peninsula, in central-southern Italy and in the Balkans and northern Greece (Blanco et al. 1992; Boitani 1992, 2000). The nearest large (> 1,000 individuals) wolf populations were found in Romania, Bulgaria, and the former USSR republics (Jedrzejewska et al. 1996). In the 1960s, European wolf populations were probably at their lowest numbers and had the smallest and most fragmented ranges (Zimen and Boitani 1979). Prey populations, such as red deer, moose, roe deer, and wild boar were also at their lowest densities (Breitenmoser 1998). Nevertheless, wolves' adaptable food ecology allowed them to survive on garbage and livestock (Peterson and Ciucci 2003).

Rapidly changing economic, social, and ecological conditions in postwar Europe allowed for wolf recovery and expansion (Breitenmoser 1998). Through different patterns and timing across European countries, we can identify at least three main economic and cultural processes that contributed to wolf recovery. First, economic and industrial development after the Second World War profoundly altered the lifestyle of most citizens, as people increasingly abandoned rural areas to move into urban centres that provided new job opportunities. Wildlife habitat thus became increasingly available to wild prey populations and their large predators. The favourable size and conditions of European wild ungulate populations that we record today have not been matched in recent centuries (Gill 1990). Second, increasing ecological conscience and interest in environmental issues beginning in the 1960s have resulted in a significant shift in attitudes within the public toward wildlife conservation, including large predators. Third, large and effective conservation campaigns have actively supported wolf recovery through innovative laws, establishment of protected areas, reintroduction of wild prey populations, public opinion management, and implementation of livestock compensation programs (Boitani 1992). Fuelled by these substantial economic and cultural changes, and their high biological resilience, wolves have increased throughout most of Europe and are still expanding their range in several countries (Schröder and Promberger 1993; Boitani 2000; Salvatori and Linnell 2005).

In this chapter, we illustrate the status of the wolf in Europe and provide an argument for conserving wolves at a pan-European scale. We urgently call for a population-level management strategy to guide the development and implementation of conservation actions at national scales. In this perspective, we emphasize the critical need to integrate policy and socio-economic drivers with ecological science.

STATUS OF EUROPEAN WOLVES

European wolves could be considered part of the same large meta-population and occasional movements of animals among the populations may occur at any time (Fig. 1.1.1). However, there are at least eight major and two smaller wolf (sub-)populations that may be considered distinct (Table 1.1.1; www.lcie.org, accessed December 2008). A distinct subspecies (*Canis lupus signatus*) lives in the northwest of the Iberian Peninsula and, with about 2,500–3,000 individuals, forms one of the largest wolf populations in Europe (Blanco et al. 2005). The range is currently expanding southward into central Spain but two small subpopulations, one in the Sierra Morena and one in Portugal south of the Duero River, may be on the verge of extinction. The Italian population was reduced to a minimum of about a hundred animals in the 1970s (Zimen and Boitani 1975). Until the late 1980s, Italian wolves were confined to the Apennines mountain range. However, they recently (from 1992 according to Poulle et al. 1999) recolonized the western Alps and the population is now firmly established in southeastern France, sending dispersing animals into the Jura and Grisons regions of Switzerland and as far as the eastern Pyrenees and into Catalonia (Valière et al. 2003). The genetic and demographic link between the two populations (Apennines and Alps) has been estimated to be on average 2.5 individuals per generation, moving from the Apennines to the Alps (Fabbri et al. 2007) and both populations share the same

Figure 1.1.1. Estimate of the current (2007) extent of occurrence of the wolf and the main populations in Europe (LCIE, 2008, www.lcie.org). Arrows indicate main direction of range expansion of source populations. (Dark grey = permanent presence; light grey = temporary presence).

unique mitochondrial DNA (Randi et al. 1995, 2000). The total population sizes in the Apennines and in the Western Alps are estimated to be about 600–800 and 150 wolves respectively (Linnell et al. 2007). From Slovenia to northern Greece, the wolf range shows substantial continuity along the Dinaric Mountains of former Yugoslavian countries and the Balkan mountains of Albania, Bulgaria, the former Yugoslavian Republic of Macedonia, and Greece, even though there are several unsuitable areas devoid of wolves (Table 1.1.1).

Table 1.1.1. – Numbers, trends, and legal status of the ten (eight large and two very small) European wolf populations in 2008. This information was obtained by assembling data from available bibliographical sources and the informed and subjective estimates provided by experts of the IUCN/SSC Wolf Specialist Group and the Large Carnivore Initiative for Europe. Most of the numerical estimates should be considered as no more than indicative of the general status of the populations.

POPULATION Country	Approximate No. Wolves	Population trend	Legal protection	Livestock damage compensation
1. IBERIAN				
Spain (*includes a distinct small sub-population in Sierra Morena*)	2,500	Incr.	Game species (protected south of the Duero river)	Yes, but varies with regional laws
Portugal	300	Stable	Yes	Yes
2. WESTERN ALPS				
Italy	30–40	Incr.	Yes	Yes, by Regional Governments
France	100–120	Incr.	Yes (5–6 wolves removed annually)	Yes
Switzerland	1–3 ?	_	Yes (but limited wolf removal allowed)	Yes, by 'region' (Cantons)
3. ITALIAN				
Italy	600–800	Incr	Yes	Yes by Regional Governments
4. DINARIC-BALKAN				
Slovenia	60–80	Incr.	Yes	Yes
Croatia	130–170	Incr.	Yes (hunting quota)	Yes
Bosnia-Herzegovina	500 ?	Stable	No	No
Serbia-Montenegro	500 ?	Stable	No	No
Macedonia	800–1,000	Incr.	No (can be hunted all year, bounty)	No
Albania	900–1,200	Stable	Yes (but legal killing can be authorized)	No

Bulgaria	1,000	Stable	Game species (hunting permitted all year, bounties)	No
Greece	500–700	Stable	Yes (fully protected only south of the 39° parallel)	Yes, 80% paid by insurance

5. CARPATHIAN

Romania	3–4,000	Incr.	Game species	No
Hungary	< 10	Stable	Yes	No
Ukraine	500	Stable	No	No
Czech Republic	10–20	Stable	Yes	No
Slovakia	500	Stable	Yes (exceptions)	Yes
Poland	300–350	Stable	Yes (hunting permits)	Yes

6. BALTIC

Poland	300–350	Stable	Yes (hunting permits)	Yes
Estonia	100–150	Stable	Game species	No
Lithuania	400–500	Incr.	Game species (closed season)	No (only if animals are insured)
Latvia	300–500	Stable	Game species (annual quota and closed season)	No
Belorussia	1,500	Incr./Stable	No	No
Ukraine	500	Stable	No	No
Russia	10,000–20,000	Incr./Stable (much variation across the range)	No	No
Germany/ Western Poland (*a distinct sub-population*)	< 50	Incr	No	Yes

7. KARELIAN

Finland	200	Incr./Stable	Yes, hunting permitted only in reindeer areas	Yes, by the State and insurance companies
Russia (Karelia)	500	Incr./Stable (much variation across the range)	No	No

8. SCANDINAVIAN

Sweden	120	Incr.	Yes	Yes
Norway	20–25	Stable	Yes (within zoning system)	Yes

The Carpathian wolf population range includes a large area from Romania up to southern Ukraine and Poland and consists of five to six thousand wolves. Numbers are better known for each country and vary from about three to four thousand wolves in Romania to perhaps less than ten in Hungary. This population crosses several national boundaries, but its biological continuity is maintained. Northern Poland, the Baltic states, Belarus, in continuity with western Russia, host a population consisting of several thousand wolves, depending on the estimates and on where the range boundary is placed across the vast Russian forests. Several small population fragments are scattered at the periphery of the Carpathian and Baltic-Russian populations and are either remnants of a previous wider distribution or formed by dispersing animals, such as in western Poland, eastern Germany, and the eastern Czech Republic (Boitani 2000).

In Scandinavia the wolf was considered functionally extinct by the late 1960s, but a Swedish-Norwegian population was founded in the late 1980s (Wabakken et al. 2001) most probably by two animals dispersing from Finland, and later joined in 1991 by another immigrant from the same country (Vilà et al. 2003a). Since 1991, this population has rapidly increased in size, expanding its range into Norway and southern Sweden (Wabakken et al. 2001), and it is currently estimated at about 130–150 wolves (Liberg et al. 2005; Salvatori and Linnell 2005). Successful dispersal of wolves from Finland has been confirmed as critical for the demographic and genetic recovery of the Scandinavian population, although evidence of dispersal is rare (Vilà et al. 2003a; Linnell et al. 2005a). In Finland, wolves occur only in the eastern part of the country in continuity with the large wolf population of Karelia and Russia. While numbers and status in Finland are well known, information on the Russian populations are not available; however, population dynamics of the Russian wolves are such that a positive balance of dispersing animals into Finland has been monitored for many years (Pullianen 1993).

The ten European wolf populations have different sizes and growing patterns, and some of them may be too small yet to be considered viable in the long term. However, these populations are showing that the general negative trend of the 1950s and 1960s (Mech 1995; Boitani 2003) has reversed.

In addition, this broad perspective on population trends does not take into consideration two critical aspects. The first is the complexity of the proximate factors which ultimately caused the positive trend in European wolf populations. Only by understanding the relative contribution and interaction of factors will we be able to project their condition and management in the future. The second is that all European populations are subdivided into artificial fragments limited by national and provincial jurisdictions. Within each jurisdiction, wolf management and conservation is largely carried out in isolation.

According to current laws and guidelines (mainly the European Union's Habitat Directive and the Council of Europe's Bern Convention; see below) wolves in Europe must be managed at the national scale. From this point of view, wolf abundance varies greatly throughout the continent: only four countries host more than a thousand wolves, eleven countries host more than five hundred, and seven countries host less than a hundred. In some countries (of which notable examples are France, Switzerland, Portugal, Germany, Czech Republic, and Hungary) wolf populations are of limited size simply because they represent marginal portions of neighbouring, larger source populations. Eleven countries have increasing populations, the others reporting stable populations – the exception being Bosnia-Herzegovina with a possibly declining population.

Official protection of wolves is provided in most European countries through the Bern Convention (Convention on the Conservation of European Wildlife and Natural Habitats, 19.9.1979), where the wolf is listed as "strictly protected species" (Appendix II), and the European Council Directive on Conservation of Natural and Wild Fauna and Flora of the European Union (known as the Habitat Directive 92/43 of 21.5.1992), although exceptions have been granted to many countries.

Even though the wolf and its habitat receive full protection under the Bern Convention, its enforcement relies on the Contracting Parties, who may not fully apply their obligations. Bulgaria, Czech Republic, Finland, Latvia, Lithuania, Poland, Slovakia, Slovenia, Spain, Macedonia, Ukraine, and Turkey are among the countries that signed the Convention but made an exception for wolf protection. In addition, among the European Union (EU) countries bounded to the Habitat Directive, several have a management regime that allows wolf hunting in certain areas/times, namely Estonia, Latvia, Lithuania, Poland, Slovakia, Greece, Finland, and Spain. In six communities of northern Spain, the wolf is a game species and, in addition to poaching, the average annual bag quota is around 19 per cent of the population (Blanco et al. 1992).

Outside the EU, Switzerland and Norway protect the species but have management protocols that allow substantial exceptions (e.g., killing wolves when livestock depredation exceeds predetermined levels). Among the Eastern European countries, Romania grants full protection to its wolf population. However, as more countries enter the EU (e.g., Bulgaria) changes regarding wolf management there are expected. Across Europe, and especially in the Mediterranean countries, illegal killings of wolves are widespread and frequent, and several forms of poaching are not actively prosecuted (e.g., Boitani and Ciucci 1993).

To address livestock depredation problems, ten European countries provide, to varying extents, damage compensation to farmers and shepherds. Estimates of the annual cost of compensation programs for wolf depredations are highly variable across Europe and in different years, and can be used as a gross approximation of actual costs (Table 1.1.2). Italy ranks highest among all European Union countries with more than €5,500/wolf/year (Boitani and Ciucci 1998; L.B. and P. C., unpublished data). Only France has comparable costs (€5,000/wolf/year). In comparison, in Minnesota average annual (1990–98) compensation paid to farmers for a population of about two thousand wolves was about US$18.50/wolf (Mech 1998a).

Due to high heterogeneity of the landscape, wolves in Europe are found in such diverse habitat as wheatfields in central Spain, alpine meadows in the Alps, forests in Scandinavia, or village outskirts in Italy and Romania. A common element is that the European landscape has been inhabited and modified by humans for millennia and there are no patches of pristine habitat where predators and prey interact free of human impacts. Accordingly, prey populations and their habitats are usually intensively managed by humans. In addition, livestock numbers are high almost everywhere and serious conflict arises between shepherds and wolves (Bibikov 1982; Blanco et al. 1990; Promberger and Schröeder 1993), which profoundly shapes the views and attitudes of local people toward wolves (Fritts et al. 2003). Given this close interrelationship between wolves and humans in Europe, we maintain that human attitudes toward wolves represent an overwhelming component acting as the ultimate factor determining the quality of wolf habitat. Although wolf populations have recovered significantly during the last thirty years, there are still large sectors of the public that oppose wolf conservation (Boitani 2000; Bath 2001; Bath and Majic 2001).

In spite of the variation of local conditions, wolf ecology in Europe has not been studied as extensively as in North America and, with some exceptions, data are still minimal for the large majority of populations. For example, food habits of wolves have been studied in several countries, mostly by means of scat analyses (Meriggi and Lovari 1996; Peterson and Ciucci 2003; Andersone and Ozoliņš 2004a; Capitani et al. 2004; Nowak et al. 2005). However, with few exceptions (e.g., in the Bialowieza Forest in Poland: Jedrzejewski et al. 2002), ecological studies of predation have

Table 1.1.2. Estimates of the cost of compensation for livestock depredation in selected European countries.

COUNTRY	WOLF/YEAR (€)	NO. WOLVES	YEAR	SOURCE
Italy	5,500	350-450	1991-95	Ciucci and Boitani 1998
France	5,000	30-40	1996	LCIE[1]
Sweden	1,800	40-50	1996	LCIE
Finland	900	150	1996	LCIE
Portugal	850	300-400	1996	LCIE
Slovenia	700	30-50	1996	LCIE
Croazia	600	50-100	1996	LCIE
Spain	250	2,000	1996	LCIE

1: Large Carnivore Initiative for Europe (www.lcie.org).

been very rare. Research based on radio-telemetry and/or snow-tracking in Spain (Vilà et al. 1995; Blanco and Cortés 2002; Blanco et al. 2005), Italy (Boitani 1986, 1992; Ciucci et al. 1997; Ciucci and Boitani 1999), Sweden and Norway (Wabakken et al. 2001), Finland (Kojola et al. 2004), and Poland (Jedrzejewska et al. 1996; Okarma et al. 1998; Jedrzejewski et al. 2002) produced valuable information on movement patterns, home range size and pack dynamics. However, we are still lacking good data on vital statistics of local populations and, in particular, there is a paucity of data on dispersal, a critical gap if we are to understand the large-scale dynamics of wolf populations across the continent.

A common trait of most European studies of wolf ecology is the limited spatial (and temporal) scale of the research, which is often confined to a small local population or to a protected area. With the exception of a few ongoing long-term monitoring schemes of the wolf population (e.g., in Fenno-scandian: Wabakken et al. 2001; Vilà et al. 2003a; Kojola et al. 2004; in the Alps: Valière et al. 2003), most ecological studies have focused on a few packs in a restricted area. Although the results are important for local management, extrapolation of these results to a broader scale is not always feasible due to the diversity of environmental conditions in which wolves live. In addition, detailed field-studies on wolf-livestock conflicts are generally lacking, which does not help development and monitoring of cost-effective and economically feasible prevention methods and strategies.

WOLF CONSERVATION ISSUES

Although an increasing number of wolves currently inhabit Europe and their overall population trend is positive, there are several reasons to be concerned about their future. In addition, on a broad scale, we face the new and complex challenge of finding functional solutions for the coexistence between humans and large, viable, and ecologically effective wolf populations. This challenge entails not only reliable biological knowledge but also familiarity with human dimension tools and deep integration at the socio-economic, political, and administrative levels.

Small Populations

The first and most important concern is that several European wolf populations are still small and highly susceptible to extinction (Table 1.1.1). Due to low numbers, wolf populations in southern Spain, Portugal, Germany, western Poland, and Scandinavia should still be considered threatened. Discussion on the minimum viable population (MVP; the minimum number necessary for population survival, Soulé 1987) for wolves has not generated consensus, and estimates vary greatly from theoretical models to empirical considerations (cf. Fritts and Carbyn 1995). For example, Fritts and Carbyn (1995) opposed MVP estimates as being based on insufficient theoretical models to account for the high resilience of small wolf populations. Nevertheless, based on widely used Population Viability Analysis, the Swedish Parliament has taken the important step of identifying a numerical target (200 wolves) to be reached by the population before any discussion on routine population control will be initiated (Linnell et al. 2005a).

Small populations are also more vulnerable to inbreeding depression (Liberg et al. 2005) and to hybridization with dogs. Given the high number of stray and feral dogs in many European countries, this may be a serious threat. Evidence of wolf-dog hybridization has been obtained in Italian field studies (Boitani 1986; Boitani and Ciucci 1993), and more recently, using molecular genetic techniques, at least 5 per cent of all examined wolf samples showed evidence of genetic introgression by dogs (Randi and Lucchini 2002; Ciucci et al. 2003; Verardi et al. 2006). The same problem has been found in other European wolf populations (Teruelo and Valverde 1992; Andersone et al. 2002; Vilà et al. 2003b; Blanco, personal communication). Concerns for small populations also apply to the more external propagules of sub-populations, which may not have continuous and firm links with the main populations. For example, the Italian wolves in the western Alps are tenuously connected to the wolves of the Apennines range (Fabbri et al. 2007). Similar concerns apply to the small populations in northern Slovenia, northern Bulgaria, and the Czech Republic.

Some of these small populations currently show negative trends (e.g., southern Spain and central Portugal), while others have recently established and are improving (e.g., eastern Germany). Artificial augmentation of small, isolated wolf populations has never been seriously suggested in Europe, their future being left solely to changes in human attitudes and habitat improvements. Survival of these populations will ultimately depend on the health of neighbouring source populations and their ability to produce a sustained flow of dispersing animals. Therefore, a functional system of connecting areas to allow for natural dispersal is required to ensure the conservation of these marginal populations.

The Process of Recolonization

Wolves travel far and fast when dispersing, easily traversing small European countries, as shown by the recent history of wolves in Scandinavia (Vilà et al. 2003a) and the Alps (Valière et al. 2003; Ciucci et al. 2005). In North America, dispersal distances up to 890 kilometres have been recorded (Van Camp and Gluckie 1979), and in Europe, distances of > 2,000 kilometres can also be inferred from dispersing wolves whose origin can be traced back using genetic data (e.g., Sweden/Norway: Vilà et al. 2003a; France and Switzerland: Valière et al. 2003). In Europe, dispersal distances > 1,000 kilometres have been found also by a limited number of GPS-telemetry studies (Ciucci et al. 2005; Kojola et al. 2006; Wabakken et al. 2007). In 2005, a male radio-marked wolf travelled more than 1,240 kilometres for a maximum dispersal distance of 217 kilometres from the northern Apennines in Italy to southern France (P. C. and L. B., unpublished data). Originating from Italian wolves settled in the western Alps by 1992, recolonizing individuals were first detected in Valais (Switzerland) in 1996, in the Massif Central (France) in 1997, in the Grisons (Switzerland) in 2004, and as far as the eastern Pyrenees (France) in 1999 (Valière et al. 2003).

Dispersing wolves often move back into areas from where the species had been exterminated by people decades ago, and recolonization is generally met with fierce opposition by local human communities. In these areas, local socio-economic conditions recently developed in the absence of a large, free-ranging predator; therefore recolonizing wolves can seriously conflict with economic interests of local communities. Specifically, livestock husbandry methods evolved under predator-free conditions (e.g., large herds are left unattended and free-ranging; guarding dogs are not used), which is less labour-intensive and yields higher economic profits.

Under these conditions, wolf recolonization not only generates economic losses but also, and perhaps most importantly, high animosity, social stress, and tense political controversies. In addition, the public and the media are intensely interested in these animosities, and conservation values clash against market values, thus resulting in misinformation and emotional debates (Fritts et al. 2003). Recent situations in Norway, France, Switzerland, and Northern Italy are examples of this pattern. There is a need to study, monitor, and manage these social reactions using a set of research tools not typically utilized by biologists. If the negative reaction of local communities in recently recolonized areas grows into organized anti-wolf movements, it could generate backlash on all efforts to maintain healthy wolf populations. While effective public opinion management is critical in this perspective, there also appears to be the need to control the recolonization process and guide it toward the most suitable areas after timely preparation of the local community of stakeholders.

Availability of Suitable Habitat

Wolves are generalist and opportunistic predators and can survive on a diverse range of food resources (Peterson and Ciucci 2003) and habitat types (Mech 1970). In Europe, there are places where wolves are known to have survived essentially on garbage and livestock and in close proximity to humans (Macdonald et al. 1980; Boitani 1982; Fonseca 1990; Cuesta et al. 1991; Ciucci and Boitani 1998a). Discussions on what is considered ecologically 'suitable' habitat for the wolf will often be of limited value because almost any habitat type which provides food and cover is good for wolves as long as they are not killed by humans (Fuller 1995). This adaptability to all habitat types has ensured wolf resiliency; however, it has also increased conflicts with human interests and made it difficult to keep wolves separated from areas used by humans.

Although wolves can utilize alternate food sources, wild prey populations are a desirable component of wolf habitat. In North America, Fuller (1989) found that ungulate densities explained more than 70 per cent of the variation in wolf densities; however, these findings apply to specific conditions seldom found in Europe. Following a modelling approach, suitable wolf habitats in North America have been broadly identified in areas where road density was below 0.45 km/km^2 (Mladenoff et al. 1995), although these estimates have been recently questioned because wolves have colonized areas with a higher road density during their southward and eastward range expansion in Minnesota (Mech 2001). In Italy, given other favourable habitat conditions, areas inhabited by wolves have no relationship with road density but rather are associated with human densities lower than 30–40 people/km^2 (Corsi et al. 1999). In Spain, recent research has shown that wolves can even thrive in areas crossed by fenced four-lane highways (Blanco et al. 2005). Finally, European protected areas are small (the majority are smaller than 1,000 km^2); therefore, they provide only partial protection to wolves, which normally have territory sizes of the same order of magnitude (Linnell et al. 2001a, 2005b).

In short, wolves can and do live in areas highly utilized by humans (Linnell et al. 2001b) and appear to be very tolerant of human disturbance. Conservation concerns arise from the need to ensure a long-term viable coexistence between wolves and humans. There is no management alternative for wolves other than to try to integrate them as much as possible within human-dominated landscapes. Segregation of large carnivores from human landscapes has been proposed by several North American authors (cf. Soulé and Terborgh 1999), but it appears scarcely feasible in that continent and certainly is not an option in Europe.

Legislation Fragmentation

The European Habitats Directive and the Bern Convention provide broad umbrellas of protection to wolves; however, they rely on national governments to implement them, and national governments have authority only on wolves living within their respective countries. Management is therefore highly fragmented in national and even sub-national units (e.g., Spain's communities, Italy's regions, Germany's Länder) that rarely coordinate their actions. Spain and Portugal, France and Italy, Sweden and Norway are all good examples of lack of political coordination between management authorities across national borders even though excellent cooperation is often in place among scientists and NGOs. Also, within a given country, wolves are often managed by several authorities without much coordination, and it is often the case that the Forestry Service, Game Boards, Regional or Provincial Boards, various ministries, as well as the Veterinary Services all have a say in wolf management. This fragmentation of authority makes any real implementation of a species conservation plan very difficult.

It is difficult to manage a species when it is protected by the Ministry of the Environment, hunted under permit from the Game Board, managed by the Ministry of Health for all health-related issues (rabies, etc.), while livestock depredation is compensated by the Ministry of Agriculture and the habitat is fragmented by infrastructure planned by the Ministry of Transport. Legal protection has to be supported by a set of integrative rules and norms that allow for flexible management, compensation for livestock depredation, and, in selected cases, wolf hunting or removal.

Livestock Conflicts

Throughout Europe, even in areas where wild prey are available, domestic animals are consumed by wolves to varying extents, depending on their relative abundance and accessibility (Castroviejo et al. 1975; Bjarvall and Isakson 1982; Reig and Jedrzejewski 1988; Lesniewicz and Perzanowski 1989; Ionescu 1993; Pullianen 1993; Papageorgiou et al. 1994; Meriggi and Lovari 1996; Ciucci and Boitani 1998a, 2005; Espuno et al. 2004). As wolf populations expand into areas where livestock protection techniques have been abandoned (see above), wolf–livestock conflicts are expected to increase further (Mech 1995, 1998a), and they cause a serious handicap to any wolf conservation effort. Damage done by wolves is compensated in most European countries, and the cost of these schemes is highly variable depending on the programs themselves (e.g., percentage paid, verification procedures, conditions) and on variables correlated of depredations events (i.e., livestock and terrain types, husbandry techniques, relative livestock-wolves-wild prey densities, etc.) (Boitani 1982, 2000; Blanco et al. 1990; Ciucci and Boitani 1998b, 2005). However, no assessment in Europe has been done to evaluate the effectiveness of compensation schemes in reducing the conflict, i.e., increasing farmers' tolerance toward wolves and reducing illegal killing of wolves (Boitani et al., unpublished report). There are indications that in some areas costly compensation programs did not appear to reach either of these two objectives (e.g., Tuscany: Ciucci and Boitani 1998b) and that, in most situations, current compensation policy tends to become an additional form of subsidy to farmers, therefore encouraging a permanent state of conflict (Cozza et al. 1996).

Compensation for livestock losses was never meant as a tool to prevent wolf depredation. Its intent was to mitigate economic losses and social conflicts at the local level and, as such, this tool can still play an essential role in reducing human–wolf conflicts. However, it must be recognized that it should be integrated in a more holistic management plan that requires adoption of preventive husbandry methods, reliable verification of alleged damages, and stakeholder participation as conditions for compensation (Blanco et al. 1990; Fernández et al. 1990; Fritts et al. 1992, 2003; Cozza et al. 1996; Ciucci and Boitani 1998b). In Sweden, an innovative compensation system provides economic incentive to reindeer breeders living in areas of wolf presence (but not in the northern reindeer husbandry areas where there are not meant to be any wolves) and is based on the principle of paying for the presence of carnivores rather than losses (Schwerdtner and Gruberb 2007; Zabel and Holm-Müller 2008). This approach provides an example of a framework for economic incentives for increasing tolerance of wolves by humans.

Economic Incentives for Livestock Producers

Compensation programs are not functionally integrated within the economic incentive policy that largely subsidizes livestock farmers in most European countries. In 1998, before the more recent revision of the European Common Agricultural Policy (C.A.P.), sheep farmers in Europe received economic subsidies up to 60 per cent of the value of their business, and up to 80–82 per cent in Switzerland and Norway as shown by the value of Producer Subsidy Equivalent (PSE) percentage in Europe. The PSE includes the market support measures (export refunds, intervention buying, etc.), direct payments (headage payments, area payments, etc.), reductions or increases in production costs (for breeding related to changes in the price of forage, etc.), and indirect support (any type of facility such as tax concessions for example). PSE measures the percentage of producer income derived from the agricultural support policy (Savelli Giannuzzi et al. 1998; Table 1.1.3). Livestock subsidy systems vary greatly across Europe. Romania, for example, lacked any financial support for the livestock industry, while substantial subsidies exist in Norway and Switzerland. In the countries of Central and Eastern Europe, livestock subsidy grants are mainly aimed toward encouraging the production of purebred animals.

On the other hand, the C.A.P. of the European Union, which draws off about half of the total budget of the European Union, provides incentives to produce high numbers of livestock and maintain high market values for meat and dairy products (Savelli Giannuzzi et al. 1998). This results in overproduction that is often incompatible with the ecological carrying capacity of the agro-pastoral system and, important to this discussion, this policy appears to be largely incongruent with large carnivore conservation goals. Unless the C.A.P. and the European Union Habitat Directive are reconciled and made compatible in their objectives and mechanisms, there are serious reasons to be concerned about the sustainability of both wolf conservation and agro-pastoral ecosystems.

Human Attitudes

Wolf management in Europe has often been highly controversial from the perspective of a variety of emotional and rational positions, which originate from old traditions and new prejudices (Boitani 1995; Fritts et al. 2003). For example, in areas of southern and eastern Europe where wolves were never exterminated, people are not concerned about potential attacks on humans, but in recently recolonized areas of central and northern Europe, the fear of wolf attacks is common and old myths and legends are again popular (Bath 2001). However, there are very few reports of healthy wolves attacking humans in Europe in the last century (Linnell et al. 2005b).

Shepherds typically have a negative attitude toward wolves, and the same holds true for hunters even where there are abundant game populations (Fritts et al. 2003). Negative attitudes are fertile ground for illegal wolf killing. Human attitude toward wolves is an aspect that cannot be ignored by any wildlife management plan. In spite of the crucial importance of human attitudes, there have been relatively few studies on the attitudes of Europeans on wolves. In the last few years, the Large Carnivore Initiative for Europe (LCIE), an independent IUCN/SSC group of experts on large carnivores, has sponsored and supported several studies on human attitudes toward wolves in France, Portugal, and Croatia (Bath 2001). Unfortunately, there is no benchmark to measure whether tolerance of wolves

Table 1.1.3. Producer Subsidy Equivalent (PSE) percentage in the European Union, in Switzerland, and in Norway (Savelli Giannuzzi et al. 1998). PSE measures the percentage of producer income derived from the agricultural support policy.

Livestock product	Producer Subsidy Equivalent (%)[1]		
	European Union	Switzerland	Norway
Milk	63%	84%	80%
Beef and veal	60%	88%	75%
Sheep meat	59%	81%	82%
Pig meat	10%	55%	45%
Poultry meat	23%	88%	59%
Eggs	5%	88%	61%
All livestock products	46%	80%	74%

[1] Return to farmers from agricultural policy support

by the public or any group of interest has recently increased or decreased, although experts dealing with wolf issues on a daily basis report that there are no indications that perceptions of wolves are improving (Bath 2001). More troublesome is that, in spite of its obvious importance to successful wolf management, experts in the fields of public opinion management, participatory management, conflict resolution, and environmental mediation have seldom been requested to support wolf-management planning.

PAN-EUROPEAN, POPULATION-LEVEL AND LOCAL SCALES OF CONSERVATION

The wolves that dispersed from the Italian population as far as the Spanish Pyrenees, the French Jura Mountains, and the Swiss Grison (cf. Valière et al. 2003; see above) provide an excellent case study to show the reason why wolf management in Europe must be approached on a continental scale. In 1999, the Bern Convention endorsed the Action Plan for the Conservation of

Wolves in Europe produced by the LCIE (Boitani 2000), which includes a detailed list of conservation actions needed for each European country. However, the Action Plan is no more than a strategic document and has no means to enforce its implementation in each country. Rather, it once again relies on individual countries to adopt the strategy and coordinate conservation actions among themselves. Almost all European countries have approved a national Action Plan or wolf-management protocol that calls for coordination of strategies and actions with adjacent countries. However, no real implementation has ever followed beyond the personal coordination of some field biologists.

Furthermore, as the European landscape is highly fragmented, there is a need for a careful and reliable broad-scale assessment and management of potential source-sink dynamics. A continental approach that considers European wolves as one large meta-population would be the optimal conservation strategy, applying consistent and coordinated conservation actions throughout the range. The European Commission, with its mandate to implement the Habitat Directive, would be the natural authority to advance and implement this approach.

Two fundamental concepts should inform wolf conservation across Europe. The first foundation should be that the management unit is not that portion of a wolf population that falls within a given country's boundaries, but rather the entire biological (sub-)population, defined regardless of its political and administrative geographical location (Boitani 2000). The strategy should therefore focus on the biological features of the management unit (viability, demography, ecology, etc.). However, management and conservation plans for each of the ten European wolf populations should take into account the diversity of ecological and socio-economic conditions in implementing locally adapted measures. This approach appears obvious to biologists when considering wolves' ecology and behaviour (long dispersal distance, high reproductive potential, adaptable food ecology, etc.) and the way European national boundaries cut across ecologically homogeneous areas (e.g., the Alps). This approach, however, is currently opposed by individual countries that want to maintain full sovereignty on their land and hesitate in empowering the European Commission. On the contrary, the population approach is well represented in the United States by the Endangered Species Act, the most important federal legislation dealing with endangered species. Recently, the recovering gray wolf populations of the lower forty-eight states have been divided into three distinct populations that are managed as if they were distinct species (Bangs et al., this volume). A similar provision by the Habitat Directive appears urgent and appropriate for an ecologically sound management of all European large carnivores, and indeed for all species whose ranges are larger than single countries. In 2006, an important step in this direction has been taken by the European Commission with the beginning of a discussion on guidelines for population-level action plans for large carnivores (Linnell et al. 2007).

In densely populated Europe, wolves are able to thrive in areas of high human density (Bibikov 1982; Boitani 1986; Blanco et al. 1990, 2005; Promberger and Schröeder 1993; Ciucci et al. 1997) and coexistence between people and wolves can be achieved essentially by reducing economic damages and increasing wildlife–society acceptance capacity (Decker et al. 2002). In line with the mission statement of the LCIE, the main goals should be maintenance and restoration, in coexistence with people, of viable populations of large carnivores as an integral part of the ecosystems and landscapes across Europe. Managing wolves in human-dominated landscapes has two important implications: the first is that wolf populations have to be continuously managed to maintain wolves at acceptable densities (cf. Mech 1995); the second is that wolves will not always be allowed to fully play the ecological role of predators because their ecosystems will often be managed for competing human interests (Linnell et al. 2005b). Nevertheless, wolf–human integration rather than segregation will allow for many more wolves in many more areas than the current ranges (Boitani 2003; Mech and Boitani 2003), with obvious benefits for a cascade of ecological relationships over broader ecological and geographical scales.

For these conservation approaches to be implemented, there is a need for adaptive management under a well-defined strategic plan. Europe is so diverse and complex, and wolf management touches on so many different ecological, cultural, and socio-economic aspects, that it is not possible to draft a management plan that can foresee all possible management actions throughout the wolf ranges. Even if such an approach could be designed, it would be too rigid to allow for changes in time and flexibility needed at the local scale. Wolf conservation could instead be articulated through population-level management plans with clear objectives and sets of criteria to choose among alternative management scenarios to be implemented at national and local levels.

Zoning (*sensu* Breitenmoser et al. 2005; Linnell et al. 2005c) is one the oldest and most widely used techniques to apply different management regimes to various sections of a population. This could represent an effective tool only if applied at the proper ecological scale. If zoning were applied to establish where European wolves would be allowed to persist, then these areas would have to be large enough, close enough, and connected among themselves enough to match consistently with the best available information on the demography and ecology of the entire wolf meta-population. In this perspective, the Natura 2000 network of protected areas throughout Europe (http://ec.europa.eu/environment/nature/home.htm) shows a substantial weakness. While the goal of Natura 2000 is the long-term conservation of biodiversity, no protected area or Natura 2000 site in Europe on its own is large enough to ensure the persistence of a viable wolf population. This, in our opinion, is a critical issue that urgently needs to be addressed by national authorities and the European Commission in their implementation of the network.

Preventing and reducing livestock losses to wolves will remain the crucial aspect in ensuring wolf–human coexistence, and it may invoke some form of wolf control or hunting. If prevention and mitigation can be applied at a local scale with a variety of techniques to suit the local socio-economic traditions, wolf control should only be contemplated within the frame of a large-scale population management plan. Demographic increases up to more than an annual average of 40–50 per cent are normal in healthy, recolonizing wolf populations, and evidence suggests harvest quotas up to 35 per cent do not impair population maintenance or growth (see Fuller et al. 2003 for a review). Therefore, removal of a smaller percentage of animals appears biologically feasible as it will have limited impact on the growth of the overall population. However, to evaluate the feasibility of removing wolves in selected areas, the demography and structure of the population must be known over large spatial and temporal scales. The approach is legally feasible as the Habitat Directive allows for lethal control of protected species if the favourable status of their populations is maintained and given sufficient justification.

Other European policies affect wolf management indirectly. The policies regarding human health and veterinary care (i.e., food processing and livestock husbandry methods), land use, economic incentives to leave uncultivated fields, and subsidies to support milk and meat production are changing the way millions of farmers do their jobs and are deeply affecting the European landscape. While it appears obvious that all of these issues are relevant to wolf management, wolf conservation programs rarely look at the cumulative effects of these broader issues. For example, the new rules on milk processing are based only on concerns for human health, but they are changing the way shepherds manage their sheep and cattle in mountain areas, which deeply affects the ecology of pastures, their herbivores, and wolves. In practice, farmers find it economically impractical to graze their stock where processing facilities are not accessible. Whether wide-scale measures like these are ultimately beneficial to wolves depends on pure chance rather then prudent planning. For example, by linking subsidies with production levels and distorting market prices, the C.A.P. has encouraged a shift toward more intensive livestock production with negative impacts on the environment, including greater use of fertilizers to increase pasture productivity, as well as problems from overgrazing and under-grazing.

The LCIE proposed a tiered system to reconcile all types of subsidies and provide the flexibility needed to respond to differences in environments and cultures among European states (Savelli Giannuzzi et al. 1998). The first tier consisted of a basic Community-wide payment for all producers (and not linked to any environmental consideration), the second tier was a payment assigned if certain types of environmentally friendly agriculture were practised, and the third tier was to be applied in particularly fragile areas where the main objective is conservation. The third tier would include economic incentives to improve systems to prevent livestock losses to wolves and to compensate for the extra costs linked to the presence of large predators. In the long term, however, it would be advisable to eliminate all compensation for stock losses and introduce incentives for the use of anti-predator techniques, especially by those livestock producers in high depredation risk zones. This approach shifts the concern on conflicts between breeders and wolves from a local to the European context (legislation and economic strategies) and encourages the development of cross-border management systems.

Wolves are charismatic animals and often attract a disproportionate amount of attention from the public and wildlife managers. It is therefore common that much discussion is focused on the ways and means to manage wolves. In doing so, a simple but essential ecological paradigm is often neglected: wolves are just one of the many elements of the European environment, and their conservation is often best accomplished not by singling them out as a special species but by managing them within several other components of the ecosystem in a holistic approach. The challenge ahead to all of us is to bring this approach to the heart of European rules and offices.

1.2 Ecological and Social Constraints of Wolf Recovery in Spain

Juan Carlos Blanco and Yolanda Cortés

INTRODUCTION

During the nineteenth and twentieth centuries, wolves were almost eradicated from Mexico and the contiguous states of the United States, and the populations of Western Europe were seriously fragmented. In recent decades, wolves have started to recover in many countries (Mech 1995), but in Western Europe, several populations remain isolated (Boitani 2000; Botani and Ciucci, this volume). In the Iberian Peninsula, the main wolf population was cornered in the northwest and reached its minimum circa 1970. Since then, however, the population has increased and spread eastward and southward (Blanco et al. 1992; Blanco and Cortés 2002). In Italy, wolves also started to recover in the 1970s, they first bred in the French Alps in 1992, and from there some individuals reached the eastern Pyrenees circa 1999 (Boitani and Ciucci 1993; Valière et al. 2003). Although the isolation of populations for more than a century led to a reduction in genetic variability (Randi et al. 2000), the re-establishment of genetic flow between populations is expected to lead to the recovery of some of the lost genetic variability. This process may also be expected in other European populations.

The ultimate causes of the ongoing recovery of wolf populations in western countries result from the ecological and social changes deriving from the urbanization of society (Mech 1995). In Spain, these changes include rural depopulation, the recovery of native vegetation, and an increase in wild ungulate populations (Blanco et al. 1992). At a regional scale, however, an understanding of why some areas have been recolonized and others have not requires a consideration of the effects of ecological and social barriers. Man-made and natural barriers can hinder wolf dispersal and recolonization (Paquet and Callaghan 1996; Carmichael et al. 2001; Blanco et al. 2005), but some social constraints, particularly damage to livestock, can impair public attitudes toward wolves, eventually jeopardizing their survival in some areas (Fritts et al. 2003).

Since 1987, we have surveyed the wolf populations in Spain, monitored their expansion, and assessed the features of the habitats recolonized by wolves (Blanco et al. 1992; Blanco 2001; Llaneza and Blanco 2005). In addition, we assessed the patterns of the damages to livestock caused by wolves in various regions, the relationship between the damage to livestock and husbandry practices, and how damage to livestock influences the public's perception of wolves (Blanco et al. 1992; Blanco and Cortés 2002; Blanco 2003). We have also radio-collared sixteen wolves in agricultural habitats to obtain general information on their ecology, including diet, territoriality, and habitat use (Cortés 2001; Blanco and Cortés 2007), and specific information on the impact of natural and man-made barriers on wolf movements and dispersal and on the population expansion (Blanco et al. 2005; Blanco and Cortés 2007). Our results demonstrate that the wolf population in Spain has increased in numbers and distribution and that ecological and social factors promote expansion in some areas and retard it in others. The ecological factors are mainly associated with habitat. Apparently, favourable habitat for wolves is little modified and has high proportions of forest and mountains, low human population density, and a high wild ungulate population density (Blanco 2001). Social factors are associated with the magnitude of damage to livestock, which depends on the husbandry practices used in different regions (Blanco et al. 1992; Blanco 2003).

In this chapter, we examine some unexpected patterns in the recent recovery of the wolf population in Spain. Wolves have expanded into some intensively modified agricultural areas previously thought unsuitable for them but have not recolonized some more natural areas, such as certain mountain ranges or the extensive wood pastures (in Spanish, *dehesas*) that extend along the border of Spain and Portugal. To understand these patterns, we studied the ecological and social factors that can affect wolf recovery. We evaluated the effect of man-made and natural barriers and of livestock damage on the patterns of wolf recovery in Spain, and we discuss the problems the Iberian population faces to further expand and join the Franco-Italian wolves that have reached the Pyrenees and to rescue the isolated southern population in the Sierra Morena. To assess the barrier effect on wolves, we have reviewed the literature in our study area, searching both for published and unpublished data. To understand the social conflicts caused by wolves, we evaluated the damage to livestock in three habitats where the recovery of the wolf population did not occur in a manner predicted, considering only the obvious ecological characteristics of the habitats.

STUDY AREA AND WOLF RECOVERY IN SPAIN

Factors Affecting Wolf Recovery in Spain

The Iberian Peninsula lies in southwestern Europe and is formed by two countries, Spain and Portugal. Spain covers 500,000 km^2 and has a human population of 44 million. With 88 inhabitants/km^2, it retains more natural areas than other nearby countries (Beaufoy 1998). The Sites of Community Importance in the Natura 2000 network occupy 22.6 per cent of Spain's territory, a much higher percentage than the European average (12.6%), only surpassed by Slovenia (33.2%) (European Commission 2006).

In 1971, under Spanish law, the status of wolves changed from "vermin" to "game species." In 1992, wolves living south of the River Duero (Fig. 1.2.1) were fully protected by the European Union's Habitat Directive. Wolves north of the River Duero are included in Annex V of the Habitat Directive (i.e., a game species). Since 2003, the European Union has permitted the autonomous region of Castile and León (Fig. 1.2.2) to

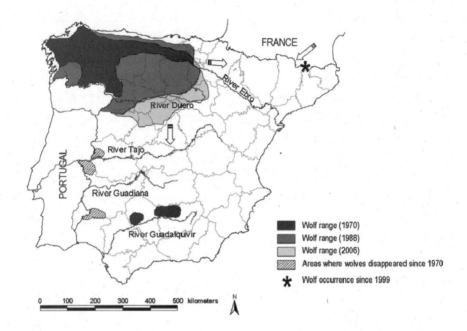

Figure 1.2.1. Wolf distribution in Spain in 1970 (Valverde 1971), 1988 (Blanco et al. 1992) and 2006 (J.C.B. and Y.C., unpublished data). In dark gray, wolf distribution in 1970; mid-gray, range increase from 1970 to 1988; light gray, range increase from 1988 to 2006. Major rivers are shown. The arrows represent the probable directions of wolf expansion.

cull wolves south of the River Duero in areas that have experienced severe damages to livestock, as long as the cull does not harm the general wolf population. Actually, the only population strictly protected is in the Sierra Morena, southern Spain (Fig. 1.2.1). In recent years, public support for wolf conservation has increased, management is predominately based on scientific data, and law enforcement has improved, but illegal killing remains widespread. Wolf management is under the jurisdiction of the autonomous regions, which make the decisions about hunting quotas, wolf control, and compensation for damage (Blanco et al. 1992). Hunting and culling intensity are generally proportional to the amount of damage to livestock (Blanco 2005). In a human dimension survey carried out in 1997 in Cantabria, 71.7 per cent of the urban people, but just 28.4 per cent of rural people, expressed positive attitudes toward wolves (Blanco and Cortés 2002).

Characteristics of Wolf Recovery

Until the late nineteenth century, wolves occupied almost the entire Iberian Peninsula. Then the population started to decline, and by about 1970, it was at its minimum. At that time, the last wolves in Spain were restricted to the northwest, particularly Galicia, the Cantabrian Mountains, and Zamora (Fig. 1.2.2). In addition, a few isolated nuclei survived along the border with Portugal and in Sierra Morena, in southern Spain (Valverde 1971). Since then, the northwestern population has recovered rapidly, but all the isolated nuclei except that of Sierra Morena became extinct. In 1987 and 1988, the first detailed nationwide survey showed that wolves had increased notably, occupying an area of 100,000 km² (Blanco et al. 1992). In 2001, a new survey showed that the distribution range of wolves had increased by another 20 per cent and had expanded southward from the River Duero (Llaneza and Blanco 2005) (Fig. 1.2.1). In 2007, Spain retained a large continuous population centred in the northwest, which occupied about 120,000 km² and consisted of at least 260 packs, probably representing some 2,000 wolves. Castile and León has 56 per cent, Galicia 25 per cent, and Asturias 14 per cent of the Spanish wolves (for details on regional surveys, see Blanco 2004). In addition, a small endangered population of some 5–10 packs persists in the Sierra Morena (R. Carrasco, personal communication), isolated since the 1970s. Since 1971, the distribution area in Spain has at least doubled and the total number of wolves has probably increased four-fold. In addition, since about 1999, a few wolves from the Franco-Italian population have colonized the eastern Pyrenees (Valière et al. 2003; J. Ruiz-Olmo, personal communication) (Fig. 1.2.1). These wolves are about 400 kilometres and 450 kilometres away from the closest Spanish and French breeding packs, respectively.

During this recovery process, wolves have expanded eastward and southward, and they have extensively colonized apparently inappropriate

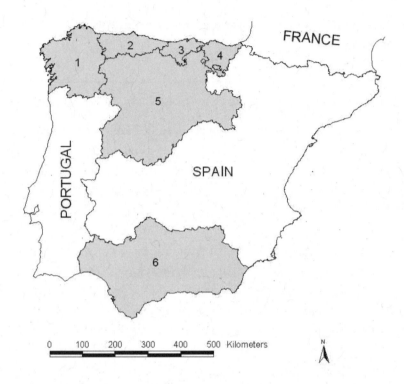

Figure 1.2.2. Autonomous regions cited in the text. (1) Galicia; (2) Asturias; (3) Cantabria; (4) Basque Country; (5) Castile and León; and (6) Andalusia.

agricultural habitats. Since 1988, however, the eastward expansion has been blocked in the Demanda Mountains and in the Basque Country (Fig. 1.2.2), which has prevented the recolonization of the Pyrenees. In addition, toward the southwest, the expansion has been blocked in the *dehesa*s of Salamanca (Fig. 1.2.3). Considering only ecological characteristics, it is difficult to explain these apparent inconsistencies. For instance, in some natural areas that have a low human population density, such as mountains and *dehesa*s, high vegetation cover and abundant populations of wild ungulates and livestock, wolves have not prospered or population expansion has stopped. By contrast, in recent years, wolves have flourished in agricultural habitats that have limited vegetation cover, very small populations of

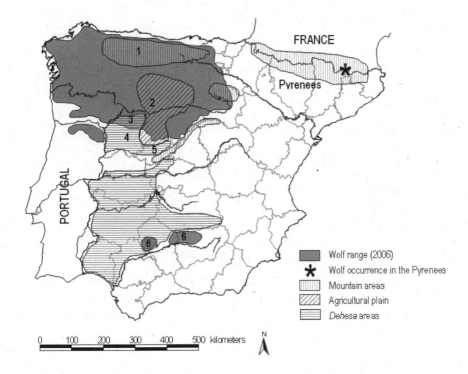

Figure 1.2.3. Current wolf range and habitats cited in the text. (1) Cantabrian Mountains; (2) study area in the agricultural plain; (3) *dehesa* area in Zamora, (4) in Salamanca, and (5) in Ávila provinces; and (6) Sierra Morena wolf population.

natural prey, and high human and road densities (Blanco et al. 2005; Boitani and Ciucci, this volume).

If ecological characteristics of areas do not seem to be responsible for these counterintuitive patterns, they may be caused by social factors associated with livestock husbandry, wolf damages to livestock, and the resulting human-caused mortality of wolves. We studied wolf–human conflicts in three areas where the patterns of wolf population recovery are inconsistent with natural habitat characteristics: the agricultural plain, where wolves prosper despite its ecological limitations, and mountain and *dehesa* areas, which constitute apparently favourable areas that wolves often fail to recolonize.

The Agricultural Plain in Castile and León

The agricultural plain (Fig. 1.2.3) is a flat, almost treeless landscape, largely comprised of cereal and maize fields, and it has a human population density of 10–40 inhabitants/km². Only 7 per cent of the area is covered by small patches (15–35 km²) of remnant forests. Wild boar (*Sus scrofa*), the only wild ungulate in the area, are common in the remnant forests (about one animal/km²) and almost absent in other areas. Livestock carrion is the staple of the wolf's diet (for a detailed description of the area, see Blanco et al. 2005).

Mountain Areas of Cantabria

The mountain area of Cantabria (800–2,000 m) has extensive beech (*Fagus sylvatica*) and oak (*Quercus* spp.) forests on abrupt terrain (Fig. 1.2.2 and 1.2.3). In 60 per cent of the area, population density is < 10 persons/km² and, elsewhere, 10–50 persons/km². Wild prey is abundant. In the nearby Somiedo Natural Park, there are 2.92 red deer (*Cervus elaphus*), 2.38 chamois (*Rupicapra pyrenaica*), 1.17 wild boar, and 0.55 roe deer (*Capreolus capreolus*)/km² (C. Nores, personal communication). Wolf diet in Cantabria comprises 60.6 per cent wild ungulates and 39.4 per cent livestock (J.C.B. and Y.C., unpublished data).

The "Dehesa" Area

This savannah-like wood pasture consists of grassland with scattered trees, containing 10–25 persons/km². The *dehesa* is a traditional type of habitat comprising temperate and rainy areas of western Spain (Fig. 1.2.3), where the rearing of livestock occurs with other land uses (e.g., crops, cork and acorn production). Livestock (cattle, sheep, and pigs) feed and sleep out in the field for most of the year, within private estates separated by stone walls, and are very vulnerable to predation by wolves. Wild boar and roe deer density is intermediate between those in the Cantabrian Mountains and those in the agricultural plain. Wolf diet has never been assessed here.

METHODS

The Effect of Man-made and Natural Barriers

To assess the barrier effect on wolves, we reviewed the published and unpublished data reported for our study area. In addition, we used the movement data from one adult female wolf fitted with a Global Position System (GPS) Global System for Mobile communications (GSM) collar in the agricultural plain (Fig. 1.2.3), thirteen kilometres away from the A-6, a four-lane, fenced highway. These kinds of radio-collars are equipped with a GPS that provides very accurate locations, which are transmitted to the scientist's computer by the GSM. We used data recorded from 31 May 2005 to 31 September 2006. The collar was programmed to obtain a minimum of two fixes per day (at 4:00 and at 12:00) and an intensive twenty-four-hour monitoring (one fix per hour) every ten days. For details on radio-collaring, monitoring, and highway characteristics, see Blanco et al. (2005).

Damage to Livestock and Wolf Surveys

To obtain a general picture of the damage to livestock caused by wolves in Spain, we estimated the annual cost in every Spanish autonomous region. In Galicia, the available statistics cover a small part of the actual damages, and our estimate is based on the opinion of regional experts and on extrapolation from similar habitats. In Asturias, Andalusia (Sierra Morena), the Basque Country, most of Cantabria, and in the hunting reserves of Castile and León (Fig. 1.2.2), the governments of the autonomous regions compensate farmers for livestock damage after verification by wardens, and reliable statistics are available, although in most cases this information is unpublished. In the autonomous region of Castile and León, south of the River Duero, the regional government provides partial compensation for losses incurred by farmers who have taken out insurance for the livestock (the insurance company pays the remainder), and the official unpublished statistics give an indication of the overall amount of damage.

Elsewhere in Castile and León, we identified three habitats in which damage patterns are rather consistent (Blanco et al. 1990; this study): 1) the mountainous areas of the Cantabrian Mountains and the east of the autonomous region; 2) the forest transition between the plain and the mountains, immediately south of the Cantabrian Mountains; 3) the agricultural plain in the centre and the south of the region. We have accurate data on the damages incurred in these three habitats collected in Zamora province by Talegón (2002), in the agricultural plain of the provinces of Valladolid and Zamora collected by the authors (see below), and in the mountainous habitat and the forest transition habitat through the statistics of the hunting reserves of several provinces (Llaneza and Blanco 2002). These data permitted us to estimate the average amount of damage caused per wolf pack in each of the three habitats. For each province, the amount of damage was estimated by multiplying these estimates by the number of wolf packs (Llaneza and Blanco 2005) in each type of habitat.

In addition, we have collected detailed data on livestock damage and wolf numbers in the three areas described in the "Study Area" section. Although the data were recorded in different years, we think they represent the general trends in these areas.

Agricultural Plain in Castile and León

In 1999, we assessed wolf-caused livestock damage by interviewing 129 sheep shepherds and three cattle owners, i.e., most of the livestock farmers living within the range of four wolf packs. To estimate the number of wolves and home range sizes, since 1997, we have monitored thirteen radio-collared wolves (Blanco et al. 2005).

Mountain Areas of Cantabria

We carried out fieldwork during 1997–98. We interviewed 84 farmers throughout the wolf range, and we analyzed the official compensation statistics from 1986 to 1997, particularly those from 1997, because they were the most accurate data and that was when we surveyed the wolf population. To estimate pack numbers, we used information on livestock damage and sightings by locals; we searched for wolf signs and used the simulated howling method to identify rendezvous sites (Harrington and Mech 1982).

Dehesa Areas in the Province of Ávila

In 2002, we assessed livestock damage by interviewing 114 farmers within the wolf range and analyzing official statistics. We estimated wolf numbers and range by monitoring one radio-collared wolf and using the same methods as those used in Cantabria.

To compare the proportions of each type of livestock that was depredated relative to their abundance, we used a chi-square test. All the monetary figures were converted into current currency in December 2005, considering inflation. In November 2006, €1 = US$1.32 = CDN$1.50.

RESULTS

Physical or social barriers might constrain wolf population recovery and range expansion. Physical barriers can be natural (e.g., high mountains, rivers) or artificial (e.g., roads or other infrastructures). In addition, there are social barriers, such as those derived from wolf persecution by man. In Europe and in other areas occupied by wolves, this persecution is mainly triggered by wolf predation on livestock. In the following sections, we assess the impact that ecological barriers and socio-economic constraints can have on wolf population recovery in Spain.

Man-made Barriers

Several studies have shown that fenced highways are not an absolute barrier for wolf dispersal. In the agricultural plain of north-central Spain, we examined the impact of a fenced, four-lane highway that runs along a flat, almost treeless area and lacks wildlife crossing facilities. From March 1997 to October 2001, the four radio-collared wolves living < 15 kilometres from the highway (including residents and dispersers, males and females, young and adults) crossed it between 4.4 and 33.3 per cent of the monitoring days, using vehicle bridges. In our study segment, there were thirty-one asphalted bridges for vehicles over the highway (0.53 bridges/km), fourteen of them (45%) connecting unpaved forest roads and seventeen (55%) connecting paved roads. All bridges were 50–70 metres long and 8–12 metres wide with no specific adaptations for wildlife crossing. Moreover, the four highways we have studied have not delayed expansion of the increasing wolf population, suggesting that highways are not an important barrier for wolves in that region (Blanco et al. 2005).

In addition, other studies carried out in Spain, France, and Italy have shown that wolves can cross four-lane highways that are also bordered by fences. During a genetic survey undertaken in the Basque Country (northern Spain, Fig. 1.2.2), Echegaray et al. (2006) collected scats from a female that had crossed the Bilbao-Zaragoza motorway at least twice, adjacent to a railway line. Mata et al. (2005) and C. Mata (personal communication) also found that wolves used the crossing structures of a highway in Zamora (northwestern Spain). Valière et al. (2003), using molecular analysis of scats, monitored the expansion of the French wolf population. Wolves were first detected in the French Alps in 1992 and in the eastern Pyrenees in 1999. To cover this 500-kilometre distance, wolves had to cross at least three major fenced highways and many other important roads. In 2004, Ciucci and Boitani (L. Boitani, personal communication) monitored a male wolf fitted with a GPS GSM collar that in a few months moved extensively across the border between Italy and France and crossed at least three fenced highways and many other important roads. In North America, specific studies have shown that wolves regularly cross the fenced, four-lane Trans-Canada highway in Banff National Park (Paquet and Callaghan 1996; Clevenger and Waltho 2005) and the unfenced, four-lane highway studied in Wisconsin by Kohn et al. (1999). In addition, long-range dispersal events have been described in which three radio-collared wolves crossed numerous interstate highways (Merrill and Mech 2000).

Nevertheless, highways can constitute a semi-permeable barrier for wolf movements (Paquet and Callaghan 1996). Sometimes, highways circumscribe wolf territories and some individuals may avoid crossing them.

This is the case of an adult female wolf that we radio-collared with a GPS GSM transmitter (Fig. 1.2.4). From June 2005 to September 2006 (1,689 locations), she was only detected once crossing the fenced, four-lane highway that other wolves crossed regularly in previous years (Blanco et al. 2005).

Natural Barriers

In Spain there appear to be no natural barriers capable of stopping the expansion of the wolf population, although some habitats are more appropriate for wolves than are others. A few decades ago, it was thought that wolves could not survive in treeless agricultural habitats that had few wild ungulates. During most of the twentieth century, even in its first half when wolves occurred throughout most of Spain, there were no wolves in agricultural areas (Valverde 1971). In places where vegetation cover is limited, wolves could be easily located and killed, which prevented the maintenance of a stable population. Thus, most of the naturalists were led to believe that these agricultural areas were unsuitable for wolves (Blanco et al. 1990). However, our research with sixteen radio-collared wolves in these habitats demonstrated that the wolves can feed on livestock carcasses, form packs that persisted at least seven years in territories with < 1 per cent tree cover, colonize most of the agricultural area with densities of 2.5–3 wolves/100 km^2, and expand into adjacent areas. Thus, a scarcity of wild prey and of natural conditions does not necessarily deter the permanent presence of wolf populations (Cortés 2001; Blanco et al. 2005; Blanco and Cortés 2007).

Mountains do not seem to be an obstacle for wolves either, as they can live at elevations higher than 4,500 metres in the Himalayas (Fox and Chundawat 1995) and even in the High Arctic (Mech 1998a). In Spain, it was previously thought that wolves were unable to survive in high mountains because throughout most of the twentieth century they were absent from the Pyrenees and the Picos de Europa Mountains (Valverde 1971). Currently, however, wolves are breeding in the Picos de Europa National Park at elevations of > 2,000 metres (Palacios 1997), in alpine habitats

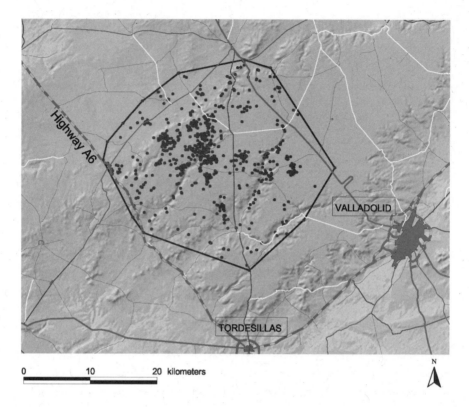

Figure 1.2.4. Home range of a radio-collared wolf in relation to a four-lane, fenced highway (A6) and other roads.

above the tree line. Similarly, the wolves from the Franco-Italian population have reached the French Pyrenees (Valière et al. 2003) and from there, the Spanish side, where they have been detected using genetic analysis of scats (J. Ruiz-Olmo, personal communication). The Spanish mountains, which peak at 3,400 metres, are unlikely to pose an obstacle for such an adaptable species as the wolf.

In other studies undertaken round the world, no topographic barriers for wolves have been found. Carmichael et al. (2001) showed that gene flow is significantly reduced across the Mackenzie River and the Amundsen Gulf, but they concluded that the migration patterns of the caribou (*Rangifer tarandus*) may be the primary determinant of wolf population structure.

Mixed Barriers

Sometimes, man-made and natural barriers occur together, and their combined effects can complicate dispersal and the expansion of wolf populations. Such is the case with the River Duero (Fig. 1.2.1), which crosses the Iberian Peninsula and, for almost two decades, has formed the southern border of wolf distribution (Blanco et al. 2005). The River Duero corridor is a good example of the addition of one natural and several man-made barriers.

From 1997 to 1999, we radio-collared eight wolves living within five kilometres from the River Duero corridor, which comprises the river itself (50–100 m wide), plus one road, one railway, and two channels that run along it and maybe multiply its barrier effect. Wolves were monitored a total of 56.8 months (mean: 7.1 months; range: 2–17 months) living < 10 kilometres from the river. Only three of the eight wolves were detected crossing the river, and two of these three started to cross it only after a week of extensive military manoeuvres carried out in the forest where the wolves had their main rendezvous sites. In addition, the River Duero corridor seems to have delayed wolf expansion in Spain for about fifteen years, which suggests that it is a semi-permeable barrier for wolves (Blanco et al. 2005). Furthermore, a recent genetic survey showed that the wolf population in Portugal is structured in two subpopulations separated by the River Duero. The genetic variability of the wolves sampled north of the River Duero (where there are fifty-four packs) was higher than that of those sampled south of the river (nine packs) (Godinho et al. 2005), which suggests that the river (and maybe the disturbed habitats alongside it) acts as a barrier for wolf dispersal and might be preventing the rescue of the small southern population by dispersers from the northern population.

These studies suggest that the combination of several small barriers can have synergistic effects, creating a much stronger barrier effect. A pattern of obstacles similar to that described along the River Duero is common along a large part of other major Iberian and European rivers, which may be important barriers for wolves and other large mammals (Blanco et al. 2005).

Wolf Depredation on Livestock in Spain

Damage to livestock is the main factor promoting the persecution of wolves worldwide (Mech 1995); thus, the knowledge of the patterns of livestock damages can help us to understand why wolves flourish in some areas and are absent from others. In 1988, annual damages caused by wolves to livestock in Spain were estimated at nearly US$1 million (US$1.94 million = €1.4 million in 2005, considering inflation) and was unevenly distributed. Mountain areas, where livestock are usually grazed unattended, suffered 77.0 per cent of the losses of the whole country but supported only 20.6 per cent of Spain's wolves (Blanco et al. 1992). We estimate that the damage in 2005 cost almost €1.9 million, although the estimate is partially based on incomplete data and contains many extrapolations (Table 1.2.1).

Considering that there are some 2,000 wolves for Spain, an average wolf would cost €940 per year.

We have also studied in detail the damages in three habitats where the patterns of wolf abundance are inconsistent with the expectations based on the ecological characteristics of the habitats. We suggest that the number of wolves in these areas is mainly determined by the persecution triggered by the damages to the livestock. If this is correct, the damages in agricultural areas, where wolves flourish despite the apparently unfavourable habitat conditions, should be lower that the national average, and the damages in the mountain and the *dehesa* areas, where wolves are less abundant than expected based on the ecological characteristics of the habitat, should be above the national average.

Livestock damage and management in the agricultural plain of Castile and León

In the agricultural plain (Fig. 1.2.3), sheep are the predominant livestock. We interviewed 129 shepherds in Valladolid and Zamora provinces who work within the territories of four packs with radio-collared wolves. The average flock size was 308.5 (±140.89) sheep and the average number of herding dogs was 1.94 (±1.00). In addition to the herding dogs, 40.2 per cent of the flocks were guarded by Spanish mastiff dogs (mean, 2.1 ±1.01),

Table 1.2.1. Cost of wolf damage to livestock and number of detected packs in the Spanish autonomous regions.

REGION[A]	DAMAGE (€)	NO. OF DETECTED PACKS[B]
GALICIA (1)	300,000	68
ASTURIAS (2)	550,000	30
CANTABRIA (2)	125,000	5
León (3)	260,000	48
Zamora (4)	130,000	39
Salamanca (2)	35,000	1
Palencia (3)	130,000	28
Burgos (3)	130,000	24
Valladolid (5)	65,000	12
Soria (3)	30,000	3
Segovia (2,5)	22,000	6
Ávila (2,5)	40,000	2
CASTILE AND LEÓN (sum)	842,000	163
BASQUE COUNTRY (2)	30,000	2
CASTILLA LA MANCHA (2)	3,600	1
ANDALUSIA (2)	30,000	5
TOTAL	1,880,600	260

Source of data: (1) estimate (official statistics cover a small part of actual damages); (2) unpublished official statistics; (3) extrapolated from Talegón (2002), Llaneza and Blanco (2002), and this study; (4) Talegón (2002); (5) estimated from interviews with shepherds (this study). Data on wolf populations, reviewed by Blanco (2004).
A In small letters, the provinces of Castile and Leon region.
B The total number does not equal the sum of the packs because some packs are shared by different provinces or regions.

Table 1.2.2. Wolf damage to livestock in the three areas considered in this study.

	Agricultural plain of Castile	Mountains of Cantabria	Dehesas of Ávila
Sheep/goat predated	61	521	227
Cattle predated	10	61	19
Horses predated	0	35	0
Total cost of damages*	10,338	78,874	27,783
No. of wolves	40	35	15
Cost per wolf per year *	258	2,254	1,852
Average sheep killed per attack	5.55 ±15.65	3.70 ± 4.88	19.95 ±14.77
Average cattle killed per attack	–	1.07 ± 0.30	1.18 ± 0.54
Average horses killed per attack	–	1.11 ± 0.40	–

* In euro, currency of 2005.

a breed specifically selected to protect the livestock against wolves. Most herds (87.9%) spent the night in indoor pens, and the others did so in corrals (outside pens), all the latter guarded by mastiff dogs. During the day, the herds grazed outside for an average of 5.9 hours (±1.92) in summer and 1.4 hours (±2.87) in winter and were always attended by shepherds and dogs. In addition, there were three herds of cattle that grazed and spent the night unattended in large pastures that were accessible to wolves.

In 1999, about forty wolves killed sixty-one sheep and ten cattle, and only 5.4 per cent of the farmers interviewed suffered losses. The average annual cost per wolf was about one-quarter the national average, and only 10–15 per cent of the cost of wolves in mountain and *dehesa* areas (Table 1.2.2). The average number of sheep killed per attack was also low. Wolves killed 0.15 per cent of the 38,961 sheep and 1.07 per cent of the 930 cattle censussed (chi square = 42.61, df = 1; $p < 0.0001$). Cattle were killed disproportionately, probably because they were less protected than sheep. From 1997 to 1999, only two wolves in the four packs we studied were legally hunted, and at least two more wolves were illegally killed.

Livestock damage and management in the mountain area of Cantabria

In this area, the predominant livestock is cattle, which graze unattended on open ranges in mountains from May to October. During the grazing season, farmers visit their flocks between once a day and once a week. They sometimes use mastiff dogs to guard the flocks but, typically, the cattle are scattered in the mountains, which reduces the effectiveness of the dogs.

In 1997, about thirty-five wolves living in Cantabria killed about 521 sheep and goats, sixty-one cattle, and thirty-five horses. The annual cost per wolf was 2.4 times greater than the national average (Table 1.2.2). In the decade 1987–96, in the most affected municipalities, 28–50 per cent of the livestock producers suffered losses caused by wolves. Within the wolf distribution area, 4.43 per cent of the enumerated sheep, 0.27 per cent of the cattle, and 1.52 per cent of the horses were killed by wolves every year. The average number of sheep killed per attack was the lowest of the three areas (Table 1.2.2). Seventy-nine per cent of the cattle and 89 per cent of the horses killed by wolves were less than one year old. In Cantabria, in 1997, seventeen wolves were killed legally, and six were found dead from other causes.

Livestock damage management in the *dehesa* area of Ávila province.

In the *dehesa* area (Fig. 1.2.3), cattle predominate but sheep are also abundant. A large part of the livestock grazes unprotected during most of day and night. Mastiff dogs are seldom used to protect the livestock. We surveyed the livestock damage in an area with one breeding wolf pack and perhaps a few wolves that were not part of the pack. In 2002, approximately 227 sheep and nineteen cattle were killed by wolves. The cost per wolf per year was 2.5 times higher than the national average. The number of sheep killed per attack was also high (Table 1.2.2). From November 2004 to October 2006, eight wolves were legally culled, and cars killed at least three wolves. In 2006, there were two known packs in the province.

DISCUSSION

Natural and man-made barriers can affect wolf movements and population recovery, e.g., the River Duero corridor (Blanco et al. 2005; Godinho et al. 2005). In other cases, stagnation of the population expansion apparently is caused by the additive effects of wolf persecution triggered by high livestock damages and severe habitat loss, as may happen in the Basque Country (Fig. 1.2.2). In many cases, however, high damages to livestock alone are enough to prevent wolves from expanding into ecologically suitable habitats, and low livestock damages favour population expansion into habitats that are apparently unsuitable for wolves. In the last twenty years, the Spanish wolf population has experienced its greatest expansion into agricultural habitats that are almost depleted of wild ungulates, have little vegetation cover, and a high density of roads and other man-made infrastructures. In contrast, in mountain areas that are free from man-made barriers, have high densities of wild ungulates, and small human populations, and in the rather well-preserved *dehesa* areas (the savannah-like wood pasture where livestock graze unguarded), wolves have hardly expanded since 1988. These counterintuitive results underscore the strong effect that social factors can have on a wolf population's recovery.

Livestock damages are estimates but, within habitats, they are quite consistent among regions and provinces. For example, in 2003, in Asturias, a region adjacent to Cantabria (Fig. 1.2.2) which has similar habitats characterized by the presence of mountains, forests, and high densities of wild ungulates, the cost of damage caused by some thirty wolf packs in 2003 was €513,000 (equivalent to €549,423 in 2005, Table 1.2.1) (Llaneza et al. 2005; O. Hernández, personal communication), i.e., an average of €2,289 per wolf per year, which is very similar to the cost per wolf in Cantabria (€2,254). Although wolves in Asturias are culled at much lower rates than they are in Cantabria, and their densities are three times higher, the damage cost per wolf differs little, which suggests that it depends on the type of livestock husbandry, rather than on wolf management or wolf population density. Another example of consistency is the damage costs incurred in three *dehesa* areas in different provinces. In Salamanca province,

Table 1.2.3. Damage to livestock caused by wolves in four countries of south-western Europe and two areas of the United States.

	SPAIN	PORTUGAL	FRANCE	ITALY	MINNESOTA	WEST USA
Damages	€1.9 M	€700,000	€1 M	€1.9 M	€61,380	€70,000*
Wolf numbers	2,000	350	100–120	500	2,500	666
Damages/wolf	€940	€2,000	€9,000	€3,800	€24.5	€105
Management	Game species	Protected No culling	Protected Culling	Protected No culling	Protected Culling	Protected Culling
Author	This study	I. Barroso, pers. comm.	Celdran and Moraud 2006	Ciucci and Boitani 2005	Mech 1998a	Bangs et al. 2005

* Estimated from data provided by Bangs et al. (2005).

in 2003–2005, the annual average damage caused by wolves was about €24,660 (regional government of Castile and León, unpublished data), i.e., some €2,055 per wolf per year (assuming twelve wolves). In the *dehesa* area of Zamora province, the cost per wolf per year was €1,803 (€63,105 and thirty-five wolves; Talegón 2002). These results are very similar to those obtained by the authors (€1,852 per wolf per year) in the *dehesa* area of Ávila province (Fig. 1.2.3, Table 1.2.2).

The annual cost per wolf in livestock damage in Spain (€940) is higher than it is in North America. For example, in the late 1980s, annual livestock losses caused by about 50,000 wolves in North America were estimated to be US$280,000–320,000 (Carbyn 1987). In 2002, 666 wolves in the northwestern United States killed just 58 cattle, 102 sheep, and 9 dogs (Bangs et al. 2005), with an estimated cost of €70,000. In addition, in

1997 in Minnesota (2,500 wolves), compensation for wolf-caused livestock damage was US$46,500 (Mech 1998b). The cost per wolf in livestock damage in Spain appears to be lower than it is in other countries in south-western Europe. For example, in Portugal (300–400 wolves), compensation for livestock damage in 2006 was about €700,000 per year (I. Barroso, personal communication), and, in 2005, in France (100–120 wolves), it was almost €1 million (Celdran and Moraud 2006). In the period 1991–95, in Italy (> 500 wolves), annual compensation payouts averaged almost €1.9 million (Ciucci and Boitani 2005) (Table 1.2.3).

In Spain, the distribution of damage to livestock is shaped by socio-ecological factors (Blanco et al. 1992). The open countryside in the mountain and *dehesa* areas of northern and western Spain, respectively, is very appropriate for letting livestock graze unattended. There, the rainy weather provides green grass during much of the year, and there is enough room for the livestock to roam without harming crops. This type of husbandry saves shepherd salaries and allows the livestock owners to have a second job, making livestock raising more profitable (Sebastián 1997; Zamora and Ortuño 2003). Guard dogs are inefficient when livestock is scattered, and other measures to prevent wolf predation are comparatively difficult to implement (Breitenmoser et al. 2005), so livestock suffer high damage rates, which in general are compensated partially or fully by regional governments. Damage compensation payments and subsidies support the farmers, but they keep the wolf–human conflict in a chronic state. To encourage habitation and economic activity in marginal agricultural habitats, the subsidies to farmers, which mainly are provided by the European Union, have increased in the last twenty years and have therefore contributed to an important increase in the numbers of livestock (Spanish Statistics Institute 2007). As a result, the percentage of livestock insufficiently guarded and vulnerable to wolf depredation has also increased, which has fuelled the conflict in some of the regions where wolves have become re-established.

In contrast, in the agricultural plain, flocks must always be attended by shepherds to prevent them from invading crops, private estates, and roads. Therefore, when wolves colonize these areas, a few minor improvements (e.g., mastiff dogs, proper protection during the night) are sufficient adjustments to the new situation without great expense for the farmers. In the presence of a shepherd, wolves rarely attack the sheep flocks during the day. In the agricultural plain, there are many sheep herds that graze near the rendezvous sites of packs with radio-collared wolves but they are seldom attacked by the wolves (J.C.B. and Y.C., unpublished data). For this reason, the livestock owners of this area are rather tolerant toward wolves, and this allows the packs to live and breed in very small forest patches or in cereal or maize fields. If the hostility toward wolves was higher, as it is in other regions of Spain, wolves would be quickly eradicated from these habitats, where there is limited protective cover.

Clearly, the amount of damage to livestock caused by wolves influences wolf survival. Livestock damages influence the attitudes of humans toward wolves, strongly influence wolf management, and, ultimately, determine the extent of human-caused wolf mortality. A human-dimensions study on the wolf conflict has shown that the hostility of livestock farmers toward wolves in three areas of Cantabria was proportional to the amount of damage to livestock. In addition, the livestock farmers of the agricultural plain of Castile and León were less hostile toward wolves than were the farmers in Cantabria, which suffered greater damage (Blanco and Cortés 2002). These attitudes are reflected in the data on wolf persecution. In our study, 1.3 per cent, 25.0 per cent, and 48.6 per cent of the estimated number of wolves were officially killed each year in the agricultural plain, the *dehesa* area of Ávila province and the autonomous region of Cantabria, respectively, where annual cost of damages per wolf were €258, €1,852, and €2,254 (Table 1.2.2). These data suggest that the higher the damage costs per wolf, the greater the proportion of wolves killed. When other detected deaths (mainly, illegal killing and traffic casualties) in each region are included in the total, minimum annual mortality rates reach 2.5 per cent, 34.3 per cent and 57.5 per cent. We had a closer look at wolf mortality by means of a radio-telemetry study, which is the only way to assess mortality accurately. In the agricultural plain of Castile and León, the annual mortality rate of the wolves fitted with radio-collars for 40.6 wolf-years was 18 per cent (Blanco and Cortés 2007). Most wolf populations decrease when annual mortality exceeds 34 per cent (Fuller et al. 2003), thus, these results illustrate why the population in the agricultural plain has increased, whereas most of the populations of mountain and *dehesa* areas have hardly expanded since 1988.

Because of its expansion, the large northwestern Iberian wolf population may rescue the small and endangered population of Sierra Morena and join the wolves that have reached the eastern Pyrenees from the Alps (Fig. 1.2.1). The recovery of the Sierra Morena population has considerable cultural and emotional value for the Spanish but has limited significance within the broader European context. Sierra Morena wolves are popular characters of many local legends and folk tales and, in Spain, they are perceived as an important ecological element in a region that maintains large natural forests, a low human population, very high densities of wild ungulates, mainly red deer (*Cervus elaphus*) (Blanco et al. 1990), and high biological diversity, including the critically endangered Iberian lynx (*Lynx pardinus*). Nevertheless, a few more wolf packs are of limited relevance to the European population, mainly because the Sierra Morena population is at a dead-end in the southwestern corner of Europe and without a possible connection to other wolf populations.

Nevertheless, the connection between the Iberian and the Franco-Italian populations would probably improve the genetic variability of both populations (Randi et al. 2000). We cannot predict whether the few wolves from the Alpine population that have been living in the eastern Pyrenees from at least 1999 to 2006 will eventually breed and expand. Even if they vanish, the wolf population in France is expanding southward (Valière et al. 2003), and it is likely that wolves will continue to appear in the Pyrenees, which would allow the formation of an intermediate outpost between the Iberian and the Alpine populations. The patterns of wolf population recovery in Spain during the last thirty years have a predictive value. If habitat conditions remain stable, we can expect that the large river corridors will hinder the expansion of wolf populations. For example, along the length of the River Ebro, there is a dense transport network and disturbed habitats that might hamper the expansion toward the Pyrenees. To a lesser extent, the River Tajo corridor might impede the rescue of the Sierra Morena endangered population (Fig. 1.2.1). That said, the greatest problems will occur in the two areas that have the highest livestock damage. The *dehesa*s in western Spain probably will retard or prevent individuals from the northern population from encountering the isolated southern population in Sierra Morena (Fig. 1.2.3). In addition, the population expansion eastward would be hindered because of the livestock damage that will be incurred in the Pyrenees, even though they are relatively unpopulated mountains, with abundant forest and natural prey. In the last sixty years, the sheep husbandry practices in these mountains has developed in a largely predator-free environment (there are just a few brown bears, *Ursus arctos*), and mimics the husbandry conditions described by Swenson and Andrén (2005) in Norway, which are greatly restricting the expansion of Scandinavian wolves and bears into Norway.

This wolf–human conflict may prevent the settlement of wolves in the Pyrenees, result in colonization only at low densities, or just permit limited interchange of dispersers between the main Iberian population and the individuals or packs that establish in the eastern Pyrenees. It is unlikely, however, that these conflicts will completely prevent the dispersal of wolves along the Pyrenees. In any case, conflicts over livestock damages probably would not be much worse than those observed in other countries in southwestern Europe, and almost certainly would be lower than those in the Scandinavia reindeer husbandry areas. In those areas, the Swedish and Norwegian management plans do not permit the permanent presence of wolves; only single wolves are permitted in the reindeer areas to allow the exchange of dispersers between the Scandinavian and the Fenno-Russian wolf populations (Wabakken et al. 2001; Swenson and Andrén 2005). However, the role of just a few dispersers can be important. The contribution of just three immigrants from Finland was enough to establish the present Scandinavian wolf population (Wabakken et al. 2001; Vilà et al. 2003a), although its genetic diversity is low and continues to decline each year (Liberg et al. 2005).

Anyway, the conflicts caused by high livestock damage may be mitigated using preventive measures (Breitenmoser et al. 2005), proper compensation for damages (Nyhus et al. 2005), and zoning (Linnell et al.

2005c) designed to minimize livestock depredation and maximize connectivity. In Spain, preventive measures, such as guarding mastiff dogs and electric fences, are being used in several regions, including the *dehesa* areas south of the River Duero, but their efficiency is very limited when the livestock is completely unattended. The regional governments partially or fully compensate for the damages to livestock (Blanco 2003), which might be reducing the animosity that farmers have toward wolves. Likewise, the region of Castilla y León is about to pass a wolf-management plan which includes zoning in which the hunting pressure will be proportional to the amount of damages to livestock.

Given the complexity of the interactions between the ecological and social factors to wolf recovery, it is crucial to integrate the ecology and the human dimension expertise to connect the currently isolated European wolf populations and, in this way, contribute to the recovery of the genetic diversity, which was lost during centuries of unrestrained persecution.

ACKNOWLEDGMENTS

We thank G. Garrote, M.A. Rodríguez, A. de la Fuente, J.M. García, and J. Rodríguez for field assistance. I. Barroso (ICN, Portugal), P. Degeorges (Ministry of the Environment, France), E. Rosa (government of Galicia), P. Cacho (government of Cantabria), L. Llaneza, and several officials from the Castile and León regional government provided unpublished data on livestock damage. C. Nores (University of Oviedo) gave us unpublished data on wild ungulate densities. B. Pliego prepared the figures, F.J. García and C. Prada corrected previous drafts of the manuscript and J. Muddeman and B. MacWhirter improved the English. The Spanish Ministry of the Environment (SME), the regional governments of Cantabria and Castile and León, and the University of Cantabria provided funding, logistical support, and unpublished information. B. Heredia and J.J. Areces helped in many aspects during this study. J.C.B. was supported by the General Directorate for Biodiversity (SME) and Tragsa during manuscript preparation.

1.3 Gray Wolf Conservation in the Great Lakes Region of the United States

Adrian P. Wydeven, Randle L. Jurewicz, Timothy R. Van Deelen, John Erb, James H. Hammill, Dean E. Beyer, Jr., Brian Roell, Jane E. Wiedenhoeft, and David A. Weitz

INTRODUCTION

The western Great Lakes region (Minnesota, Wisconsin, and Michigan) is the only portion of the United States south of Canada where gray wolves (*Canis lupus*) avoided extirpation during the twentieth century. Wolves persisted due to large areas of remote public forest, minimal human conflict (and hence less eradication effort), and connectivity to the adjacent and abundant Canadian wolf population. Additionally, modern conservation's earliest and most eloquent champions, including Sigurd Olson (Backes 1997), Aldo Leopold (Meine 1988), Milt Stenlund (Stenlund 1955), and Durward Allen (Allen 1979), took up the cause of recovery for Great Lakes wolves. Though never extirpated, wolf populations reached very low numbers in the mid-1900s. Efforts by these early wolf conservationists, and others who followed, saw a tremendous recovery of wolf populations during 1980s and 1990s in the region.

Wolves in Michigan, Minnesota, and Wisconsin share a similar history. Wolves likely colonized the Great Lakes when the glaciers retreated ten thousand years ago, following large grazing mammals, as did early human hunters. Un-glaciated regions in southwest Wisconsin and southeast Minnesota may have been continually occupied by gray wolves for most of the Pleistocene. Extensive settlement by Europeans began in the early 1800s. Southern Great Lakes forests were oak and maple-basswood interspersed with savannas in the east, and tall grass prairie in the west. Northern portions of the region were covered by mixed hardwood-conifer, and boreal forests. Wolf populations prior to European settlement were probably higher in the south where savannas and prairies supported higher biomass of ungulates including white-tailed deer (*Odocoileus virginianus*), elk (*Cervus elaphus*), and bison (*Bison bison*). Deer occurred as far north as Lake Superior, but at much lower densities. The mature forests of the north with their high conifer component and more severe winters contained low to moderate densities of moose (*Alces alces*) and sporadic small populations of woodland caribou (*Rangifer tarandus*). At the time of European settlement, the region may have contained 10,000–18,000 wolves (3,000–5,000 in Wisconsin [Wydeven et al. 1995]; 3,000–5,000 in Michigan based on similar sized area, and 4,000–8,000 in Minnesota [Mech 2000]).

European settlement spread westward in the early 1800s, and harvest of the northern forest enabled settlers to move north into the cutover land in the late 1800s and early 1900s. The U.S. Congress passed a wolf bounty in 1817 for the Northwest Territories that included the western Great Lakes region. Additional territory bounties were established for the Wisconsin territory in 1839 (Thiel 1993) and Minnesota territory in 1849 (Mech 2000). State bounties often began soon after statehood, beginning in 1838 in Michigan (Michigan Department of Natural Resources [DNR] 1997), and 1865 in Wisconsin (Thiel 1993). These bounties encouraged wolf killing, and, along with drastic reductions in wild ungulates due to year-round human hunting, caused intense declines in the wolf population. Wolves reached their lowest level in the 1950s and early 1960s, when the population in Minnesota fell to 350–700 (Fuller et al. 1992), wolves were extirpated in Wisconsin (Thiel 1993), and only a few scattered individuals remained in Michigan (Hendrickson et al. 1975).

Wolves were considered unprotected predators up to the 1950s throughout the region. The State of Wisconsin eliminated bounties and designated the gray wolf as a protected animal in 1957 (Thiel 1993), probably the first time the gray wolf was given regulatory protection in the United States.

Michigan followed suit with eliminations of its bounty in 1960 and full legal protection in 1965. Minnesota ended its bounty in 1965. Elimination of bounties and financial incentives for wolf control may have initiated recovery of the Great Lakes wolf population.

The eastern gray wolf was designated a federally endangered species in 1967 on the first list of endangered species created by the U.S. Fish and Wildlife Service, and again listed in 1974 under the 1973 federal Endangered Species Act (U.S. Fish and Wildlife Service 1992). Wolves were listed as state endangered species in 1975 in Wisconsin and in 1976 in Michigan. Wolves were listed as state threatened in Minnesota in 1984. The federal government downlisted wolves in Minnesota to threatened status in 1978 and downlisted in Michigan and Wisconsin in 2003. Wolves were returned to federally endangered status in Michigan and Wisconsin in 2005 due to a federal court decision in response to a suit by environmental groups who opposed the means for wolf reclassification used by the U.S. Fish and Wildlife Service. Thus throughout the last three decades wolves in the Great Lakes region have been managed under varying levels of federal and state legal classifications. Wolf classification and management are still uncertain in the region. The U.S. Fish and Wildlife Service delisted wolves from the federal list of endangered and threatened species in March 2007 and returned management authority to the three states. However, in September 2008 the U.S. District Court ruled in favor of the Humane Society and annulled the 2007 rule to delist the Gray Wolf in its Western Great Lakes Distinct Population Segment (DPS). Thus, authority on wolf management was remanded back to the U.S. Fish and Wildlife Service. Finally, in April 2009 the U.S. Fish and Wildlife Service published a Final Rule to delist the Gray Wolf - Western Great Lakes DPS.

Here, we examine the population growth and recolonization process of wolves in the western Great Lakes (Fig. 1.3.1) and the role that various conservation measures played in wolf recovery. We also summarize demographic data obtained through numerous research projects, and the use of such information in developing conservation and management plans for wolves.

STUDY AREA

The prairie, savannah, and oak forests of the southern Michigan, Minnesota, and Wisconsin have been converted to agricultural land with scattered woodlots and urban development. Most of the northern forest in the region was logged by the early 1900s. Efforts to convert these cut-over areas into agricultural land largely failed and most of the area reverted into second growth forest. Substantial portions are now under public ownership, particularly, national, state, and county forests, state and national wildlife areas, and state and national parks. The Boundary Waters Canoe Area Wilderness (BWCA) comprises 417,000 hectares in northeast Minnesota, along the Ontario boundary, and represents the largest wilderness area in the region. This area, along with adjacent protected areas in Minnesota and Ontario, provided core habitat for the residual wolf population that persisted into the 1950s and 1960s. Extensive second-growth forest across the rest of the northern Great Lakes held deer at relatively high numbers and allowed wolves to expand their range (Fig. 1.3.1). Moose populations also occur in northern parts of the region, predominately northern Minnesota, and were reintroduced to Upper Michigan in the mid-1980s. Small reintroduced populations of elk exist in local areas of northwest Minnesota and were reintroduced to northwest Wisconsin in 1995. Beaver (*Castor canadensis*) populations have recovered throughout the region from low numbers in the 1800s.

METHODS

Because of the different legal and demographic history, wolf conservation activities have varied among the three states. We compared wolf management within the three state areas, highlighting examples of successful recovery, but also exploring pitfalls to sound conservation. Minnesota's population was downlisted to federally threatened status in 1978; consequently, flexible management of wolf depredation occurred much earlier in

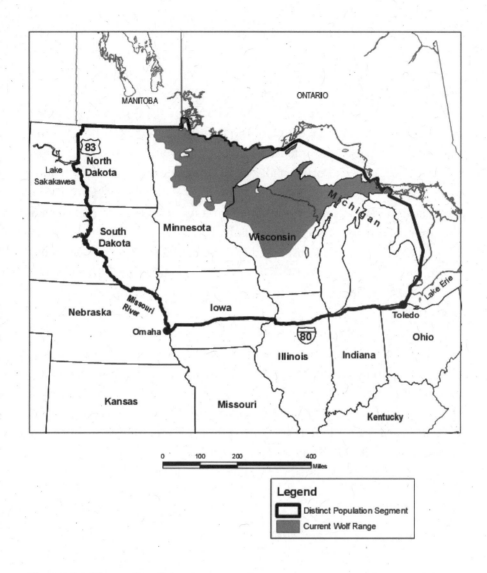

Figure 1.3.1. Western Great Lakes distinct population segment.

that state. Similar flexibility was not available in Wisconsin and Michigan until 2003.

We also compared the methods of estimating wolf numbers. Wolf populations have been surveyed annually since 1979 in Wisconsin (Wydeven et al. 1995) and since 1992 in Michigan (Potvin et al. 2005). In Wisconsin and Michigan, wolves are counted using a combination of radio-tracking on a subset of packs and intense snow track surveys on unmarked packs (Wydeven et al. 1995; Potvin et al. 2005). Complete counts of all individuals in the population were attempted based on aerial observations of collared packs and tracks in the snow from ground surveys. These represented minimum estimates of the population but probably under-estimated lone wolves. Counts in both states relied mainly on wildlife agency personnel, but in 1995 the Wisconsin DNR also created a volunteer carnivore tracking program to supplement data collected by agency personnel (Wydeven et al. 1996).

Minnesota DNR initially conducted extensive wolf surveys at about ten-year intervals, and more recently at about five-year intervals (Fuller et al. 1992; Erb and Benson 2004). Personnel from federal, state, county, and tribal conservation agencies were asked to report all observations of wolves and wolf signs during winter. These wolf observations, along with habitat information (human and road density), were used to estimate occupied wolf range in Minnesota. A sample of radio-collared individuals from research projects, across the wolf range, was used to estimate average pack and territory size, and eventually wolf densities within the estimated wolf range. Unlike minimum population estimates obtained in Wisconsin and Michigan, the methodology used in Minnesota produces confidence intervals by using observed variability in some of the survey parameters.

The labour-intensive radio-telemetry monitoring used in the Great Lakes allowed researchers to assess mortality factors affecting wolves across wolf range. Detecting mortalities during early years of the monitoring were dependent on repeated location of wolves at a discrete location, but since the early 1990s motion-sensitive mortality detectors were incorporated within radio-collars.

These detectors generally allowed recovery of dead wolves within one week of death, whereas early mortalities remained in the field for weeks before recovery and assessment. Death rates of actively monitored collared wolves were assumed to be the most unbiased assessment of overall population-level mortality. We used a combination of survival estimates on methods that assumed constant mortality within pre-defined time intervals (Heisey and Fuller 1985), and Kaplan-Meier methods that do not assume constant survival within a time intervals (Pollock et al. 1989).

Pup survival was determined in Wisconsin (Wisconsin DNR, unpublished data) from the estimated number of pups surviving to be counted during their first winter, number of breeding females, and a foetal rate of 5.2 foetuses/breeding female.

$$\check{S}_{pups} = N \div (N_{bf} \times 5.2)$$

Where $\check{S}_{pups}$ = pup survival through their first winter

N = pups alive during the first winter

N_{bf} = estimated number of breeding females the previous winter

Pups in winter were determined by knowledge of pack compositions from previous live-trapping, changes in pack composition between surveys, summer howl surveys, and reported observations of pack members. Breeding females were determined from winter surveys of packs showing breeding activity and assuming one breeding female per pack.

We examined the methods and assessment of wolf habitat across the region. Although presence of adequate prey and lack of human persecution are critical to survival for wolves (Fuller et al. 2003), road density often served as a reliable descriptor of suitable wolf habitat (Thiel 1985; Fuller et al. 1992; Mladenoff et al. 1995; Wydeven et al. 2001; Potvin et al. 2005). Road density by itself or in combination with human population density, deer density, and landscape composition were examined for predicting amount of suitable habitat for wolves in the Great Lakes region (Fuller et al. 1992; Mladenoff et al. 1995; Potvin et al. 2005) and were used to predict potential wolf numbers (Mladenoff et al. 1997).

Depredation management has been handled differently in the three states due to differences in legal status and wolf population size. Federal downlisting to threatened status in Minnesota enabled use of lethal control in 1978, but similar authority was not granted to Wisconsin and Michigan until 2003. Depredation management was examined by Fritts (1982) and Fritts et al. (1992) for Minnesota and by Treves et al. (2002) for Wisconsin. We compared depredation management and discuss recent developments for the three-state area.

State wolf-management plans were developed in Michigan in 1997 (Michigan DNR 1997), Wisconsin in 1999 (Wisconsin DNR 1999), and Minnesota in 2001 (Minnesota DNR 2001). In the United States, management of terrestrial mammals is the authority of the states unless species are designated federally endangered or threatened. We will examine the similarity and differences of the state plans because state plans will determine the long-term management of wolves once removed from federal designation.

RESULTS

Population Estimates and Growth Rates

The population of wolves in the western Great Lakes reached its lowest levels in the 1960s, near the end of the bounty systems, but showed continual, and at times rapid growth from the 1970s through to the 2000s (Table 1.3.1). Wolf populations in the region have experienced exponential growth and the Wisconsin and Michigan populations for the most part behaved as a single population (Fig. 1.3.2). Annual population growth in the 1990s was 37.4 per cent in Michigan (1990–99), 22.1 per cent in Wisconsin (1990–99), and 4.6 per cent in Minnesota (1989–98). The higher

Table 1.3.1. Gray Wolf Populations in the Great Lakes states, 1950–2005.

YEAR	MICHIGAN	MINNESOTA	WISCONSIN
1950	40–50[a]	430–637[c]	48[d]
1963	12–20[b]	350–700[c]	0?
1973	6[a]	500–1,000[c]	0?
1976	< 6	1,000–1,200[c]	2+
1979	?	1,235[c]	?
1980	?	~1,300	25
1989	3	1,521–1,710[c]	31
1998	139	2,450 ±500	178–184
2004	361	3,020 ±700	373–410
2005	405	~3,000	435–465

[a] Hendrickson et al. 1975.
[b] Mech 1970.
[c] Fuller et al. 1992.
[d] Thiel 1993.

growth rates in Michigan and Wisconsin reflected the rapid recolonization by wolves into previously vacant but suitable habitat (Mladenoff et al.
1995). Wolves in Minnesota were well-established by the 1990s, with less
vacant habitat to colonize, more intra-specific competition, and subject
to regular depredation control activities. Annual growth rates slowed in
the 2000s, to 12.3 per cent in Michigan (2000–2006), 11.1 per cent in
Wisconsin (2000–2006) and to 3.6 per cent in Minnesota (1998–2004).
Slower rates of population growth may indicate that wolves were beginning to fill most areas of suitable habitat.

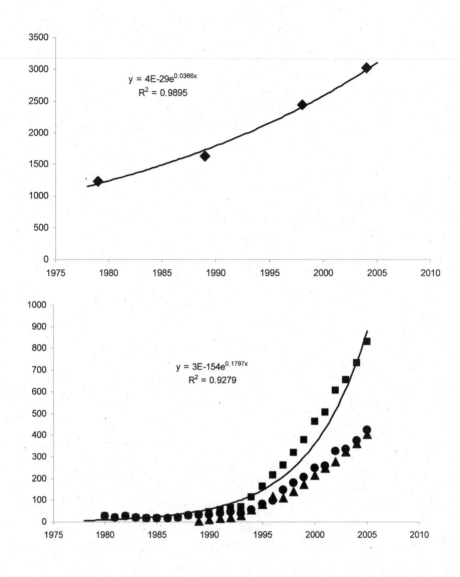

Figure 1.3.2. Time series of recent population growth of wolves in Minnesota (diamonds), northern Wisconsin (circles), and upper Michigan (triangles). Wisconsin and Michigan wolves likely comprise a single biological population (squares). Trend lines illustrate simple exponential growth in the discrete populations of Minnesota and combined regions of Wisconsin and Michigan.

The distribution of wolves in Minnesota had stopped expanding by the late 1990s. The estimated increase in the population estimate from 1998 to 2004 suggested an increase in wolf density, likely due to higher deer densities (Erb and Benson 2004). However, the Minnesota population estimates in 1998 and 2004 had coefficients of variation of about 18 per cent and 23 per cent, respectively, therefore limiting the strength of conclusions regarding population growth.

Because the Wisconsin and Michigan population estimates were based only on wolves detected, they represent minimum counts at a given point in time. These estimates were obtained in mid- to late winter, during the low point of the annual population cycle, and wolf numbers probably double each spring when pups are born.

Annual population estimates for Wisconsin (1980–2006) showed a population decline in the mid-1980s, coincident with a similar decline of wolves on Isle Royale (Peterson 1977). Population declines in both areas were believed to be due to outbreaks of canine parvovirus (Wydeven et al. 1995; Peterson et al. 1998). Minor declines occurred in Wisconsin in 1993 and in Michigan in 1997 and may have been linked to outbreaks of Sarcoptic mange, which was first detected in the Great Lakes region in 1991. Yearly fluctuations linked to mange were impossible to detect for Minnesota without annual surveys, but track-based indices indicate a mange related decline may have occurred in 2000–2001 (Minnesota DNR, unpublished data).

Survival Rates

Annual survival of adult wolves in Wisconsin averaged 0.71 (1979–94), and 0.76 (1995–2003). Earlier work in Wisconsin showed annual survival of wolves > 1 year to average 0.61 during population decline (1979–85), but increased to 0.82 during a three-fold increase in the population (1986–92; Wydeven et al. 1995). Illegal killing by humans accounted for 72 per cent of mortality of radio-collared wolves in Wisconsin prior to 1986, but from 1990 through 2002 the proportion of mortality attributed to illegal killing had declined to 26 per cent. Survival of wolves > 5 months old averaged

0.67 in north central Minnesota in the 1980s in a population that was relatively stable (Fuller 1989), and survival rates were 0.72 in the 1970s in Northwest Minnesota where wolves were increasing at 13 per cent annually (Fritts and Mech 1981). From 1999 to 2004, annual survival of radio-collared wolves in Upper Michigan (0.76) was similar to observed rates in Wisconsin about the same time and illegal killing accounted for 41 per cent of the observed mortality (Huntzinger et al. 2005).

Pup survival (as defined above) in Wisconsin averaged 0.30 (range 0.16 to 0.57). Lowest pup survival occurred in 1985 and 1986 when the wolf population declined due to parvovirus, and in 1993 when the population declined from high infestation rates of Sarcoptic mange. In recent years (1996–2004), a mean of 28 per cent of packs (range 19 to 37%) had no surviving pups by late winter in Wisconsin. Fuller (1989) estimated an annual survival rate of 0.37 for pups in north central Minnesota.

Habitat Predictors

Road density was demonstrated as a useful measure for predicting distribution of wolf pack territories in the Great Lakes region (Thiel 1985; Fuller et al. 1992; Mladenoff et al. 1995, 1997; Wydeven et al. 2001; Potvin et al. 2005). Road density generally correlates closely to human density and extent of forest cover, factors that also relate to wolf pack presence. Fuller et al. (1992) found that 88 per cent of wolf packs in Minnesota occurred either in townships with < 0.70 km roads/km^2 and < 4 humans/km^2, or < 0.50 km roads/km^2 and < 8 humans/km^2. Mladenoff et al. (1995) found that all wolf packs occurred in areas with a mean density of ≤ 0.45 km of road/km^2 in Wisconsin through the early 1990s. Potvin et al. (2005) found a mean road density of 0.30 km/km^2 for wolf packs in Michigan through the early 2000s, and determined a threshold density of 0.7 km/km^2 if deer density was adequate. Road density alone was not a good predictor of wolf occupancy in areas where prey density is limiting such as the deep snow regions of Upper Michigan (Potvin et al. 2005).

In the early 1990s Mladenoff et al. (1995) predicted future wolf distribution in the Great Lakes and by 2004 wolf distribution largely mirrored those predictions. The distribution of wolves in Minnesota stabilized by about 1998 (J. Erb, personal communication), close to the boundaries predicted by Mladenoff et al. (1995). Some areas that were predicted as poor quality habitat have been occupied by wolves, particularly in fragmented forest adjacent to suitable habitat, a pattern also described by Boitani and Ciucci and Blanco and Cortés for Europe (this volume). Although some packs in Wisconsin and Minnesota have moved into areas of mixed farmland and forest, most packs continued to occur in heavily forested areas.

Depredation Management

Management of wolf depredation became a major activity in Minnesota in 1975 following federal classification of wolves as endangered (Fritts 1982). Depredation management in Wisconsin became a major activity in the late 1990s (Treves et al. 2002) and only recently became important in Michigan. Prior to reclassification to threatened status in 1978, lethal control of wolves in Minnesota was prohibited; thus live-trapping and translocations were used on 108 wolves between 1975 and 1977 (Fritts 1982). After 1977, only pups captured prior to 1 August were released back to the wild. Consequently most wolves trapped at depredation sites were euthanized. From 1979 through 2006, the number of verified complaints in Minnesota ranged from 16 to 145 annually, and the number of farms experiencing wolf depredations on livestock or poultry ranged from 12 to 99. Verified complaints and farms with depredation in Minnesota peaked in 1998 and declined thereafter. Government trappers removed 38 wolves from depredation sites in Wisconsin between 1991 and 2002; 32 were translocated 52–277 kilometres away, 3 were released locally (< 10 km), 2 died in captivity, and 1 was euthanized. Annually, 0–67 verified depredation complaints were received from < 25 farms and from attacks on dogs in Wisconsin (1976–2006). Depredations in Wisconsin increased during the late 1990s and 2000s. In Michigan, 24 wolves associated with verified livestock depredations were trapped and relocated from 1998–2002; 14 were moved from 58–79 kilometres and 9 were moved > 160 kilometres. Fifty-six livestock depredation events were verified in Upper Michigan from 1998 to 2006, ranging from 0 to 13 annually and tending to be lower than rates observed in Wisconsin and Minnesota.

In Minnesota, the total number and percentage (based on linear interpolation between periodic population estimates) of wolves killed for depredation control increased from the late 1970s until it peaked in 1997 and ranged from 6 to 216 wolves or 0.5 per cent to 9.2 per cent of the winter population (Table 1.3.2). The mean percentage of previous winter wolf population killed annually at depredations was 2.5 per cent (SD 1.09) from 1978 to 1989, 6.3 per cent (SD 1.89) from 1990 to 1999, and 4.2 per cent (SD 0.86) from 2000 to 2006. Numbers of wolves trapped and killed at depredation sites (1979–2005) correlated with numbers of farms with wolf depredations ($R^2 = 0.95$, $P < 0.001$), and numbers of verified depredations ($R^2 = 0.93$, $P < 0.001$). Lethal controls of depredating wolves became a regular activity after 2002 in Wisconsin and Michigan, and during the period 2003–2006, an average of 5.5 per cent (SD 1.29) of the previous winter population were killed in Wisconsin and 1.2 per cent (SD 0.54) in Michigan. The number of wolves killed at depredations sites would probably have been higher in Wisconsin in 2006, but the state lost authority for lethal controls during summer due to a lawsuit by animal welfare groups. Compared to Michigan, more wolf conflict occurred in Wisconsin, due to higher density of livestock operations, especially at the edge of wolf range (Treves et al. 2004).

State Plans

Management plans to address wolf conservation following federal delisting of endangered or threatened status varied among the three states (Table 1.3.3). Population goals associated with federal delisting were much higher for Minnesota because a viable wolf population already existed when a federal recovery plan was developed (U.S. Fish and Wildlife Service 1992). Minimum population goals for the state's plans were 100–200 wolves higher than minimum federal goals. Only Wisconsin's plan included a management goal, a level at which government proactive population controls and public harvest could be considered. Wisconsin was also the only state to

Table 1.3.2. Wolf population growth and wolves killed in depredation control activities in Michigan, Minnesota and Wisconsin 1979–2005. Non-italic numbers are actual counts or population estimations, and italic numbers are interpolations based on average annual population growth between actual population estimations.

	MICHIGAN			MINNESOTA			WISCONSIN		
	Wolf Kill		Population	Wolf Kill		Population	Wolf Kill		Population
	No.	%	Estimation	No.	%	Estimation	No.	%	Estimation
1978	–	–	?	26	2.2	*1,200*	–	–	?
1979	–	–	?	6	0.5	1,235	–	–	?
1980	–	–	?	21	1.7	*1,269*	–	–	25
1981	–	–	?	29	2.2	*1,305*	–	–	21
1982	–	–	?	20	1.5	*1,341*	–	–	23
1983	–	–	?	42	3.1	*1,378*	–	–	19
1984	–	–	?	36	2.5	*1,416*	–	–	18
1985	–	–	?	31	2.1	*1,456*	–	–	14
1986	–	–	?	31	2.1	*1,496*	–	–	15
1987	–	–	?	43	2.8	*1,538*	–	–	18
1988	–	–	?	59	3.7	*1,581*	–	–	26
1989	–	–	3	81	5.0	1,625	–	–	31
1990	–	–	10	91	5.4	*1,700*	–	–	34
1991	–	–	17	54	3.0	*1,779*	–	–	39
1992	–	–	21	118	6.3	*1,862*	–	–	45
1993	–	–	30	139	7.1	*1,948*	–	–	40
1994	–	–	57	172	8.4	*2,039*	–	–	54
1995	–	–	80	78	3.7	*2,133*	–	–	83
1996	–	–	116	154	6.9	*2,232*	–	–	99
1997	–	–	112	216	9.2	*2,336*	–	–	148
1998	–	–	140	161	6.6	*2,445*	1	0.6	178
1999	–	–	174	163	6.4	*2,533*	1	0.5	204
2000	–	–	216	148	5.6	*2,623*	–	–	248
2001	–	–	249	109	4.0	*2,717*	–	–	257
2002	–	–	278	146	5.2	*2,814*	–	–	327
2003	4	1.2	321	125	4.3	*2,915*	17	5.1	335
2004	6	1.7	360	105	3.5	*3,020*	24	6.4	373
2005	2	0.5	405	102	3.3	*3,128*	29	6.7	435
2006	7	1.6	434	122	3.8	~3,200	18	3.9	467

Table 1.3.3. Comparisons of Gray Wolf Management Plans for Great Lakes States.

MANAGEMENT ACTIVITIES	MINNESOTA	MICHIGAN	WISCONSIN
Federal delisting goal	1,250–1,400	100 with WI	100 with MI
Minimum state population goal	1,600	200 for 5+ years	250 outside Indian reservations
Management Zones	2	1	4
Management goal*	None	not currently	350 outside Ind. res.
Shooting in the act	Yes	no	Yes
Permits to landowners	Yes	Not addressed	Yes
Government lethal controls on verified depredators	Yes	Yes	Yes
Pro-active government controls	Some	Not addressed	Yes
Public harvest	Possible 5 years after federal delisting	Not addressed	Possible if > 350 wolves
Road-density management	No	Yes	Yes
Den site protection	No	Yes	Yes
Reimbursement for losses to livestock	Yes	Yes	Yes
Reimbursement for losses to pets and hunting dogs	No	No	Yes
Frequency of population estimations	Every 5 years	Annually	Annually
Annual track and telemetry surveys	No	Yes	Yes
Volunteer tracking program	No	No	Yes
Pre-plan roundtable Involvement	Extensive	None	Minor
Pre-plan public meetings	Yes	Yes	Yes
Plan implementation stakeholders	No	No	Yes
Technical recovery team	Yes	No	Yes
Technical management team	No	No	Yes
Program manager	Yes	Yes	Yes
Plan approval	State legislature	Director, MDNR	Natural Resource Board

*Level at which government population controls and public harvest could be considered.

designate population goals specifically outside of Indian reservations because states do not have authority over wildlife on lands of native peoples; generally 2 to 6 per cent of Wisconsin's wolf count included wolves living on reservations. Public hunting and trapping seasons were not considered for the first five years following delisting for Minnesota, not addressed in Michigan's plan, and considered a possible tool for wolf management in Wisconsin when the population exceeded the state management goal of 350 wolves outside of Indian reservations, a level achieved by 2004.

Minnesota and Wisconsin use federally employed professional trappers to remove problem wolves after depredations are verified. Michigan uses both federal and state-employed trappers to control depredating wolves. Minnesota and Wisconsin plans have provisions for landowners to control problem wolves on their land. Wolf plans in Wisconsin and Michigan also put more emphasis on habitat protection, including maintaining low road density areas and protecting den sites on public forest land because of their relatively small wolf populations.

State plans also varied in terms of public involvement and management oversight. All used extensive public meetings to develop plans, but only Minnesota relied extensively on a roundtable group to develop the plan, and only Wisconsin used a stakeholders group to help implement the plan. Plan approval differed among states. Wisconsin's plan was approved by the Natural Resources Board, Michigan's by the Director of the Department of Natural Resources, and Minnesota's by the legislature. Wisconsin's plan requires legislative approval to implement public harvest. Michigan is currently revising the state's wolf-management plan with the assistance of a roundtable group.

DISCUSSION

Population Surveys

Intense population monitoring was effective for annual population estimates in Wisconsin and Michigan following recolonization by wolves. Minimum late-winter counts provided standardized and consistent measures of wolf numbers for assessing growth of the population, success toward achievement of population goals, and potential impacts on other ecosystem components. A weakness of minimum counts is that the variance properties are poorly understood for the techniques used and calculations of confidence intervals, as done in Minnesota, were not attempted for Michigan and Wisconsin. We do believe the proportion of undetected wolves is low and that inferences regarding population growth or relationships between wolf numbers and other parameters are reliable.

The periodic wolf population survey in Minnesota was deemed more appropriate for this larger wolf population, which had never been near extirpation. Intense annual surveys conducted in Wisconsin and Michigan were more feasible in part because they were initiated when numbers were very low. As wolf populations increase, intensive surveys such as minimum counts will likely become logistically infeasible and prohibitively expensive for state wildlife agencies. Modifications under consideration include sampling strategies using existing survey methods (Potvin et al. 2005), use of a Minnesota type survey (Fuller et al. 1992), and/or use of various population indices, including sex, age, and reproductive data that may be collected from wolves in future harvest or control actions.

The highest rate of population growth (> 50% per year) occurred in Michigan, shortly after wolves apparently recolonized the state in the late 1980s. Infrequent reports of wolves suggested that complete extirpation may never have happened (Hendrickson et al. 1975; Thiel and Hammill 1988); nonetheless, 1989 is regarded as the date of the functional colonization of the extant population. Recolonization occurred in Michigan about fifteen years after it had occurred in Wisconsin, and the Michigan population escaped the outbreak of canine parvovirus that hit Wisconsin's population in the 1980s. The Michigan wolf population likely benefited from education efforts begun in Wisconsin and Minnesota in the late 1980s and possibly intensified enforcement of endangered species laws.

Survival Rates and Population Growth

Wolf populations may decline if human-caused mortality exceeds 35 per cent (Fuller 1989; Fuller et al. 2003). The Wisconsin population suffered high human-caused mortality and annual population mortality of 0.39 in the early 1980s, but reduced human-caused mortality and annual population mortality rates of 0.18 in the late 1980s and early 1990s (Wydeven et al. 1995) resulted in improved population growth in Wisconsin and perhaps facilitated recolonization of Michigan. Higher adult survival continued through the 1990s and early 2000s, and, despite low average pup survival to winter (~0.30), rapid population growth occurred throughout the 1990s and 2000s, in Wisconsin and apparently as well in Michigan.

High populations of white-tailed deer occurred throughout much of the region since the early 1990s, likely benefiting wolves. Although ungulate diversity had somewhat declined, ungulate biomass was at historical high levels, promoting survival of wolves and reducing competition from human hunters.

Suitable Habitat Assessment

Similar to what is described for Europe by Boitani and Ciucci and by Blanco and Cortés in this volume, suitable habitat for wolves contains adequate prey and low levels of human-caused mortality, enabling sufficient numbers of wolves to survive and reproduce. Road-density measurement by itself or in combination with human population density (Fuller et al.1992), landscape spatial indices (Mladenoff et al. 1995), or prey density (Potvin et al. 2005) have been useful for describing favourable wolf habitat in the Great Lakes. Road density predicts frequency of human encounters, and, in turn, likeliness of human-related mortalities (Fuller 1989; Wydeven et al. 2001). Road density is less useful for predicting presence of wolves in areas with limited public access such as military bases (Merrill 2000).

Mladenoff et al. (1995) predicted the extent of favourable wolf habitat based on road densities to be 50,168 km² in Minnesota, 29,348 km² in Michigan, and 14,864 km² in Wisconsin. Occupied wolf range in the early 2000s was 67,852 km² in Minnesota (Erb and Benson 2004), 26,000 km² in Michigan (Potvin et al. 2005), and 16,500 km² in Wisconsin (Wydeven and Wiedenhoeft 2005). Mladenoff et al. (1995) only analyzed areas within Recovery Zones 1–4 in Minnesota (U.S. Fish and Wildlife Service 1992) and did not include potential areas of habitat outside these zones (Fuller et al. 1992) that have since been occupied by wolf packs.

Mladenoff et al. (1997) used habitat and prey models to predict equilibrium populations of 262 to 662 wolves for Wisconsin, and 581 to 1357 wolves in Michigan. By 2005 the Wisconsin wolf population was near the mid-point of these projections. While the Michigan population in 2005 was nearing the lower projections, the eventual population may be at the lower end of this predicted equilibrium. Limited deer availability and larger home range areas perhaps will not allow as large a wolf population as originally projected (Potvin et al. 2005).

Predictions of suitable wolf habitat based on road density compared closely to areas occupied by wolf packs by the mid-2000s, and the Wisconsin's wolf population was at the midpoint of projected population levels. While it remains to be seen where wolf distribution and abundances stabilize in the Great Lakes, these habitat and population predictions have been useful in determine management zones and other aspects of state management plans.

Mech (2006) challenged that landscape models based on road densities did not adequately predict wolf colonization patterns in Wisconsin because areas of predicted poor habitat were still occupied by wolves. In general, he believed that the models did not fully appreciate the adaptability of wolves. Mladenoff et al. (2006) countered that Mech's methods for assessing actual habitat use by wolves were inadequate. Probably, Mech failed to recognize that Mladenoff et al. (1995, 1997) had indicated that wolves were adaptable and that future landscape selection by wolves may change.

It is also possible that in some regions of Wisconsin the wolf population saturated the best habitats and started occupying sub-optimal habitats. In facts, packs that occupied less favourable habitat occurred mainly in northwest and north-central Wisconsin, where the more suitable areas were mostly saturated. Other wolves may have occupied portions of more favourable habitat (according to the spatial model); however, Mech may not have detected wolf occupancy of such portions.

Depredation Management

Wolf depredation management has a long history in Minnesota, and by the 2000s it had also become an important component of wolf conservation in Michigan and Wisconsin. There are about 8,500 farms in Minnesota wolf range (International Wolf Center web site), about 6,500 farms in Wisconsin's occupied wolf range and about 1,900 farms in Upper Michigan (National Agriculture Statistical Services 2002). In general the farm count illustrates that potential wolf problems are likely to be greater in Minnesota and Wisconsin than in Michigan. Levels of wolf depredation in Wisconsin during mid-2000s seemed similar to rates in Minnesota during the early 1980s (Fritts et al. 1992). The percentage of wolves trapped and euthanized in Wisconsin (6.1%, 2003–2005) was similar to the percentage removed in Minnesota (6.3%, 1990–1999) but much higher than the percentage removed in Michigan (1.1%, 2003–2005). Michigan's wolf range contains few farms and is restricted to the Upper Peninsula, which is bounded by Lakes Superior and Michigan, hence Michigan is unlikely to experience dramatically increased depredations with future population growth, unless wolves recolonize Michigan's lower peninsula. Wolves have been verified in Lower Michigan, but survey efforts in 2005 and 2006 did not document any established territories. Minnesota's wolf range evidently has stabilized since 1998, and rates of depredation have declined. Reported wolf depredation rates in Wisconsin are growing more quickly than the wolf population, and between 2001 and 2005 the wolf population grew at an average rate of 13 per cent annually, but numbers of farms with wolf depredation grew 50 per cent annually (Wisconsin DNR, unpublished data). Wolves in northwestern Wisconsin have filled suitable wolf habitat as identified by Mladenoff et al. (1995) and are expanding into more agricultural landscapes; thus, additional wolf depredation is likely and will depend on the spatial extent of wolves once stabilized (Treves et al. 2004).

Wolf Conservation Plans

The three Great Lakes states have developed different management plans to address future wolf conservation as the federal government delegates management authority to each state. Plans were designed for the states' unique characteristics of potential habitat, potential wolf population levels, and anticipated depredation problems. Habitat modelling and wolf population surveys figure prominently in development of these plans. Education and outreach programs, which were similar to those described for Europe by Taylor (this volume), were critical to sound wolf conservation in the region. Challenges for the future include stabilization of wolf populations to areas of suitable habitat, maintaining viable and ecologically significant numbers, and reducing rates of depredation and wolf–human conflicts. Public harvests may be desirable to manage the wolf population in the future but will be highly controversial and will require carefully planned citizen involvement. We expect plans to be modified and adapted as wolf-management dynamics change (an updated plan is being developed in Michigan at the time of this writing), but plans will continue to emphasize long-term conservation of wolves.

The Future of Wolf Conservation in the Great Lakes

With the federal delisting of wolves on 12 March 2007, wolf management was transferred to the states of Michigan, Wisconsin, and Minnesota. In the future, wolves in other parts of the United States that are currently listed federally as threatened or endangered may also be returned to the management of state wildlife agencies. Although the federal government, through U.S. Fish and Wildlife Service and U.S. Geological Survey, was very involved in wolf research and management in Minnesota, most wolf monitoring and management activities in Wisconsin and Michigan were done by state wildlife agencies under authority and some funding by the U.S. Fish and Wildlife Service. Following federal delisting, involvement in wolf management by the U.S. Fish and Wildlife service will mostly disappear. USDA–Wildlife Services will continue wolf depredation management as agents of the state and the U.S. Forest Service will continue to protect wolf habitat. The state department of natural resources will be responsible for wolf management.

Minnesota, Wisconsin, and Michigan have been meeting together annually since the late 1980s, along with federal agencies, university researchers, non-government agencies, and private individuals such as the Midwest Wolf Stewards. This group will likely continue to meet regularly to discuss, cooperate, and coordinate wolf management throughout the region.

Wolf populations in the Great Lakes region are not likely to expand much beyond the heavily forested areas currently occupied. The distribution of wolf packs in Minnesota seems to have stabilized. In comparison, Wisconsin still has some unoccupied or sparsely occupied habitat in the northeast portions of the state, although viable populations of wolves are unlikely to become established much beyond the northern forest region (Zone 1) or the central forest area (Zone 2). Wolves in the Upper Peninsula of Michigan may be able to occupy fully the central and eastern portions of the peninsula, but most of the region is saturated. If wolves in Michigan are able to recolonize the Lower Peninsula, areas of favourable habitat could support an additional 40 to 105 wolves (Gehring and Potter 2005).

Future management actions will continue to affect wolf numbers and distribution. Zones 3 and 4 in Wisconsin and zone B in Minnesota represent agricultural and urban areas with poor to marginal wolf habitat. Both state plans provide liberal controls on nuisance and depredating wolves in these zones. Government trapper controls and controls by private land owners would likely reduce abundance of wolves in areas near farms and residential areas, as projected by Haight et al. (2002). Wolf populations in these zones would likely decline or remain at low levels.

Wolf populations in wolf zones (Zone A in Minnesota, Zones 1 and 2 in Wisconsin, and Upper Michigan) will likely reach carrying capacity in the near future and will fluctuate annually depending on prey abundance. Packs living near farms or urban areas may be subject to control actions by government trappers. Public forestlands will likely continue to provide favourable habitat in these wolf zones but future housing developments on private land may reduce favourable habitat by eliminating some private land and fragmenting some public forestland (Radeloff et al. 2005).

The hunting and trapping of wolves by the public is likely to engender a major debate in the Great Lakes states in the near future. Such harvests are not likely to endanger wolf populations and might help stabilize wolves to areas of suitable habitat and away from areas of conflict (Mech 2001; Haight et al. 2002). However, acceptance of public hunting or trapping seasons is low for many members of the public (Naughton et al. 2005). Although public harvests have high acceptance in wolf range and may improve local attitudes toward wolves (Mech 1995), the debate over hunting is likely to be very divisive (Nie 2003). The hunters' negative attitudes toward wolves as well as the public's objection to wolf hunting seem comparable in North America and Western Europe (Bath, this volume). However, in Europe most wolves are found in Eastern Europe, where wolf hunting is maintained and may contribute to public acceptance of wolves (Boitaini and Ciucci, this volume). Nie (2003) has suggested: "The issue of hunting and trapping – a public take – after they become delisted is perhaps the most divisive and potentially explosive issue in the entire wolf debate." He further states: "Conflict between hunters and animal rights and welfare interests over the issue of wolf management and possible public hunting or trapping of wolves will become only more evident and embittered in the future." (Nie 2003).

The conservation of wolves in the Great Lakes region is a wildlife management success story. Wolf populations in the region are now secure and unlikely to become endangered in the near future. Wolves are again and will remain important elements of forest ecosystems. Unfortunately, wolf-management issues will continue to be divisive, especially as state wildlife agencies begin consideration of public hunting or trapping seasons.

ACKNOWLEDGMENTS

Many people have helped with conservation efforts of wolves in the three-state area, and some of the more notable include the following: Dave Mech, Rolf Peterson, Bill Paul, Steve Fritts, Dick Thiel, Ron Schultz, Nancy Thomas, Bill Berg, David Kuehn, Todd Fuller, Mike Nelson, Dave Mladenoff, Bob Willging, Dave Ruid, Sarah Boles, Pam Troxell, Kerry Beheler, Grace McLaughlin, Kathy Converse, Bruce Kohn, Julie Langenberg, Ron Refsnider, Mike Don Carlos, Don Lonsway, and many others.

1.4 The Art of Wolf Restoration in the Northwestern United States: Where to Now?

Ed Bangs, Mike Jimenez, Carolyn Sime, Steve Nadeau, and Curt Mack

INTRODUCTION

As Europeans settled North America, they poisoned, trapped, and shot gray wolves (*Canis lupus*), causing this once-widespread species to be eradicated from most of its range in the contiguous United States (Mech 1970; McIntyre 1995). Wolf populations were eliminated from Montana, Idaho, and Wyoming, as well as adjacent southwestern Canada by the 1930s in deference to other social objectives such as intensive livestock production (Young and Goldman 1944). Thereafter, only isolated observations of individual wolves were reported (Ream and Mattson 1982; Weaver 1978). After human-caused mortality of wolves in southwestern Canada was regulated in the 1960s, populations expanded southward (Pletscher et al. 1991). Dispersing individuals occasionally reached the northern Rocky Mountains (NRM) of the United States (Ream and Mattson 1982) but lacked legal protection there until 1974, when wolves were listed as endangered under the Endangered Species Act of 1973, as amended (ESA) (39 FR 1171), and the U.S. Fish and Wildlife Service (USFWS) was charged with their recovery and management.

With increased urbanization, society began to place more value on wildlands, wildlife, and natural processes. Consequently, public interest in wolves shifted from persecution to restoration. Naturally dispersing wolves from Canada denned in northwestern Montana in 1986 (Ream and

Table 1.4.1. Minimum estimated December 31st wolf population, annual confirmed wolf depredation, and annual agency wolf removal in the northern Rocky Mountains of Montana, Idaho, and Wyoming, 1987–2006.

YEAR	# WOLVES	CATTLE	SHEEP	OTHER[1]	DOGS	WOLVES MOVED	WOLVES KILLED[2]
1987	10	6	10	0	0	0	4
1988	14	0	0	0	0	0	0
1989	12	3	0	0	0	4	1
1990	33	5	0	0	1	0	1
1991	29	2	2	0	0	3	0
1992	41	1	0	0	0	0	0
1993	55	0	0	0	0	0	0
1994	48	6	0	0	0	2	0
1995	101	3	0	0	4	8	0
1996	152	11	37	0	2	23	6
1997	213	22	126	0	4	21	21
1998	275	21	12	0	5	3	7
1999	337	33	89	1	15	19	23
2000	437	32	80	0	11	16	20
2001	563	40	138	4	6	18	19
2002	663	52	99	5	9	0	46
2003	761	64	211	10	6	0	59
2004	846	130	270	5	9	0	86
2005	1,020	97	244	2	11	0	103
2006	1,300	184	247	3	8	0	142
TOTAL		712	1,565	30	91	117	538

[1] Total livestock other than cattle and sheep confirmed killed by wolves, 1987–2006: 11 llamas, 12 goats and 7 horses.
[2] Includes wolves legally shot by livestock producers. Others killed in government control efforts.

Mattson 1982). Reintroduction into Yellowstone National Park (YNP) and central Idaho in 1995 and 1996 greatly accelerated wolf population growth in southwestern Montana, central Idaho, and northwestern Wyoming (Bangs and Fritts 1996; Fritts et al. 1997). By 2006 the NRM wolf population contained 1,300 wolves (USFWS et al. 2007; Table 1.4.1).

Our wolf restoration program attempted to maintain adequate public tolerance for wolves by minimizing damage to livestock. We used three primary tools to accomplish this goal. First, our wolf restoration efforts were focused on the highest quality wolf habitat to reduce the costs of wolf restoration (livestock depredation, agency costs, and wolf removal) and increase its benefits (positive public perceptions of wolves, public enjoyment and viewing, and ecological restoration). Secondly, we implemented an interagency wolf control program that included removal of wolves that chronically depredated on livestock to reduce the risk of further livestock depredation. Lastly, as the wolf population increased and suitable wolf habitat became saturated, we transferred more management authority to the affected states, tribes, and local livestock producers and more aggressively removed problem wolves. Although population recovery and removal from the ESA's protection was our ultimate goal, our interim objective was to reduce controversy over federal authority and move wolves into the more familiar North American model of state-led conservation of wildlife (Geist 2006). Within the biological limits of wolf populations, that conservation model included reducing property damage through agency management and defence of private property regulations and eventually would include regulated public harvest.

Our success had more to do with decisions made decades ago (establishment of public lands, restoration of native ungulate populations, changes in human attitudes, and increased local public tolerance of wolves and wolf damage) than with wolf biology. We discuss the role of wolf removal as one component of an integrated program of wolf restoration in the NRM and the additional management tools that may be required to conserve and maintain public support for a recovered wolf population in the future.

STUDY AREA

Shortly after wolves became protected by the ESA, we formed an inter-agency team to complete recovery planning for wolves in the NRM (US-FWS 1980, 1987). We concluded that wolf restoration should be focused in large contiguous blocks of federal public land with high wild ungulate populations and low numbers of livestock. Three distinct recovery areas were identified – (1) northwestern Montana (Glacier National Park and adjacent wilderness areas and public lands), (2) central Idaho (wilderness areas and adjacent public lands), and (3) the Greater Yellowstone area (GYA) (including YNP and adjacent wilderness areas and public lands).

Cattle production in the NRM was widespread and intensive. Some sheep were raised but other livestock were uncommon (Bangs et al. 2005). Livestock were fed throughout the winter on private land, where calving and lambing also usually occurred in late winter and early spring. During summer, livestock were grazed on vast remote private and public land grazing allotments. Livestock were gathered and the young shipped to market in fall. Breeding stock were returned to private land to winter. Wild ungulates also followed that season pattern of habitat use. Many herds summered at higher elevations on public land but wintered in valleys on private land.

Early assessments of potential suitable wolf habitat included large blocks of public land and relatively high levels of native prey and low levels of livestock grazing (USFWS 1980, 1987, 1994). Recently, we examined models of suitable wolf habitat in Montana, Idaho, and Wyoming (Oakleaf et al. 2006) and the western United States (Carroll et al. 2003, 2006) to determine how much suitable habitat might be left for wolves in the NRM. Those models compared the biological and physical characteristics of areas occupied by wolf packs with adjacent areas that were unoccupied. Suitable wolf habitat in the NRM was characterized as public land with mountainous forested habitat having abundant year-round wild ungulate populations, low road density, low numbers of domestic livestock that were only present seasonally, few domestic sheep, low agricultural use, and few people. Unsuitable wolf habitat was typically just the opposite. A mix of

Table 1.4.2. A matrix of generalized environmental attributes and an illustration of the relative probability of them occurring in the different types of areas used by wolf packs in the northern Rocky Mountains (NRM) of the United States.

	LAND STATUS WITHIN SUITABLE HABITAT USED BY WOLVES IN THE NRM				
Attribute	Park	Wilderness	Public Land	Public/ Private Land	Private
Ecological integrity	high	high-moderate	moderate	sporadic	low
Pack Size	large	large-moderate	moderate	small	pairs
Pack persistence	high	high-moderate	moderate	moderate-low	low
Pack distribution	contiguous	contiguous-uniform	uniform	fragmented	sporadic
Wolf density	high	high-moderate	moderate	low	low
Dispersing wolves	source	source	mainly source	mainly sink	sink
Rate of mortality	low	moderate-low	moderate	moderate-high	high
Livestock density	none	low and seasonal	low and seasonal	seasonal/ moderate	high and all year
Livestock vulnerability	low	moderate-low	moderate	moderate-high	high
Rate of conflict	none	low	moderate	moderate-high	high
Management options	none	few	non-lethal to lethal	non-lethal to lethal	mainly lethal
Management intensity	low	moderate-low	moderate	moderate-high	high
Management cost	low	moderate-low	moderate	moderate-high	high
Public tolerance	high	high-moderate	moderate	moderate-low	low
Public enjoyment	high	high-moderate	moderate	moderate-low	low
Public access	low	moderate-low	moderate	moderate-high	high

these characteristics produced varying degrees of suitability, ranging from highly suitable (i.e., the northern range of YNP or the vast wilderness of central Idaho) to highly unsuitable (i.e., a city or a sheep ranch in eastern Montana) and various levels of suitability between the two extremes (Table 1.4.2).

There were large blocks of suitable wolf habitat in central Idaho and the GYA and to a lesser extent in northwestern Montana (Carroll et al. 2006; Oakleaf et al. 2006). Those areas were atypical in the western United States because nowhere else did habitat with suitable characteristics occur in such large contiguous blocks. These findings supported the recovery planning (USFWS 1987) that identified those three areas as the most likely to support a wolf population. However, there was only limited and fragmented suitable habitat in the remainder of Montana, Idaho, and Wyoming and adjacent portions of Washington, Oregon, Nevada, Utah, and Colorado (Carroll et al. 2003, 2006).

METHODS

As wolves began their natural recolonization, we formed an interagency wolf working group, composed of federal, state, and tribal agency personnel (USFWS et al. 2007). We conducted four basic recovery tasks (monitoring, control, research, and outreach), in addition to the standard law enforcement functions associated with the take of a federally listed species.

1) The size and distribution of the wolf population was estimated each year (USFWS 2007; Table 1.4.1). We used standard capture techniques (foot-hold trapping and helicopter darting) to radio-collar (with standard mortality sensors) and release adult-sized wolves. We typically located radio-collared wolves 1–3 times monthly, unless other circumstances (livestock damage, wolf control, or research) required more frequent

monitoring. We documented location, if the wolf was alive, presence of other wolves, denning activity and pup survival, and special events such as kills made by wolves or livestock conflict. Since the early 1980s, we have radio-collared and monitored over nine hundred wolves in the NRM to assess population status, conduct research, and to reduce/resolve conflicts with livestock. Radio-collared wolves were located thousands of times, primarily from the air.

2) In the NRM, suspected wolf-caused damage to livestock was investigated by United States Department of Agriculture–Wildlife Services (USDA–WS) specialists using standard techniques (Roy and Dorrance 1976; Paul and Gipson 1994). Most reports were investigated within twenty-four hours. If the investigation confirmed wolf involvement, we authorized USDA–WS to initiate the appropriate control action. We, and various cooperators, used numerous non-lethal and lethal tools to reduce the risk to livestock (Bangs et al. 2006a). The federal government attempted to mitigate, but did not pay for, wolf-caused damage.

A private program compensated ranchers the full market value of confirmed, and one-half market value of probable, wolf damage to livestock and livestock guarding animals (Fischer 1989; Defenders of Wildlife 2007; Stone, this volume). It relied on standard USDA–WS field investigation reports to validate wolf damage but dealt directly with the affected livestock producer to negotiate compensation. The program has paid nearly $800,000 since 1987 and about $100,000 annually from 2001 to 2006. However, compensation was only partial because many livestock producers complained they were missing several times more livestock after the summer grazing season than the 2–3 per cent they were missing before wolf packs became established in their remote grazing allotments (Oakleaf et al. 2003). Despite its shortcomings (Montag 2003), compensation redistributed some of the economic costs of wolves and was politically popular (Woodroffe et al. 2005; Stone, this volume).

3) We and a host of federal, state, tribal, university co-operators, and private groups conducted and helped to initiate, fund, and facilitate various research projects on wolf relationships to ungulate prey, other carnivores and scavengers, livestock, and people (USFWS et al. 2007).

4) We provided accurate science-based information through reports and mass media so the public could develop their opinions about wolves and wolf management from an informed perspective. We consistently published and made this information available on our website (http://westerngraywolf.fws.gov), including weekly wolf reports (USFWS 2006a), annual interagency wolf reports (USFWS et al. 2007), and numerous popular and scientific publications. We gave over a thousand local, national, and international public and professional presentations and thousands of interviews to all forms of public media, including film, video, television, internet, radio, books, magazines, and newspapers. During certain phases of the project, we conducted substantial and massive public outreach programs (USFWS 1994; Bangs and Fritts 1996).

RESULTS

Wolf Population Statistics

In late 2006, we estimated there were 1,300 wolves in 173 packs (for the purpose of this survey a pack comprised > 2 wolves occupying distinct territories). Out of these surveyed packs, 86 packs also qualified as breeding pairs (packs with an adult male and female that raised at least 2 pups to December 31) (USFWS et al. 2007; Tab. 1). The average annual increase from 1995 to 2006 was 24 per cent. In 2006, wolves were most numerous in Idaho (643 wolves in 40 packs with breeding pairs) with equal numbers present in Montana (316 in 21 breeding pairs) and Wyoming (311 in 25 breeding pairs). The wolf population first achieved its ESA recovery goal (a minimum of 30 breeding pairs and 300 wolves equitably distributed in Montana, Idaho, and Wyoming for a minimum of three successive years) in 2002 and has exceeded it every year since (USFWS et al. 2007).

As part of the interagency wolf monitoring and control program and various research projects, up to 30 per cent of the NRM wolf population was radio-collared since the 1980s and that caused a 3 per cent mortality rate among all wolves handled (USFWS et al. 2007). The annual survival rate of mature wolves in northwestern Montana and adjacent Canada from 1984 to 1995 was 80 per cent (Pletscher et al. 1997); 84 per cent for resident wolves and 66 per cent for dispersers, and 84 per cent of it was human-caused. Bangs et al. (1998) reported similar statistics for the NRM. For the past ten years, radio-collared wolves in the largest blocks of remote suitable habitat with few livestock, such as central Idaho and YNP, had annual survival rates around 80 per cent (Smith et al. 2006). Preliminary analysis of wolf telemetry data from 1980 to 2006 indicated that wolves outside of these large remote areas had annual survival rates as low as 54 per cent (D. Smith et al., unpublished data), near the minimum that an isolated wolf population can sustain (Fuller et al. 2003). The two largest causes of radio-collared wolf mortality in the NRM were agency control and illegal killing, each removed an estimated 10 per cent of the radio-collared wolves annually (D. Smith et al., unpublished data). All other causes of mortality combined (i.e., inter- and intraspecies conflict, accidental killing by humans, disease, parasites, and accidents) killed about 4 per cent of the radioed wolves annually.

WOLF HABITAT

The area currently occupied by the NRM wolf population was calculated by drawing a line around the outer points of radio-telemetry locations of all known wolf pack (n = 132) territories in 2005 (Fig. 1.4.1) (USFWS 2006a). The overall distribution of wolf packs was similar from 2000 to 2005 (USFWS 2006a) at around 100,000 mi^2 (261,331 km^2). Nearly 90 per cent of this area was Temperate Steppe Forest (Bailey 1995). Although this area included some prairie (2%) and some high desert (9%), no wolf packs have persisted in those habitat types in the past twenty years because of high levels of wolf control and illegal killing. Landownership in the occupied habitat area was 66,745 mi^2 (172,870 km^2) federal (66%); 5,457 mi^2 (14,133 km^2) state (5.4%); 1,523 mi^2 (3,944 km^2) tribal (1.5%); and 27,176 mi^2 (70,386 km^2) private (27%). We included some habitat between the core recovery areas within our occupied wolf habitat designation even though wolf packs did not use it because those areas were often traversed by dispersing wolves (USFWS 1994). Oakleaf et al. (2006) predicted 65,725 mi^2 (170,227 km^2) of suitable wolf habitat in Montana, Idaho, and Wyoming. Roughly 57,374 mi^2 (148,599 km^2) or 87 per cent was within the area currently occupied by the NRM wolf population. There was little suitable wolf habitat unoccupied by packs, and to avoid resident packs, lone wolves increasingly dispersed to, and tried to form new packs in, unsuitable habitat. An example of this occurred in 2006 when three packs established home ranges in Wyoming east and south of previously occupied habitat in the GYA. However, only one survived long enough to qualify as a breeding pair and by spring 2007 all had been removed due to conflicts with livestock.

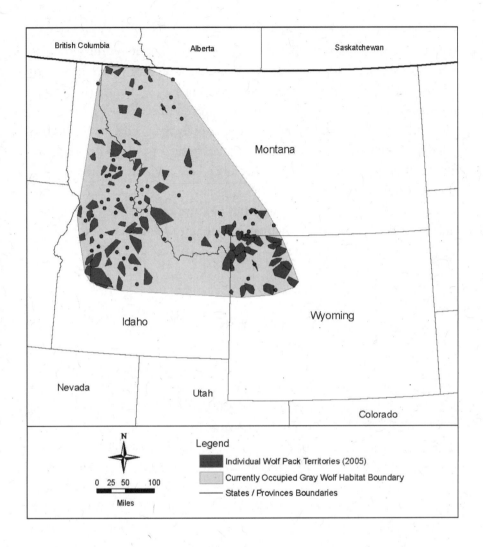

Figure 1.4.1. Currently occupied gray wolf habitat in the northern Rocky Mountains of Montana, Idaho, and Wyoming that encompasses all 132 individual wolf pack territories documented in 2005 (USFWS 2006a).

Strips and smaller patches (> 1,000 mi² [2,600 km²]) of theoretically suitable habitat (typically isolated mountain ranges) often resulted in higher wolf mortality than otherwise predicted because they were surrounded by areas of high mortality risk. This phenomenon, in which the quality and quantity of suitable habitat was diminished because of interactions with surrounding less suitable habitat, is known as an "edge effect" (Mills 1995). Edge effects are exacerbated in small habitat patches with high perimeter to area ratios (i.e., those that were long and narrow like isolated mountain ranges) and in wide-ranging species, like wolves, because they were more likely to encounter surrounding unsuitable habitat (Woodroffe and Ginsberg 1998). While habitat models indicated that some isolated mountain ranges were theoretically suitable wolf habitat, to date no wolf packs have persisted in them.

LIVESTOCK DEPREDATION

From 1987 to 2006, wolves in the NRM were confirmed to have killed 712 cattle, 1,565 sheep, 91 dogs (primarily livestock guard and herding dogs and hunting hounds; Bangs et al. 2006b), 12 goats, 11 llamas, and 7 horses (USFWS et al. 2007; Tab. 1). Wolf depredation caused about 0.04 per cent and 0.01 per cent of all annual cattle and sheep losses in the NRM (Bangs et al. 2005). Over 67 per cent of confirmed cattle depredations and 75 per cent of confirmed sheep depredations occur during the April–September summer grazing season (Bangs et al. 2005). About 75 per cent of the cattle killed by wolves were calves and about 30 per cent of confirmed cattle depredations occurred on public grazing allotments. About 64 per cent of the sheep killed were adults. Unlike cattle, sheep typically wintered outside of occupied wolf habitat and 52 per cent were killed on public grazing allotments (Bangs et al. 2005).

WOLF REMOVAL

While wolf depredation was a minor cause of livestock death in the NRM, it was inordinately controversial (Bangs et al. 2004, 2005). In response to confirmed livestock depredation, we relocated wolves 117 times (Bradley et al. 2005) and killed 538 (USFWS et al. 2007). A comparison of wolf population estimates and agency removal indicated that we killed an average of 7 per cent of the NRM wolf population annually from 1987 to 2006 (USFWS et al. 2007; Tab. 1). Agency control did not prevent wolf population growth, but, along with other causes of human-caused mortality, it limited breeding pairs to suitable habitat.

WOLF-MANAGEMENT STRATEGIES

Biologists recognized that conflict with livestock was the major reason that wolves were extirpated, and control of problem wolves was necessary to maintain local public tolerance of wolves (USFWS 1980, 1987, 1994). In 1988, the USFWS developed a control plan for wolves in northwestern Montana (USFWS 1988) and revised it in 1999 (USFWS 1999). Evidence showed that most wolves did not attack livestock, especially adult horses and cattle, but wolf presence around livestock always resulted in some level of depredation (Bangs et al. 2005). We developed guidelines for when depredating wolves could be harassed, moved, or killed by agency officials to minimize the risk of chronic livestock depredation. The control plans were based on evidence that wolf populations can sustain up to 30–50 per cent annual rate of human-caused mortality (Fuller et al. 2003) and that agency wolf control actions would only affect a small number of wolves. We believed that professional control of problem wolves would help sustain public tolerance for non-depredating wolves, reduce illegal killing, and thus enhance the opportunity for successful population recovery (Mech 1995; Fritts et al. 1994, 2003; USFWS 1999). Removal was dependent on the overall level of the wolf population. Wolf removal was the last resort during lower population levels because every individual wolf was potentially valuable to population recovery, but, as wolves became more numerous, removal was liberalized.

When we reintroduced wolves to central Idaho and the GYA, we established that special regulations offered more flexibility for lethal take than was normally allowed for federally listed species (USFWS 1994; Bangs and Fritts 1996). Those regulations allowed private landowners to shoot wolves that were seen physically attacking cattle, sheep, horses, and mules. In addition, we trained, provided rubber bullets and cracker shells, and issued permits to landowners to shoot wolves with less-than-lethal munitions to increase wolf wariness. On ranches with chronic depredations, in addition to lethal agency control, we issued shoot-on-sight permits to those affected landowners. In recognition of the impact of a larger wolf population and the development of state wolf-management plans that were approved by the USFWS, we further liberalized and expanded those special regulations in 2005 (USFWS 2005a). Landowners in Montana and Idaho can now shoot wolves seen attacking or chasing their livestock, livestock herding and guarding animals, and dogs. On federal grazing allotments, permittees (including guides and outfitters that use livestock) can shoot wolves that are attacking or chasing their livestock and herding and guarding animals. Since 1995, only forty-three wolves (8% of all problem wolves killed from 1995 to 2006) were legally shot by private landowners. We believed that empowering local landowners to protect their own livestock and pets increased local tolerance of wolves. The take by private landowners targeted individual problem wolves, reduced wolf density where the potential for conflict was highest, made surviving wolves more wary, and reduced agency costs. In addition, we transferred the authority to implement federal regulations to the state Fish and Game agencies in Montana and Idaho who had more and better-distributed professional staff to implement wildlife management programs than the USFWS (USFWS et al. 2006a). Unfortunately, we couldn't extend those more flexible rules to Wyoming because they did not have a state regulatory framework for wolf management that the USFWS could approve (USFWS 2006b).

Incremental agency wolf control took the minimum action believed necessary to reduce further depredation and included a wide variety of non-lethal and lethal control measures (Bangs and Shivik 2001; Bangs et al. 2004, 2005, 2006a, 2006b). However, non-lethal methods to reduce wolf/livestock conflict were often only temporarily effective (Bangs and Shivik 2001; Bangs et al. 2005, 2006b; Breitenmoser et al. 2005) and by themselves did not offer effective long-term solutions to chronic damage to livestock. For instance, relocation typically did not promote wolf recovery unless vacant suitable habitat was available (Bradley et al. 2005). After 2001, most suitable habitat was occupied by resident packs and problem wolves were not relocated (USFWS et al. 2006a). In 2005 and 2006, under the new more liberal regulations and increased use of lethal control, 9 and 10 per cent respectively of the wolf population was killed to reduce conflict with livestock (USFWS et al. 2007; Table 1.4.1). Most problem wolves were killed by agency aerial gunning, trapping, and shooting from the ground.

Killing problem wolves arguably reduced conflict because it:

- enhanced the effectiveness of non-lethal control measures (as described for Europe by Brietenmoser et al. 2005),
- interrupted use of livestock as food by surviving wolves,
- removed offending individuals,
- reduced wolf density in conflict areas,
- eliminated packs where chronic livestock depredations occurred,
- helped to keep wolf packs out of unsuitable habitat,
- made surviving pack members temporarily avoid or be more wary of people and/or areas with livestock,
- reduced the pack's overall need for food,
- made it more difficult for the fewer remaining pack members to kill larger prey like adult cattle or attack calves protected by cows,
- increased the detection rate of subsequent depredations because livestock carcasses were consumed more slowly (so additional control could be applied more rapidly),
- reduced compensation and control costs, and
- moderated some of the public anger over livestock depredation.

We implemented lethal control after we determined that non-lethal methods were unlikely to prevent additional depredations, livestock were clearly killed by wolves, and there was no evidence of intentional feeding or unnatural attraction of wolves. In addition, lethal control was reactive and incremental. For example, if a pack of eight wolves was confirmed to have killed livestock, and lethal removal was warranted, we removed 1–3 wolves, often specific individuals or age classes, and then waited to see if the problem continued. If more confirmed depredations occurred, we removed a few more individuals. Often depredations stopped before the entire pack was removed. This cycle was normally allowed to repeat itself 3–4 times before the entire pack was eventually removed, which has occurred in about twenty cases since 1987.

Reactive incremental removal of problem wolves resulted in control being commensurate with the level of confirmed livestock depredation. Incremental removal resulted in higher levels of livestock damage than would have occurred if entire packs were removed immediately. However, since all wolf packs in the NRM exposed to livestock occasionally depredated, this incremental approach allowed most wolf packs to survive the summer grazing season and to reproduce the following winter, thus sustaining the wolf population. This approach often eliminated lone dispersing problem wolves and newly formed pairs from unsuitable habitat but left larger packs in suitable habitat. The most important element of this reactive incremental approach to lethal control was that it allowed wolves to determine what habitat was suitable. Wolves were allowed to establish packs anywhere they could and were only removed after chronic livestock depredation.

Critical to our control philosophy was the seasonality of livestock grazing in the NRM and the full range of suitable habitat types, ranging from national parks to private lands that were available for wolf occupancy (Table 1.4.1). Often simply preventing or delaying further livestock damage by non-lethal tools or reducing the rate of problem wolf removal through incremental killing resulted in reduced livestock vulnerability because calves were larger (Oakleaf et al. 2003) or because livestock were moved out of remote summer grazing pastures. If livestock had been more vulnerable (smaller or younger livestock, longer calving/lambing seasons, longer grazing seasons, or more livestock grazed in Temperate Steppe Forest), our current strategy for wolf removal might have exceeded the wolf population's ability to sustain itself. The reverse was also true, if wolf packs expanded into areas with less or smaller blocks of suitable habitat and more vulnerable livestock, a much higher level of chronic wolf depredation and control occurred. The level of conflict that the local and national public will tolerate is unknown, but few people question that there are areas where wolf packs will not be allowed to live under current conditions and public attitudes (Fritts et al. 1994, 2003; Fritts and Carbyn 1995). However, as it is also highlighted for Europe and North America by Bath (this volume), human attitudes and tolerance for wolves are known to vary at local, regional, and national scales as well as with time. Thus, the specific areas and times where wolves will be accepted are difficult to predict.

DISCUSSION

In all areas where livestock and large carnivores coexist, some predators are killed by people to reduce conflicts (Fritts et al. 2003; Woodroffe et al. 2005). In the thick forests of the Midwest United States, or the wilds of Alaska or Canada, it is difficult for people to kill many wolves by shooting them. However, wolves in the NRM seem susceptible to human-caused mortality because of the open and fragmented landscapes in the western United States (Bangs et al. 2004). Mountain topography concentrated both wolf and human activity in valley bottoms (Boyd and Pletscher 1999), especially in winter, which further increased wolf vulnerability to humans, making wolf conservation in the NRM dependent on local human-tolerance. The removal of problem wolves was required to maintain enough local public tolerance of wolves for populations to persist (USFWS 1994; Fritts et al. 1994, 2003; Fritts and Carbyn 1995; Mech 1995a; Boitani 2003; Bangs et al. 2004, 2005).

In an attempt to reduce livestock damage, maintain local tolerance of wolves, and reduce the rate of illegal killing, we killed problem wolves and occasionally entire packs. Killing problem wolves immediately reduced depredation risk in that area. It also reduced wolf density and pack size in high conflict areas, theoretically reduced wolf dispersal and pack formation in unsuitable habitat by providing social vacancies in suitable habitat, reduced the overall rate of livestock damage, and was infrequent enough (7–10% removed through control on average per year) to allow the NRM wolf population to grow an average of 24 per cent per year from 1995 to 2006. We perceived that killing wolves that attacked livestock was generally a widely supported concept in the NRM, as long as wolf populations were not jeopardized. Removal was a common and accepted management practice to reduce private property damage caused by other predators and ungulates in the NRM.

Wolves limited their own density even in highly suitable habitat like YNP (Smith et al. 2006). Thus some wolves dispersed into intensive livestock grazing areas. Managers will need additional tools to address wolf dispersal into marginal or unsuitable wolf habitat because this only resulted in an unproductive cycle of dead livestock and dead wolves. While non-lethal tools were temporarily helpful in some situations, they were generally ineffective, particularly in areas that simply had too many livestock for wolf packs to persist (Bangs et al. 2006a). However, it is crucial to underline how this chapter evaluates a limited set of non-lethal alternatives, and this critique refers to non-lethal methods directed at wolves, rather than to the use of non-lethal mitigation measures aimed at other sources of conflict. For example, changing livestock husbandry practices on a large scale may make livestock less accessible to wolves.

Conversely, in many situations wolf removal only resolved conflict until the following grazing season (Bradley 2004) because dispersing wolves simply recolonized those areas and perpetuated the annual cycle of depredation and wolf removal. This negative cycle eroded tolerance for wolves from those incurring the damage, those that opposed killing of wolves, and the general public and media who were interested in all aspects of wolf-related issues.

The North American wildlife management model holds that wildlife is public property, managed in trust by the government, and that the most positive, cost-effective, and politically popular method for surplus wildlife to be utilized is through regulated public harvest programs (Geist 2006). Consequently, we believed that a recovered wolf population would best be managed by state and tribal fish and game agencies (Bangs et al. 2004). Regulated public harvest may increase tolerance for wolves in suitable habitat because local people can legally and voluntarily participate in wolf management. They, in turn, have a reason to advocate on behalf of wolves. Public harvest would also likely remove the wolves that were most accessible and boldest, and consequently those most likely to be involved in conflicts with people and their domestic animals. Public harvest would reduce damage to livestock, the need for reactive agency control of problem wolves, and illegal killing. Public harvest would provide some positive aspects (reduced damage, hunting opportunity, trophies, and public ownership in wolf management) to wolf removal in an otherwise intractable management situation. The model of regulated public harvest to utilize surplus wildlife has been hugely successful in the conservation and management of a host of other North American wildlife species, including mountain lions, black bears, elk, and deer, and we believe it is an appropriate model for management of a recovered wolf population.

However, we caution that the successful application of wolf removal in the NRM may not be feasible in other areas or for other large carnivore conservation programs (Woodroffe et al. 2005). Habitat can be changed from unsuitable to suitable and vice versa by changes in public tolerance of wolves and wolf-caused damage, the public's ability and desire to illegally kill wolves, level of agency or public control authorized, changing livestock density, type, and grazing practices, the rate and type of other conflicts, distance or barriers from occupied core refugia, human presence and access, and/or density of wild ungulates (Table 1.4.1). For species less biologically resilient than wolves or in situations without core recovery areas like YNP or the wildlands of central Idaho, or with lesser amounts or more fragmented suitable habitat, and/or a greater ability and desire by the local public to illegally kill wolves, other strategies than the ones we used may be required to conserve wolf populations. In addition, we caution not to confuse the methodologies successfully used for the rapid restoration of wolves in the NRM under the ESA with those that might be needed for the conservation of NRM wolf populations in the long term.

Section II –
Human Cultures and Ethics Influencing Recovering Wolves

2.1 Ethical Reflections on Wolf Recovery and Conservation: A Practical Approach for Making Room for Wolves

Camilla H. Fox and Marc Bekoff

INTRODUCTION

> Ethics in our Western world has hitherto been largely limited to the relations of man to man. But that is a limited ethics. We need a boundless ethics which will include the animals also.... [T]he time is coming when people will be amazed that the human race existed so long before it recognized that thoughtless injury to life is incompatible with real ethics. Ethics is in its unqualified form extended responsibility to everything that has life. – Albert Schweitzer, 1924

In the United States, few animals provoke as wide a range of emotions as wolves. For some, wolves are icons of a lost wilderness; their return symbolizes the return of wild nature and the integrity of healthy ecosystems. For others, wolves are viewed as vicious predators with malicious intentions and are better off dead. Such deeply held beliefs about a large carnivorous mammal that was exterminated throughout most of its historic range in the conterminous United States in the nineteenth and twentieth centuries have stirred an impassioned debate that is bound to become even more heated as the U.S. government considers removing wolves from the federal endangered species list and turning management over to the states.

Prior to the arrival of European settlers in the 1600s, wolves existed throughout much of the North American continent. European colonists, however, sought to eradicate wolves and other large carnivores, viewing them as dangerous and blood-thirsty predators and an impediment to progress (Young and Goldman 1944; Mech 1970; Casey and Clark 1996; Smith and Ferguson 2005). As early as the seventeenth century, bounties were placed on wolves by U.S. government agencies, and by the 1930s, gray wolf populations were extirpated from the western United States (Mech 1970). A small pocket of wolves remained in the Great Lakes region of Minnesota, despite concerted efforts to eliminate them with poisons, bounties, and intensive trapping efforts (Mech 1970; Robinson 2005; Wydeven et al., this volume). Subsequently, public attitudes toward predators gradually changed, and in 1973 wolves received legal protection with the passage of the Endangered Species Act (ESA). With federal protection, wolves began to recolonize northwest Montana, and in 1995 the U.S. Fish and Wildlife Service (USFWS) began a controversial wolf reintroduction program in the Northern Rockies (see Bangs et al. and Stone, this volume). In recent years, wolf numbers increased in the northern Rocky Mountains and in the western Great Lakes states of Minnesota, Michigan, and Wisconsin (see Bangs et al. and Wydeven et al., this volume). Deeming the gray wolf adequately recovered, in 2003, the USFWS reclassified gray wolves from endangered to threatened status in the lower forty-eight states (with the exception of the Southwest designated population segment, which remained endangered). The reclassification rule was considered the first step in the eventual elimination of all federal protections for gray wolves in the contiguous states. Animal protection and conservation organizations challenged the ruling, however, arguing that it was premature to remove federal protections for gray wolves and that the USFWS's actions subverted the intent of the ESA to restore listed species to a significant portion of their historic range (Fox 2006a). In 2005, a U.S. District Court ruled in the plaintiffs' favour and overturned the 2003 USFWS rule, restoring the endangered status to gray wolves (except in Minnesota, where they are listed as "threatened" under the ESA). Despite this ruling, the U.S. federal government, under the Bush administration, continued to seek delisting of gray wolves in the lower forty-eight states, and animal advocacy and conservation organizations continue to challenge the proposed delisting, arguing that the federal government has failed to develop a comprehensive range-wide strategy for recovering gray wolves (Fox 2006a).

Because the return of the wolf to the conterminous states is so laden with human values, attitudes, and beliefs (see chapter by Bath, this volume), we argue that this historical moment presents a unique opportunity for reflection about the ethical issues involved in wolf restoration and the development of practical models for how humans can learn to coexist with wolves in an increasingly humanized landscape. By beginning with an ethical framework and dialogue that considers the interests and values of all stakeholders, including the wolves, who also are entitled to a point of view, we can ensure the process of wolf conservation and management is inclusive and democratic and better serves all affected. We also argue for less invasive and more humane methods of management and control when and where management and control are deemed necessary.

Wolf recovery and conservation requires a sustained commitment toward building human tolerance for the presence of large carnivores. It also requires proactive outreach aimed at educating the public about the vital ecological role wolves (Ripple et al. 2001) and other large carnivores play in maintaining species diversity and the integrity of ecosystems (Berger 1999; Terborgh et al. 1999, 2001; Soulé et al. 2003). Wolves are the consummate keystone carnivore in North America.

If those communities most affected by reintroduction and recovery efforts are to accept wolves and other large carnivores, conservationists must work toward public education and information dissemination to address real and perceived fears held by members of these communities. The principles followed in wolf education initiatives are described in this volume by Taylor, who also highlights the risks of indoctrination of the public and of 'propaganda' by the wolf experts. Integrating ethics into large carnivore recovery also mandates that we listen to community concerns and invest the necessary resources to build tolerance and dispel misinformation. Wolf conservation in general demands a collaborative process among parties who often do not speak to one another. A comprehensive wolf recovery and conservation agenda deals with animal protection, ecological concerns, and socio-political processes.

ETHICAL QUESTIONS TO PONDER

"WOLVES – government Sponsored TERRORISTS"
– Bumper sticker from www.savethe-usa.com

"A crucial point is that good science rests on good ethics. What scientists do matters; it counts ethically." – Jickling and Paquet (2005)

"The whale in the sea, like the wolf on land, constituted not only a symbol of wildness but also a fulcrum for projecting attitudes of conquest and utilitarianism and, eventually, more contemporary perceptions of preservation and protection." – Kellert (1996)

Wolves are a prototypical example of an animal whose reputation precedes them. They bring out extremes in human emotions from almost romanticized idolatry and reverence to blatant contempt and hate (as reflected in the bumper sticker slogan above) that have deep historical roots (Young and Goldman 1944; Lopez 1978; Casey and Clark 1996; Smith and Ferguson 2005). Prehistorically, in oral tradition, human fears of wolves and other large carnivores were reflected in fairy and folktales such as *Little Red Riding Hood*, a story in which a wolf follows Little Red Riding Hood home, eats her grandmother, and, according to some interpretations, rapes her. This is a story that is still read to young children throughout the world. Historically, people have viewed wolves as threats to livestock and as competitors in the human hunt for food or sport (Young and Goldman 1944). As a result of such conflicts, humans are usually the most important cause of mortality of adult wolves and other large carnivores, even within protected areas (Woodroffe and Ginsberg 1998).

Ethical reflection is needed in attempting to recover wolf populations on lands where abundant domesticated prey (i.e., unprotected livestock on the open range) bring them into conflict with livestock (Robinson 2005; Smith and Ferguson 2005). Can we really blame them for taking advantage of an accessible meal? Should we be moving predators around if we cannot let them be the animals that they have evolved to be, when recovery means intensive management, or when the areas into which we place them are increasingly developed, fragmented, and hostile? Can we call wolf recovery a success in the United States when we have confined recovery efforts to less than 5 per cent of the wolf's historical range and when approximately 80 per cent of all known wolf mortalities in the tri-state area of Montana, Idaho, and Wyoming are intentional removals by the U.S. federal government?

SOME GUIDING PRINCIPLES: THE IMPORTANCE OF ETHICS

The authors' guiding principles for how we interact with other animals are simple and straightforward: do no intentional harm, treat all individuals with respect and compassion, and recognize that all animals have intrinsic value or worth, irrespective of their utility to other animals, including humans. We recognize and acknowledge that our ethical principles and framework reflect not only our cultural backgrounds, biases, and education but also our deeper Greco-Roman ethical heritage dating back to Socrates, Plato, and even earlier to Indo-European cultures. Ethical positions within human societies differ profoundly across cultures and time. Hence, when we speak of our guiding ethical principles, we do so knowing that they reflect only a few cultural perspectives amongst a broad array of perspectives that come into play when discussing wolf recovery and conservation.

While very few people in any culture attempt to cause intentional harm or delight in doing so in their efforts to conserve and restore ecosystems and biodiversity, the other principles that call for treating individuals with respect and compassion and recognizing an individual's intrinsic value or worth are all too easily overridden because they are too difficult to consistently adhere to regardless of cultural biases. In some cases, while it clearly is not one's intention to cause harm to other animals, the very design of some studies or perhaps the very reality of some conservation efforts means that inevitably some animals will suffer or die. We must ensure that we do everything we can to minimize pain and suffering and cause the least amount of harm.

The recognition that wolves and other individual animals have intrinsic value demands that we consider ethics when we conduct projects and practices that impact them. When we use the term "ethics," we are referring to Socrates' notion of 'how we ought to live' (Irwin 1995). Hadidian et al. (2006) also note: "ethics is a conversation about the moral values that inform (or should inform) our thoughts and actions ... ethics is not only a critique of who we are as individuals and a society today, it is a vision of what our future may be if we act with ethical sensibilities in mind ... ethics is meant to help us refine our knowledge and action, to distinguish better from worse arguments, methods, data and facts." While many agree that ethics must play a central role in any project involving the use of animals (Bekoff and Jamieson 1996; Bekoff 2001; Jickling and Paquet 2005; Hadidian et al. 2006), it is interesting to note that in many books on human–animal interactions and carnivore conservation there is often no mention of ethics. This needs to change.

We assert that recovery and conservation efforts for wolves and other carnivores should be firmly rooted in ethical principles. And yet, when we look at current wolf management in the United States, consideration of ethics is largely ignored. For example, as we write this, the United States Forest Service is planning to ease restrictions on killing predators in protected wilderness areas within the western United States, allowing expanded use of aerial gunning and certain poisons (Knickerbocker 2006). And the USFWS recently issued lethal control permits to the states of

Wisconsin and Michigan that authorize officials to kill up to fifty-four gray wolves annually if the wolves are perceived as threatening livestock or pets (Fox 2006a). However, animal and environmental organizations sued to stop the killing and in August 2006 the federal court ruled in the plaintiffs' favour, stating that the issuance of lethal kill permits violates the ESA. The state of Wisconsin argued the kill permits were "necessary to maintain social tolerance for the wolves" (Frommer 2006). In her court decision, the judge responded by saying, "The recovery of the gray wolf is not supported by killing 43 gray wolves" (Frommer 2006).

Furthermore, there are examples of "Judas wolves" (Robbins 2005), individuals who are collared and then followed back to their pack so that other pack members can be located. The Judas wolf, having unknowingly betrayed its pack-mates, is then killed along with the entire pack, including pups. Despite the fact that gray wolves remain federally listed under the ESA, more than three hundred have been killed by the U.S. federal government since 1987, most for preying on livestock (Robbins 2005). Lethal removal of wolves continues while we know, and have known, that eliminating predators does little to increase economic gains for livestock ranchers (Berger 2006) or to reduce attacks over the long term (Musiani et al. 2005). On the other hand, Bangs et al. in this volume list the benefits of wolf control campaigns, whose effects are mainly in diminishing conflicts perceived by local residents.

Discussions about ethics and animals can make people uncomfortable. Surely, they exclaim, there are more important things to talk about. While ignorance may be bliss, ignoring questions about our ethical responsibilities to animals not only compromises their lives and our integrity but also can compromise the quality of scientific research. More and more students and practising scientists recognize that asking questions about ethics is in the best interests of "good science," and increasing numbers of non-researchers are also keenly interested in animal well-being (Schmidt 1989; Schmidt and Salmon 1991; Broom 1999; Eggleston et al. 2003; Soulé et al. 2005; Bekoff 2006a, 2007a, 2007b; Rollin 2006). Wildlife managers and scientists are under growing scrutiny by a concerned public who not only question how funds are used to support wildlife management practices and various scientific research projects but also want wildlife managers and scientists to be less arrogant and authoritarian and more accountable to those who support them (Kirkwood et al. 1994; Kellert 1996; Broom 1999; Bekoff 2006a, 2006b; Rollin 2006). Furthermore, science, including conservation biology, is not value-free (Soulé 1985; Bekoff 2001; Jickling and Paquet 2005; Rollin 2006). Soulé (1985) argued that conservation biology must be based on a set of ethical axioms. Personal views held by scientists influence funding and the dissemination (or withholding) of certain results. Indeed, dealing with personal sentiments and emotional conflicts makes questions about what we ought to do extremely difficult. Complicating the situation is the fact that values and sentiments change with time and are sensitive to demographic, political, and social-economic variation, as well as to personal whims. However, regardless of changes in values and sentiments, if we remain loyal to doing no intentional harm, treating all individuals with respect and compassion, and recognizing that all animals have intrinsic value and worth irrespective of their utility (the authors' guiding principles expresses above), we will ensure high ethical standards in our discussions on interaction with other species and in our actions which impact them.

CONSIDERING ALL PERSPECTIVES

As we try to repatriate and restore wolves to the landscape, we have a duty to consider the broad impacts of such efforts from all angles: on the wolf packs, the populations and ecosystems from which they are taken, and on the human, animal, and ecological communities in which they are placed. In discussing the social dynamics affecting wolf conservation in Yellowstone National Park, for example, Clark et al. (2005) aptly state, "Understanding the human participants is essential to understanding what has happened, why, and what is likely to happen." While it is imperative to consider and negotiate differing perspectives and values amongst various human stakeholder groups in wolf recovery efforts, we contend one viewpoint is often missing in this discussion: the wolf's. This chapter focuses on under-represented perspectives in wolf-recovery efforts (e.g., the wolf's viewpoint) and does not attempt at understanding the viewpoints of all interest groups (for this, also see Bath, this volume). The growing body of literature on animal cognition and emotions demonstrates undeniably that animals have interests and points of view (Masson and McCarthy 1995; Bekoff 2006a, 2006b, 2007a). Like us, they avoid pain and suffering and seek pleasure. They form close social relationships, cooperate with other individuals, and likely miss their friends when they are apart (M. W. Fox 1992; Masson and McCarthy 1995; Bekoff 2006a, 2006b). Emotions have evolved, serving as "social glue," and playing major roles in the formation and maintenance of social relationships among individuals (Masson and McCarthy 1995). Emotions also serve as "social catalysts," regulating behaviours that guide the course of social encounters when individuals follow different courses of action, depending on their situations (Masson and McCarthy 1995; Bekoff 2002, 2006a, 2006b, 2007a). If we carefully study animal behaviour, we can better understand what animals are experiencing and feeling and how this factors into how we treat them.

Recognizing that wolves and other animals have emotional lives forces us to consider their needs and interests as individuals, as families, and as members of a community. Because the wolf is a species with complex social structures and tight family bonds, we must consider the ethical implications of our actions when we disrupt family packs through management and control programs. We need to consider the wolf's point of view in our overall conservation and recovery efforts.

WOLF PERSECUTION: REPEATING THE CYCLE?

Consider the case of the Mexican wolf reintroduction program. Mexican wolves once ranged from central Mexico up into Arizona and New Mexico (Povilitis et al. 2006). They were exterminated throughout most of their historic range by the U.S. Bureau of Biological Survey and its successor agency, the U.S. Department of Agriculture Animal Damage Control program (now called "Wildlife Services") (Parsons 1998). In 1976, the subspecies was placed on the endangered species list, and a reintroduction effort was initiated in 1998. While approximately 90 captive wolves were reintroduced over the course of eight years in New Mexico and Arizona, as few as 35 (estimated range: 35–49; mean estimate: 42; USFWS 2006c) wolves remained in the wild population by the end of 2005. From 1998 through 2005, illegal shooting (23), lethal agency control (3), vehicle collisions (9), and capture complications (1) accounted for the human-caused deaths of 36 wolves; and 83 wolves were captured and either removed or translocated at the agencies' discretion for management purposes, which included 31 wolves involved in livestock losses (Adaptive Management Oversight Committee [AMOC] 2005; USFWS 2005b, 2006c). High wolf "failure rates" (mortalities + removals) are precluding population growth, causing population declines in 2004 and 2005, despite continued releases of wolves during those years (AMOC 2005; USFWS 2005b, 2006c). The program has been criticized for poor management, bureaucratic processes that hinder effective recovery, and unrealistic political boundaries that do not allow wolves to colonize public lands outside of the defined recovery zones (Robinson 2005; Povilitis et al. 2006). Moreover, ranchers are not required to improve or alter their livestock husbandry practices to reduce predation even after a wolf is removed or killed (which is the case throughout the United States, not just in the Mexican wolf reintroduction program). And, in July 2006, the USFWS announced its acceptance of a set of recommendations that, if implemented, will allow the government, tribes, and private individuals to trap or kill Mexican wolves with few restraints when the combined populations in New Mexico and Arizona exceed 125 wolves (AMOC 2005), a cap that cannot be considered either viable over the long term or ecologically effective for the region (Soulé et al. 2003; Soulé et al. 2005). We simply must ask, "What are we doing and why are we doing it?" This sort of bureaucratic mismanagement and shameless killing must be stopped if we are ever to extricate ourselves from the persecute/eliminate/try-to-recover-the-species cycle. How can we get out of this loop and constructively facilitate coexistence with this sentient, social mammal?

TRADE-OFFS: INDIVIDUALS VS. SPECIES

In conservation biology, the interests and rights of individuals are sometimes traded off against perceived benefits that accrue to higher levels of
organization: populations, species, and ecosystems. Animal protection
advocates who prioritize the welfare of individual animals are often mar-
ginalized because their perspectives are perceived as obstacles to conservation efforts. Estes (1998) poignantly and succinctly gets to the heart of the
matter in his discussion of whether or not to rehabilitate oiled wildlife,
specifically California sea otters (*Enhydra lutris*):

> The differing views between those who value the welfare
> of individuals and those who value the welfare of populations
> should be a real concern to conservation biology because they are
> taking people with an ostensibly common goal in different di-
> rections. Can these views be reconciled for the common good of
> nature? I'm not sure, although I believe the populationists have
> it wrong in trying to convince the individualists to see the errors
> of their ways. The challenge is not so much for individualists to
> build a program that is compatible with conservation – to date
> they haven't had to – but for conservationists to somehow build
> a program that embraces the goals and values of individualists
> because the majority of our society has such a deep emotional
> attachment to the welfare of individual animals…. As much
> as many populationists may be offended by this argument, it
> is surely an issue that must be dealt with if we are to build an
> effective conservation program.

Some of the main issues concerning trade-offs among individuals, populations, species, and ecosystems are highlighted when considering reintroduction programs. Such efforts raise questions about when and whether
it is permissible to override an individual's life for the good of its species
– when can individuals be traded off for conservation gains? Consider the
reintroduction of gray wolves into Yellowstone National Park (YNP). All

of the wolves who were reintroduced into YNP were translocated from Canada. Some were separated from their family packs; some died shortly after their release (Smith and Ferguson 2005). Currently, those that venture out of the protective zones of YNP may be lethally removed if they prey on livestock. Our view is that individuals count and that jumping among different levels of organization is not as seamless as some make it out to be (for discussion, see Aitken's [2004] development of what she calls the "new conservation"). We believe that carnivore recovery programs are essential to restoring ecosystem integrity and diversity, but we also believe that in so doing we must be rigorous in the questions we ask, mindful of the individual animals we are translocating and of their progeny, and ethical in the way we conduct such programs. Researchers have an obligation to attempt to fully understand the effects of reintroduction programs on life history strategies, demography, behaviour, and animals' lives (Bekoff 2001 and references therein).

REINTRODUCTION VERSUS NATURAL RECOVERY: THE ROLE OF FEAR

Recovering native species through reintroduction programs requires massive human effort and large sums of money. Humans and human society are major factors in what goes right or wrong, and people who are most affected at the local level are sometimes resentful and hostile at having to share land and space with a large predator that their forefathers purposefully eradicated. This is easy to understand especially when they have been living their lives and making their livelihoods in the absence of these predators. Moreover, the myth of the savage wolf persists and this also makes it difficult for some people to accept their presence. Fear is a powerful motivator, so those who advocate the reintroduction of wolves must work toward alleviating unfounded concern about their danger, allocate the necessary resources to build tolerance for wolves through public education and outreach programs, and help reduce conflicts where real conflicts exist.

Natural recovery of wolves also presents challenges as seen in Minnesota, Michigan, and Wisconsin (Wydeven et al., this volume); but perhaps more people would be open to the presence of wolves if they return on their own. Those less receptive would be given more time to get accustomed to the fact that wolves are on the way, and those who dislike government intervention might be open to wolves if there were less bureaucratic interference. Yet there's no denying that wolves – whether from reintroduced or naturally recolonizing populations – face tough odds when attempting to venture beyond the political boundaries in which they've been confined. For example, in September 2006, a wolf likely dispersing from one of the Yellowstone or central Idaho packs was found dead in a leghold trap on private land in Utah (Baird 2006). Four years earlier, another wolf was discovered in the state – also found in a leghold trap (Baird 2006). In Maine and Vermont where gray wolves historically roamed, at least three wolf-like canids believed to have dispersed from Canada have been shot or trapped before their presence in the states was even acknowledged (Crawford 2006). So a high tolerance level among the general public does not necessarily translate to safety for wolves if a few key humans (e.g., trappers, hunters, ranchers) have low tolerance; thus, dispersing wolves often find a lethal human environment where basic survival becomes a challenge. While there is certainly no guarantee that natural recovery will increase tolerance for wolves over reintroduction programs, the costs and benefits of both should be weighed before recovery efforts are implemented.

We also need to reconcile the disparity in the status of wolves who are reintroduced and those who appear on their own. The former are granted "experimental, non-essential status" under section 10(j) of the ESA and are subject to being killed for being the predators that they are (when they predate livestock), whereas naturally occurring individuals are ostensibly granted full protection under the ESA. While some argue reducing federal protections for reintroduced wolves was a necessary concession to garner acceptance from the ranching community (Smith and Ferguson 2005), we must ask if it is acceptable to continue to designate wolves "experimental, non-essential" and then kill them when they prey on livestock while not requiring ranchers to take some responsibility to reduce losses by removing livestock carcasses and improving their animal husbandry techniques. Caring properly for livestock is and should be one of the costs of doing business and should be reflected in the price of meat at the supermarket. Unfortunately, the current system in the United States externalizes the costs of livestock predation, and it is the American taxpaying public that bears these costs through subsidies for government predator control programs and livestock grazing subsidies. The wolves also pay with their lives when they are lethally "removed" for preying on livestock.

THE FUTURE OF WOLF CONSERVATION AND MANAGEMENT IN THE UNITED STATES

In the United States, as the federal government evaluates the opportunity to delist wolves (see Wydeven et al. and Stone, this volume), we can expect the debate about wolf conservation and management to intensify with ethics and human–wolf conflict mitigation moving front and centre to the debate. When delisting occurs, wolves will no longer be federally protected under the Endangered Species Act; management will revert to the states and tribes. Heated debates have already begun about how wolves will be managed and whether traditional forms of management, including trophy hunting and commercial and recreational fur trapping, will be allowed, as they are for some species of large carnivores. For example, Minnesota's state management plan would allow wolves to be killed to protect domestic animals, even if attacks or threatening behaviour have not occurred (USFWS 2006d), and eventually allow for the commissioner to "prescribe open seasons" on wolves, thereby legalizing trophy hunting and fur trapping (Minnesota Department of Natural Resources [MNDNR] 2001). The Minnesota state law also allows for paying "certified gray wolf predator controllers" $150 for each individual killed.[1]

---

1 Section 97B.671 Predator control program of Minnesota State Law.

Wyoming's proposed management plan calls for wolves to be classified with "dual status" (Wyoming Game and Fish Department [WGFD] 2003), allowing them to be managed as trophy game in national parks and wilderness areas and as a "predatory animal" outside of these designated areas, allowing them to be killed at any time. The USFWS, however, has rejected Wyoming's plan, stating it is inadequate to ensure long-term viability of wolf populations (Nie 2004). Despite this, in January 2007, the Wyoming legislature introduced a bill that would authorize the killing of almost two-thirds of the wolves in the state. Wildlife and animal advocates have already begun to challenge both the delisting process and the state management plans, which has served to increase public debate about the future of wolf management in the United States (Fox 2006a).

One need only look at Alaska to see why there is significant concern about how wolf management may unfold in the lower forty-eight states. In Alaska, wolves are not considered endangered and receive none of the legal protections under the ESA that their counterparts do in the rest of the United States. They can be legally trapped, trophy hunted, and aerially gunned where they are chased to exhaustion by low-flying aircraft and then shot. Between 2003 and 2006, more than 550 wolves have been killed through aerial gunning in Alaska, despite the fact that Alaskans have twice voted to ban the practice (1996 and 2000) in state-wide ballot measures (the Alaska legislature then overturned those bans). In some areas, the Alaska Board of Game has approved the killing of up to 75 per cent of the wolf population, ostensibly to boost moose and caribou populations for big-game hunters. In 1998, a citizens group called "Alaskans Against Snaring Wolves," sought to prohibit the use of snares for capturing wolves through an unsuccessful public ballot initiative after photos of severely injured snared wolves were published in local and national media outlets. The grassroots effort and the ensuing public debate it generated on the use of snares and other control methods supported by the Alaska Board of Game highlighted the growing controversy over the ethics of wolf management and individual management techniques, and the way that management decisions are made.

Some have argued that decisions made in Alaska regarding wolves cannot be compared to decisions made in the lower forty-eight states. However, when states like Idaho take an official position that the federal government must forcibly remove all wolves from the state (adopted as House Joint Memorial No. 5 in 2001) and Wyoming wants to declare open season on wolves, it becomes apparent that a similar, firmly rooted anti-wolf sentiment amongst some sectors of the public is not limited to Alaska.

INTEGRATING ETHICS INTO WOLF AND CARNIVORE CONSERVATION

While strong anti-wolf sentiments persist in some areas of the United States, particularly in more rural regions, such attitudes are rapidly changing as the populace becomes more urban and educated (Kellert 1996; Kellert et al. 2000). In this volume, Bath describes human attitudes toward wolves in Europe and North America, whereas this chapter focuses on the ethical implications of human attitudes and of changes in attitudes. Over the last century, we have seen a shift in the public's attitudes toward wildlife and nature, moving from a primarily dominionistic/utilitarian valuation toward one that is more humanistic/moralistic oriented (Kellert 1996; Kellert et al. 2000; Teel et al. 2002). With this shift in public values has come an increased demand for humane, socially acceptable, and ecologically sound management strategies for addressing conflicts between people and wild animals (Kellert 1985b; Braband and Clark 1992; Haber 1996; Reiter et al. 1999). One national study on public attitudes toward wildlife management concluded that a majority of Americans favour the use of non-lethal methods over lethal in managing wildlife (Reiter et al. 1999). In this study, survey respondents were asked to rank the importance of factors to be considered when selecting management techniques; human safety, animal suffering, effectiveness, and environmental impacts ranked highest. Less important was monetary cost, suggesting a willingness amongst the public to invest more money to develop methods that ensure public safety and mitigate animal suffering. If lethal controls must be employed, the public would like those methods to be humane and selective (Kellert 1985b; Reiter et al. 1999). Yet one study that looked at lethal carnivore management programs across the globe found that between 30 and 81.3 per cent of the carnivores killed in control operations bore no evidence of involvement in conflicts (Treves and Naughton-Treves 2005), despite the efforts to target so-called 'problem animals' such as those described for wolves by Bangs et al. (this volume).

Strong objections to U.S. government-funded lethal predator control programs have also been expressed by professional scientists with the American Society of Mammalogists (ASM). In 1999, the ASM passed a resolution stating that the "common methods of predator control are often indiscriminate, pre-emptive, lethal measures, particularly in relation to state- and federally funded livestock protection programs ... and often result in the needless killing of animals that are not contributing to the problem, as well as many non-target species" (ASM 1999). They called on the U.S. Department of Agriculture's Wildlife Services Program and other federal and state wildlife management agencies to "cease indiscriminate, pre-emptive, lethal control programs ... and to focus on the implementation of non-lethal control strategies, compensatory measures, and sound animal husbandry techniques" (ASM 1999).

If ethics, societal values, and animal welfare are not fully vetted and incorporated into wildlife management policies and programs, what are some potential consequences? Increasing use of the public ballot initiative process is one possible outcome if a large segment of the public continues to feel their values and opinions are not considered in decision-making processes. Similarly, if wolf opponents feel their concerns and values continue to go unheard, we may see an increase in illegal killings as have been documented in Idaho where a number of wolves were intentionally poisoned with the deadly poison Compound 1080 after wolves were reintroduced in the region (USFWS 2004).

A first step toward mitigating reactionary responses to wolf conservation policies and practices is for state and federal wildlife agencies to create greater opportunities for public participation in the decision-making process. In the United States, many state and federal wildlife management agencies have been criticized as operating in bureaucratic, self-serving ways that ensure their continued control and power over wildlife management while largely excluding the public from meaningful participation (Clark et al. 2005). These institutions often fail to change strategies and policies to reflect new and more holistic ecosystem approaches to wildlife conservation that incorporate adaptive management practices (Clark et al. 2005; Povilitis et al. 2006). They also tend to shun discussion or consideration of ethics, public attitudes, and values by deeming such concerns as unscientific and contrary to traditional approaches to wildlife management. The current problems with the Mexican wolf reintroduction program reflect this bureaucratic institutional system that largely disregards public input, particularly from the conservation and animal protection communities, and fails to ensure transparency in its processes, policies, and practices (Robinson 2005; Povilitis et al. 2006).

So, what is the solution to this entrenched systemic problem? As Clark et al. (2005) state, "Expanding confused bureaucracies is not the answer, although this is what we often do.... To improve wildlife conservation, especially large carnivore management, bureaucracies must be reformed." A first step toward wildlife management agency reform is to create models and processes that promote integration and inclusion – where people feel heard, where they feel their values are considered, and where they feel they can have a meaningful say in the matter. Such civic-minded processes will also help foster mutual understanding and common ground and counter the dominant wildlife management paradigm in the United States, which tends to promote divisiveness instead of cooperative problem solving (Clark et al. 2005).

PRACTICAL MODELS OF CARNIVORE COEXISTENCE

In addition to new modes of civic processes that foster inclusion and integration, we also need practical on-the-ground carnivore coexistence model programs that promote large carnivore conservation and cooperative community-based problem solving. Clark et al. (2005) call this "practice-based improvements," the application of which use actual experience and adaptive management practices to address site-specific conflict areas rather than theoretical principles as the basis for making improvements. Musiani and Paquet (2004) argue that such efforts should focus on rural areas where human–wolf conflicts are more likely to occur. We argue that such programs should also incorporate ethics and humane concerns. Globally an increasing number of "practice-based improvement" models provide examples of practices that foster large carnivore conservation and promote coexistence. For example, in Bulgaria, non-governmental organizations have implemented a program aimed at reducing conflicts between livestock and wolves non-lethally and building tolerance for the presence of wolves by supplying shepherds with Karakachan guarding dogs (Rigg 2001). They have also conducted a broad public awareness campaign that includes outreach to ranchers, students, and the general public (Tsingarska 1997). In Sweden, a government-run program provides ranchers with financial support to implement electric fencing and other non-lethal predation deterrents (Swenson and Andrén 2005); ranchers are compensated for the presence of carnivores on their property at predetermined rates, fostering better animal husbandry and carnivore conservation (Linnell et al. 1996). To date, the program appears to have been successful in reducing losses and building tolerance for the presence of wolves and other large carnivores (Swenson and Andrén 2005; Linnell et al. 1996). In Ethiopia, the Ethiopian Wolf Conservation Program employs people from the local communities to protect the wolf, conducts outreach to ranchers to improve livestock and agricultural practices, vaccinates domestic dogs to help prevent the spread of canid diseases, and has an extensive educational program aimed at building local understanding of the important role that the wolf plays in the Bale mountain ecosystem (Sillero-Zubiri and Laurenson 2001).

Isolated models of carnivore coexistence programs that integrate ethics and ecological concerns are beginning to appear in the United States as well. For example, in Marin County, California, a non-lethal cost-share program funded by the county provides qualified ranchers with financial assistance to implement non-lethal deterrents including guard dogs, llamas, improved fencing, and lambing sheds (Fox and Papouchis 2005; Fox 2006b). A cost-share indemnification program was later added to the program to compensate qualified ranchers for verified livestock losses resulting from predation; to qualify for compensation, ranchers must participate in the cost-share component of the program and have at least two non-lethal deterrents in place. Importantly, the program was adopted as a result of public opposition to the use of poisons, snares, and other lethal methods employed by a taxpayer-subsidized government trapper under the USDA–Wildlife Services program (Fox 2001). The debate centred around ethics, animal welfare, and the use of taxpayer monies to support the killing of native carnivores to protect ranching interests. The program has garnered national attention, and initial data from the County Agricultural Commissioner's office indicate it has been effective at helping to reduce livestock losses for some ranchers (Brenner 2005; Carlsen 2005; Agocs 2007).

Hence, new models of predator/livestock coexistence strategies combined with traditional techniques that historically proved effective in many parts of the world, such as shepherding and the use of guard dogs, have the potential to improve wolf conservation efforts globally (Linnell et al. 1996; Ciucci and Boitani 1998a; Musiani and Paquet 2004).

LOOKING TO THE FUTURE AND LEARNING FROM THE PAST: WE CAN ALWAYS DO BETTER

As conservationists struggle to stem the hastening global biodiversity crises, we face many ethical challenges. How do we balance the urgent need to restore ecosystem health through large carnivore recovery with our obligation to consider ethics and animal well-being? These are difficult questions with no simple answers. Nonetheless, serious ethical reflection, public education, and dialogue are needed before deciding to restore a previously extirpated species such as the wolf. Ultimately, it is unlikely that a quick fix is the best way to proceed, especially when a lack of understanding of the complex and interrelated socio-political, economic, and ecological variables involved can make or break a recovery project. For example, the very early stages of Canada lynx reintroduction into southwestern Colorado were marred by the death of four reintroduced individuals soon after they were released because there was not enough food (Bekoff 2001). Some state officials, independent wildlife biologists, and animal advocates had argued that the available data suggested that the habitat was unsuitable to support viable lynx populations; yet lynx were released using what some called a "dump and pray" strategy (Bekoff 2001). The hasty and politically motivated "quick fix" clearly did not work; however, when reintroduction protocols were changed and attention was given to the scientific data concerning food availability and habitat suitability, fewer deaths by starvation resulted, and ultimately some of the reintroduced lynx went on to breed.

As we attempt to restore wolves and other large carnivores in a human-dominated world where fragmentation – environmental and spiritual – and accelerating urban sprawl threaten to undermine such efforts, it would behoove us to look back on history and gauge where we have come from and where we are going. Less than sixty years ago, the last remaining Mexican wolves in Mexico were eliminated by the very same agency that is leading the wolf recovery effort in the United States today; less than thirty-five years ago, wolves were hunted without restrictions in many states (Mech 1970). What have we learned since then?

Aldo Leopold, who is considered by many as the father of wildlife conservation in North America, had an epiphany watching a wolf die (after having slaughtered this one and many others himself), and for the first time connected with an individual wolf in a way he had never experienced before. Through this experience, Leopold stepped beyond seeing the world from a myopic anthropocentric lens and recognized that another species had its own wants and needs – its own intrinsic worth – and a desire to live free and unfettered. Out of this and other experiences, Leopold (1949) developed what he termed "The Land Ethic." In his words:

The land ethic simply enlarges the boundaries of the community to include soils, waters, plants, and animals, or collectively: the land – and it affirms the right of all to continued existence. The extension of ethics to land and to the animals and plants which is an evolutionary possibility and an ecological necessity. In short, a land ethic changes the role of Homo sapiens from conqueror of the land-community to plain member and citizen of it. It implies respect for his fellow-members, and also respect for the community as such.

Ultimately Leopold's Land Ethic was a call to action to create a new paradigm for the way we interact with and coexist with native carnivores – indeed all living beings – one that recognizes the ecological importance of these other species and life forms as well as their intrinsic value. As we struggle to rectify the wrongs of our past and as we gauge our almost limitless power to both create and destroy – and then recreate, restore, and recover other species and ecosystems – we must, like Leopold, take a long moment to reflect upon our actions. As also highlighted by Taylor in this volume's chapter on wolf education, we must be willing to ask difficult ethical questions and learn from our past mistakes. Ultimately, we must always challenge ourselves: should we be doing what we are doing and, if so, can we do it better?

Michael Soulé, a founder of the field of conservation biology, perhaps said it best:

> We're certainly a dominant species, but that's not the same as a keystone species. A keystone species is one that, when you remove it, the diversity collapses; we're a species that when you add us, the diversity collapses. We can change everything, dictate everything and destroy everything. (Soulé 2002)

Soulé is right. As big-brained and often self-centred and arrogant mammals, we can do anything we want anywhere, anytime, and to any other beings or landscapes. We must recognize that this unprecedented power comes with enormous and compelling ethical responsibilities to do the best we can. Let us remember that in most cases we can do better; and in all cases we have an obligation to strive to do better than our predecessors.

ACKNOWLEDGMENTS

We thank Dave Parsons, Michael Soulé, and Bonnie Fox for their helpful comments on an earlier version of this chapter.

2.2 Compensation and Non-lethal Deterrent Programs: Building Tolerance for Wolf Restoration in the Rockies

Suzanne A. Stone

INTRODUCTION: WOLVES IN THE NORTHERN ROCKIES

In 1993, the U.S. Fish and Wildlife Service (USFWS) proposed five alternative plans ranging from "no wolves" to reintroduction of wolves with full-endangered species status and protection, which received more than 160,000 comments from all fifty U.S. states and forty countries, one of the largest public comment responses received on any wildlife restoration action ever proposed by the agency. Among the alternatives for reintroducing wolves was a "non-essential" status allowed under section 10(j) of the Endangered Species Act. This alternative, the most favoured of all the plans, included a provision that would allow wolves that preyed on livestock to be moved or killed, in order to protect regional livestock producers. During 1995 and 1996, wolves were reintroduced to central Idaho and Yellowstone National Park (USFWS et al. 2007; Bangs et al., this volume). Naturally recolonizing wolves are also present in northwest Montana. Finally, dispersing wolves have been found in Oregon, Washington, Utah, and, most recently, Colorado, although there is no confirmation that wolves are forming packs or reproducing in these states.

As wolf populations increase, their effect on the ecosystems becomes stronger, as shown by the wolf's role in culling weak and old elk and other ungulates (Smith et al. 2003) and reducing the long-term concentration of elk herds on sensitive meadows and wetlands (Ripple and Beshta 2004). With less grazing pressure from elk, streambed vegetation such as willow and aspen appear to be regenerating after decades of over-browsing. As the vegetation regrows, it improves habitat for native birds, fish, beaver, and other species.

However, as wolves returned in the northern Rockies, the age-old conflicts that led to their original demise also re-emerged. First among these conflicts is the issue of livestock losses to wolves. Annually, wolves kill less than 0.1 per cent of livestock within their range (Bangs et al., this volume). According to the National Agricultural Statistics Service (2006) report, 95.3 per cent of livestock death losses were due to disease, bad weather, theft, poisoning, etc. In regard to predation losses, "Coyotes and dogs caused the majority of cattle and calf [predator] losses, accounting for 51.1% and 11.5% respectively." Wolves attributed less than 3 per cent of the estimated overall predator losses. However, wolf conflicts are commonly sensationalized by local media and these stories rarely report on other causes of loss, heightening the perceived damages by wolves and undermining public support for wolf conservation. Livestock owners also experience anxiety over the added threat of livestock losses posed by the presence of wolves (Fritts et al. 2003). To minimize conflict, government agencies often kill wolves that prey on livestock to prevent additional depredations (Bangs et al., this volume). Often agency managers attempt to target individual "problem" wolves that develop a penchant for killing.

COMPENSATION TO ADDRESS WOLF AND HUMAN CONFLICTS

Wolf compensation programs to reimburse livestock owners for their losses are aimed at reducing conflicts associated with livestock losses. Most programs are administered and funded by government agencies and are, in some countries, the only means of addressing conflicts with wolves. These programs generally function to reimburse farmers and ranchers for livestock losses that are attributed to wolves but vary in type of animals covered, amount of compensation paid, compensation recipients, proof required for verification, sources of funding, and government versus private administration.

The issue of compensation was addressed during the 2003 World Wolf Congress held in Banff, Canada. Biologists reported that the Spanish government expends more than US$1 million annually for a population of less than three thousand wolves, the Italian government program reimbursement includes losses to bears, wolves, and feral dogs, and in Sweden, most livestock are compensated at market value with a standard compensation for hunting dogs at US$1,000. Some Swedish villages receive a fixed amount (normally US$100,000–US$150,000 annually) for reindeer depredation losses based on the presence of wolves. Though nearly all sheep are kept in fenced enclosures, there is increased interest in using electric fencing to reduce predation, which would in turn reduce funding needed for compensation. The Swedish government subsidizes about US$300,000 of electric fencing costs for farmers. In Slovakia, approximately 85 per cent of the country's 300,000 plus domestic sheep are raised within range of the country's more than a thousand wolves. The traditional system for raising sheep is in pastures, and sheep are gathered at night to be milked. Flocks average four to five hundred sheep with four to six shepherds per flock who work on a rotational system. Until 2002, there was no compensation for losses, but a new law was recently established allowing for compensation to livestock owners but remained unfunded when the program was initiated. An estimated four to six hundred sheep are killed by wolves annually, equal to US$25,000–50,000. Several countries, including for example Bulgaria, Romania, and India, do not have compensation programs and wolf conflicts remain largely addressed through lethal control of wolves or are not addressed at all (see India, where wolves are protected).[1]

---

1 Wolves in India are accorded schedule '1' endangered species status under the Indian Wildlife
   Protection Act of 1972 and the Convention on International Trade in Endangered Species
   (CITES).

In 1987, Defenders of Wildlife, an American-based environmental organization, initiated the first privately funded livestock compensation program of its kind in North America to reimburse livestock owners for wolf-caused losses while wolves are under federal protection. The idea originated from William Mott, a former National Park Service director, who in 1985 encouraged Defenders of Wildlife to consider private compensation for livestock losses as a way to build tolerance for wolves. While other types of compensation programs worldwide are typically administered by government agencies, none of the federal agencies involved in wolf restoration had legal authority to create a compensation program to reimburse private livestock owners. To date, the Bailey Wildlife Foundation Wolf Compensation Fund, named in honour of its largest contributor, has reimbursed ranchers more than $700,000 in the northern Rockies for their livestock losses to wolves.

By acknowledging that wolf conservation is largely dependent on the tolerance of local residents, the compensation program has achieved success in maintaining more local acceptance of wolves than would exist without the program. Ranchers, biologists, conservationists, local government leaders, and others actively endorse the intent and effectiveness of the program, but there are still concerns about its limitations. For example, it is not possible to document every wolf depredation, which is necessary for receiving compensation, and some undetected losses may still have significant impacts for some ranchers (Oakleaf et al. 2003). In a study conducted on a cattle allotment in a mountainous region of Idaho with high vegetation and low human presence, researchers determined that under these remote conditions less than one in six wolf kills may be documented by investigators (ibid.).

Another common allegation made against compensation programs is that most ranchers either refuse or are denied compensation for confirmed depredations. However, this is not borne out by the facts. Since the program's inception in 1987, USFWS reports that wolves were "confirmed" to have killed 528 cattle, 1,318 sheep, 83 dogs, 12 goats, 9 llamas, and 6 horses. During that same period, Defenders of Wildlife has paid livestock owners for 488 cattle, 1,418 sheep, 30 dogs (Defenders of Wildlife pays only for livestock guard and herding dogs), 10 goats, 6 llamas, and 5 horses. Defenders of Wildlife's program also pays 50 per cent of the market value for "probable" losses, which have included an additional 102 cattle, 228 sheep, and 4 dogs. These statistics demonstrate that most livestock owners who experience verified depredation losses to wolves do seek and receive compensation for their confirmed losses. The additional sheep losses paid by Defenders of Wildlife represent a hundred sheep that either died later of injuries or mature unborn lambs, which were not reported to USFWS.

EVALUATING THE WOLF COMPENSATION PROGRAM

In an effort to determine the effectiveness of this compensation program as a tool for promoting wolf conservation, data were gathered from a survey sent to all wolf compensation recipients in the U.S. northern Rockies during 2002 to 2004 (n = 138). By comparing livestock losses reported by the USFWS with those submitted to Defenders of Wildlife for compensation over this time period, it was determined that the losses suffered by these compensation recipients represent approximately 90 per cent of total documented losses during this three-year period. These survey recipients also represented a majority of the livestock owners with verified livestock losses to wolves from 1987 to 2004. These surveys were only sent to individuals who received compensation, which restricted the scope of the research findings to those with verified losses. Because wolf restoration is highly controversial in the region, attempts to contact recipients were limited to a single survey solicitation in order to reduce the likelihood that local media or word of mouth communication about the survey may influence its results. Despite limited solicitation, 44 per cent (n = 61) of those surveyed returned their completed questionnaires, demonstrating high interest in the issue.

COMPONENTS OF THE COMPENSATION PROGRAM

Defenders of Wildlife's compensation program is structured to reimburse livestock owners for the fair market value of verified livestock lost to wolves and to offer these payments in a timely manner. The program relies on the assistance of the United States Department of Agriculture–Wildlife Services (USDA–WS) agency, to professionally investigate claims of losses and accurately report their findings. That agency's mission is to provide federal leadership for resolving conflicts with wildlife (USDA–WS 2003). In cooperation with USFWS, state and tribal agencies, USDA–WS field investigators determine the cause of death of livestock and can implement non-lethal and lethal control measures to avoid or reduce depredation losses.

Livestock owners who seek compensation and meet the criteria for confirmed losses are paid 100 per cent of the market value (typically the peak price) up to $3,000 per animal, at an average expected weight (Defenders of Wildlife 2004). For example, a young calf has a reduced value, compared to when it matures months later, as most beef cattle are purchased by the pound. For losses that are determined to be "probable" wolf depredations, the program compensates livestock owners for 50 per cent of the market value. Under the definitions established by USDA–WS, "confirmed" depredations occur when there is "reasonable physical evidence that an animal was actually attacked" by wolves and "probable" depredations are classified as "some reasonable evidence exists but not enough to clearly confirm the cause of the species that killed or injured the animal" (USDA–WS 2003). Livestock currently covered by the program include cattle, sheep, goats, llamas, mules, horses, donkeys, pigs, fowl, and livestock guarding and herding dogs (Defenders of Wildlife 2004).

DISCUSSION OF FINDINGS

Cattle owners represented 71 per cent (n = 44) of the total survey respondents, followed by 18 per cent sheep producers (n = 11), and 5 per cent horse owners (n = 3). Single respondents reported losses for a goat, llama, and a livestock dog (n = 3). Although sheep losses to wolves are greater numerically than cattle losses, these figures reflect a representative proportion of livestock owners experiencing wolf depredations (i.e., more cattle producers experience wolf depredations than sheep producers, but more sheep are typically killed per depredation occurrence). Seventy per cent of respondents stated that they have raised livestock for more than thirty years (n = 43). The survey respondents reported receiving information about the compensation program from USFWS (29%), USDA–WS (28%), a state agency (19%), or news media (10%). Almost all (98%) stated that they received adequate information in order to file their compensation claim.

The survey recipients also held quite strong opposition to wolves, with 80 per cent objecting to wolves in their area (n = 49). Despite their animosity toward the species, more than two-thirds (69%) stated that they were "somewhat satisfied" (n = 28) or "highly satisfied" (n = 14) with the amount of compensation that they received for their losses, while only 23 per cent stated they were "somewhat dissatisfied" (n = 9) or "highly dissatisfied" (n = 5; Fig. 2.2.1).

Those who expressed dissatisfaction most commonly identified lack of compensation for unconfirmed or missing livestock as their primary concern. The issue of missing livestock is often raised as the leading complaint about the existing compensation program and is one of the most difficult to address as these losses cannot be attributed exclusively to wolves. Livestock commonly went missing before wolves returned to the region, and there is no reliable method to distinguish wolf losses from other causes, such as disease, poisoning, old age, birth defects, straying, or theft.

Most respondents (80%) asserted that they were using non-lethal preventative methods. The most common methods they reported were increased human surveillance, such as range riders, and shepherds (66%), carcass removal (39%), alternate grazing (26%), and use of guard dogs

Please indicate your level of satisfaction with the amount of compensation you received for your most recent depredation loss

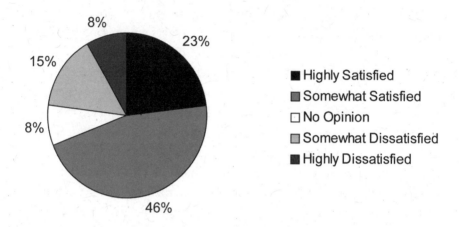

Figure 2.2.1. Responses obtained on level of satisfaction with amount compensated from a survey sent to wolf compensation recipients in the U.S. northern Rockies during 2002 to 2004 (*n* = 61).

(21%). With the exception of carcass removal, respondents rated these and non-lethal munitions (cracker shells, rubber bullets) as the most effective deterrents in reducing wolf depredations. Most respondents (59%) stated that they wanted more information about non-lethal deterrents. These survey findings revealed an important social factor for the wolf reintroduction program, as they indicated that even the people strongly opposed to wolves are still willing to try ways to co-exist with them.

Other studies have suggested that compensation does not necessarily increase tolerance for wolves (Linnell and Brøseth 2003; Naughton-Treves et al. 2003; Nemtzov 2003) and addressing this issue was a particularly important aspect of the survey. In the first question regarding tolerance, survey respondents were asked if receiving compensation increased their tolerance for wolves. More than 60 per cent said it *did not* increase their

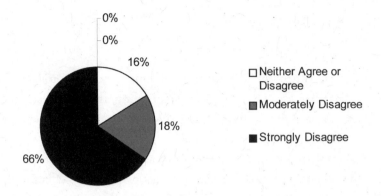

0%

0%

16%

18%

66%

☐ Neither Agree or Disagree

■ Moderately Disagree

■ Strongly Disagree

Statement: Defenders' compensation program should be continued even if wolves are moved from federal management to state management.

Figure 2.2.2. Responses obtained on continuation of a compensation program from a survey sent to wolf compensation recipients in the U.S. northern Rockies during 2002 to 2004 (*n* = 61).

tolerance for wolves. However, a second question asked how their tolerance toward wolves would be affected if the compensation program were to end. This time, nearly the exact same ratio (59%) stated that their tolerance for wolves would *decrease* from "lower" (7%) to "significantly lower" (52%), marking a sharp decline in tolerance toward wolves by nearly two-thirds of the survey respondents. Lastly, survey respondents were asked if they agreed that Defenders of Wildlife's compensation program should be ended. Not a single respondent agreed, with 66 per cent strongly disagreeing, and, in fact, nearly all respondents (80%) wanted to see the compensation program continue after wolf management passes from federal to state management (Fig. 2.2.2).

Compensation for losses has a beneficial impact on livestock owners' tolerance toward wolves as well as providing important economic relief to those bearing the direct losses of wolf restoration. At a minimum, these survey results demonstrate that compensation can prevent erosion of tolerance among the stakeholder group most opposed to (and most affected by) wolf restoration.

CONSIDERATIONS FOR COMPENSATION PROGRAMS

Administering Defenders of Wildlife's wolf compensation program is extremely challenging. Unlike many government programs, it relies exclusively on donations and grants for funding. Wolves are currently popular, which makes raising these funds easier than for less charismatic species but still requires significant organizational resources. However, the public's attraction to charismatic species waxes and wanes, which may affect long-term support for the compensation program. This is also a limiting factor that could weigh in favour of government-administered programs that may be capable of relying on more stable funding sources.

Laws and management decisions affecting wolf conservation change as a result of new administrations, growth in wolf population numbers, and new management personnel. These changes have impacted Defenders of Wildlife's compensation program by reducing incentives to maintain conservation objectives. For example, under the original reintroduction section 10(j) rule established through the Endangered Species Act, federal wolf managers were legally required to "exhaust all non-lethal control" before being allowed to use lethal control. In 2005, this rule was modified and the USFWS entirely dropped the requirement to exhaust non-lethal control in Idaho and Montana. Wolves in the reintroduction areas of these states have significantly less legal protection than those generations before them, but the criterion for our compensation program remained unchanged: recipients are still required to utilize reasonable non-lethal methods in order to qualify. If a livestock owner or agency representative were to kill wolves without attempting reasonable non-lethal alternatives, the livestock owner may be ineligible to receive compensation. Consequently, compensation may provide an incentive for non-lethal alternatives and improved animal husbandry.

One of the most important elements of any compensation program is protecting against fraudulent or misidentified claims. Agency field investigators use a wide range of reporting forms and submit varying degrees of detail about the investigations, making it harder to evaluate claims in a consistent manner. On occasion, reports are submitted without the necessary details to determine whether the report meets the standard criteria for confirmed or probable depredations. These problems delay or can prevent payments, which increases conflict and undermines the value of the compensation program. It is critically important that problems like these are carefully monitored and addressed; otherwise a program's success can be jeopardized.

Compensation programs must be carefully structured to avoid adversely impacting the species they are meant to benefit. Theoretically, the availability of compensation could be detrimental to wildlife conservation in certain situations by preserving economically unsustainable livestock producers or by creating new economic opportunities that encourage loss of wildlife habitat (Bulte and Rondeau 2005). Another potential pitfall is encouraging irresponsible animal husbandry practices when livestock owners know they will be paid for losses, even when they don't adequately protect their livestock from predation. Like the requirement for reasonable use of non-lethal methods, these programs should be structured to promote the use of best management practices by landowners. Compensation programs also need adequate insulation from political pressures that may undermine conservation objectives in lieu of economic or social perceptions and objectives.

It is not possible to document every wolf depredation and this continues to be a most contentious problem. While intensive agency investigations and wolf monitoring likely result in a lower rate of undetected wolf losses compared to other types of livestock losses, confirmed wolf losses should still be considered minimum numbers (Oakleaf et al. 2003). However, fear of wolves tends to promote exaggerated estimates of wolf–livestock depredations. Kills by other carnivores (especially coyote, *Canis latrans*) are misattributed to wolves, and missing animals (especially calves, lambs) are falsely blamed on wolves (Fritts 1982). Without close investigative scrutiny, wolves may account for only 20–50 per cent of depredations for which they are held liable (Zimen and Boitani 1979), which could diminish the effectiveness of a compensation program with respect to both economic affordability and public trust in the program.

In isolated areas with limited resources, a recently developed pilot incentive program for snow leopards in south and central Asia operates much like an insurance program by requiring local livestock owners to contribute part of the program's funding base. The program is also subsidized by international contributions from snow leopard conservation supporters, which provides for the majority of funding for compensation and deterrents to help farmers avoid depredations (Charudutt et al. 2003). As the livestock owners' participation requires a personal investment, they have greater incentives to report any fraudulent depredation claims, which helps reduce a major challenge with compensation administration. If an individual livestock owner chronically loses livestock, there is also more community pressure to help implement preventative methods to avoid depleting the insurance funding (M. Charudutt, personal communication). While this program is still in its early stages, it offers interesting alternative strategies to several components of standard compensation programs, which will be important to study as the program matures.

NON-LETHAL, PROACTIVE CONFLICT MANAGEMENT

The optimal way to manage conflicts between livestock owners and wolf conservationists is to proactively prevent wolf depredations on livestock by non-lethal means. This goal led to the creation of the Bailey Wildlife Foundation Proactive Carnivore Conservation Fund in 1998, which supports the use of non-lethal deterrents and preventative animal husbandry practices, including guard dogs, electric night pens, fladry, task-specific range riders, a volunteer program called "Wolf Guardians," and other methods. Many of these deterrents were developed in partnership with tribal and federal agencies.

Working with landowners, resource managers, and others to prevent or reduce predator problems has important conservation benefits. The single leading cause of wolf mortality in the northern Rockies and the American Southwest is government lethal control actions to stop livestock losses. Reducing conflicts can help protect wolves from being unnecessarily killed. Additionally, addressing these conflicts and implementing solutions creates opportunities for collaboration, which can help relieve social tension and encourage behavioural changes toward achieving co-existence.

A recent example of the effective nature of this program began in the spring of 2003 when ranchers in Clayton, Idaho, contacted wildlife agencies and Defenders of Wildlife for assistance in avoiding wolf predation on newborn calves. The ranchers were aware of the presence of the Buffalo Ridge pack's den near their grazing pastures. Pack members were frequenting the area to eat young fish released by Idaho Fish and Game in the creeks adjacent to the pastures. Many of these young fish were dying and the wolves learned they were a new source of protein. However, the ranchers expected the wolves would begin killing their young calves once the cattle were moved into these pastures for grazing. Several agencies, including the Nez Perce tribal wolf program, the USFWS, USDA–WS, the Salmon Challis and the Sawtooth National Forests, all contributed to purchasing hay and providing alternative grazing for the cattle until the wolf pups matured and the pack moved to a more remote rendezvous site. In subsequent years, the rancher replaced cows and young calves with older cattle that were less vulnerable to predation and used fladry to help deter wolves from the pastures. This project became the first test site for "turbo-fladry," which incorporated solar electric fencing in its design. Researchers placed the turbo-fladry around a pond that attracted wolves to nightly fishing raids in its shallow waters. The wolves did not cross the turbo-fladry while it was installed but instead circled around the outside perimeter, apparently afraid to cross the barrier. This test also led to the first development of turbo-fladry as a night corral for sheep.

The success of the project hinged on the willingness of the ranchers to adopt using non-lethal methods, and from 2003 through 2006 not a single calf was killed by wolves and the pack remained intact. Not every situation will be resolved using non-lethal methods, but this one occurred in a community where a sign posted in a window of its major store read: "Kill all the Goddamn Wolves and all the people who brought them here."

The sign was later removed and communication improved between ranchers, wolf managers, and conservationists, demonstrating that the spirit of these collaborative efforts can help reduce local animosity over wolves by allowing individual stakeholders to help manage the process. Success at maintaining and restoring healthy wolf populations across the American West and elsewhere will be directly comparative to reducing conflict in situations like this.

CRITERIA FOR NON-LETHAL, PROACTIVE PROJECTS

Over the course of the program, we have conducted a wide range of proactive and non-lethal wolf projects throughout the region, including several range rider projects in Montana (riders on horseback that patrol cattle grazing areas and implement non-lethal methods to help prevent wolves from preying on livestock); turbo-fladry development in central Idaho, grazing allotment retirement near Yellowstone National Park; supplementing livestock guard dogs on Idaho's Boise, Payette and Sawtooth National Forests; and building predator-proof fencing for llama protection near Missoula, Montana, and sheep enclosures in the Paradise Valley in Montana. From these efforts, we developed a list of general guidelines to help prioritize potential projects. In brief, project development should include consideration of location, level of cooperation, feasibility, agreements, evaluation, and limitations.

Location

It is important to determine that the proposed project area is adjacent to or directly provides suitable wolf habitat or involves areas where other wolves will continue to attempt re-establishment if removed. Additionally, the project area should have an existing or strong potential of depredation conflicts due to the regular legal presence of livestock. Local attitudes toward wolves should be included in the overall evaluation process for potential projects. If the local opposition has hampered important wolf conservation efforts in the area, it indicates a possible opportunity for constructive communication and conflict management and should be considered a higher priority. Even a small investment, like installing a temporary electric fencing system, can produce large benefits in local goodwill toward the species because the livestock owner and other members of the community are more cooperative when they feel their concerns are validated, especially when the measures implemented to address those concerns are clearly effective.

Cooperation

The attitude of the livestock owner and managers are highly important to a successful project. However, even the most ardent anti-wolf ranchers have made significant changes to prevent conflicts with wolves, so while they may be cooperative, their attitudes toward wolves may not change. They must, however, be either practising or willing to implement proper animal husbandry techniques that discourage predators, such as removing sick or injured animals or properly disposing of carcasses. When appropriate, the livestock owner should share the costs of expenses as this increases their personal investment in the project's success. This could include time and private resources in addition to, or instead of, financial contributions.

Feasibility

When assessing the project, appropriate non-lethal techniques should be reasonably applicable to the situation (e.g., range riders, livestock guard dogs, wolf deterrent fencing, fladry, Radio-Activated Guard (RAG) boxes, non-lethal munitions, etc). Project assessment should include the number, age, and type of livestock, the season(s), the availability of human presence and the size of the area to be protected. For example, fencing priority should be given to night corrals and smaller-scale projects that offer greater protection to livestock. Proposals to construct fences around large multi-acre settings would seldom be adopted as most would be prohibitively expensive. Livestock guard dogs should only be provided if they are kept in groups of two or more in order to help protect the dogs from being killed by wolves. The initial costs and maintenance are important factors to determine in advance. Projects should be practical, ideally allowing for neighbouring ranches to duplicate methods in order to widen protection from depredations. Project staff in direct communication with livestock owners should also be skilled in social conflict management and reconciliatory communication to avoid escalating the conflicts.

Agreements

When possible, a signed agreement outlining the expectations, cost estimates, and responsibilities of each cooperator should be established at the beginning of projects. These agreements should include the livestock owner's commitment for evaluation of the project, the anticipated timeline, division of labour, and an estimate of labour, equipment, and materials before the project begins. Our agreements are typically based on continued use of non-lethal methods, and funding can be withdrawn upon the use of lethal control of wolves.

Evaluation

Some projects can provide research opportunities and, when possible, should incorporate some level of evaluation during and after the project, which includes the livestock producer's comments regarding any concerns, challenges, benefits, and suggestions for improvement. It is also important to record failures as they can help improve future projects by increasing overall understanding of why some methods fare better than others in certain circumstances.

Limitations

Wolves can become habituated to almost any non-lethal method or tool. It is very important that non-lethal projects be adaptive according to the length of exposure to wolves. For example, projects relying on livestock guarding dogs have alternately used electrified fladry with successful short-term success. Other limitations include cost, project maintenance and supervision, negative impacts to neighbouring ranches, illegal killing of wolves, and more.

FUTURE OF WOLVES

In the last ten years, wolf numbers in the northern Rockies region have grown from 132 to more than a thousand animals, surpassing original recovery population goals (USFWS et al. 2005a). This growth clearly demonstrates the biological success of the wolf reintroduction program. It also shows the willingness of wolf opponents to adopt new methods and strategies to co-exist with wolves under the current federal management rules, a significant social achievement for the program. An essential component to this achievement is enhancing tolerance toward wolves, which in the northern Rockies, has at least partially been accomplished by paying compensation for livestock losses. Successful compensation programs must be structured to be viable in the long-term, reliably funded, and protected from fraud and must engage the cooperation of livestock owners and wildlife managers. The states of Montana and Idaho are developing state-managed wolf compensation programs that will reimburse livestock owners for wolf-related losses, once wolves are delisted from federal management. As the states move forward with their programs, Defenders of Wildlife will focus on increasing the non-lethal, proactive deterrents that help reduce or avoid conflict between wolves and livestock owners. Additionally, livestock owners and conservationists are finding more ways to collaboratively address conflicts, which decreases conflicts and reduces polarization. Several western ranchers are now serving on a newly created Livestock Producers Advisory Council to help evaluate Defenders of Wildlife's compensation and proactive programs. As Lane Adamson, Montana Ranchlands Group director and founding council member, stated: "The collaborative process works and can help those with divergent opinions resolve misunderstandings without damaging the value of one another as human beings.... The direction we are pursuing now regarding living with wolves is a great place to start this effort."

As envisioned back in 1985, the northern Rockies wolf compensation program has improved local tolerance toward wolves by shifting part of the economic responsibility from livestock producers to the public that supports wolf restoration. Before the USFWS removes wolves from federal protection, the agency must consider how social tolerance can be best retained under state wildlife management programs. The fate of wolves in the region will be largely dependent on the adequacy of state wolf-management plans to guarantee long-term protection for the species in balance with the interests of local residents.

ACKNOWLEDGMENTS

I wish to acknowledge the contributions of the following organizations and individuals: The Bailey Wildlife Foundation; Marco Musiani; Hawk Stone; Chris Haney; Nina Fascione; Gina Shrader; Laura Jones, Carter Niemeyer; Doug Smith, Rick and Carol Williamson; Linda Thurston; Levi Holt, Tom Gehring, Paul Sneed, Steve Fritts, Kim Holt, Amaroq Weiss; Ralph Maughan, Jan Holder; Stewart Breck, John Shivik, Mark D. Duda, and Responsive Management; the U.S. Fish and Wildlife Service; USDA–Wildlife Services; the Nez Perce tribe, and western livestock producers who are tolerating the return of the wolf including Defenders of Wildlife's Livestock Advisory Council members Lane Adamson, Jael Kampfe, John Hayne, Clint Krebs, Mike Stevens, and Tim Tew.

2.3 Education as a Conservation Strategy: Exploring Perspective Transformation

Denise Taylor

INTRODUCTION: EDUCATION FOR WOLF CONSERVATION

Although it is increasingly recognized that education can play a vital role in conservation, it would seem very little has been presented about the concepts, processes, and theories of education. There are numerous examples of good practice in wolf conservation education; the challenge now lies in the application of theory to practice within the context of the socio-political and cultural frameworks. This chapter explores transformation theory as one approach for conservation educators to employ in their efforts to try and change negative attitudes and behaviours toward wolves. Before looking at transformation theory and how we can apply this in practice, we need to consider some of the general concepts of education in relation to the stakeholders involved in wolf conservation education programs (WCEPs).

One of the main aims of education is "the development of the pupil or student as a relatively autonomous thinker and learner, who is moving through his life towards the independent exercise of his own reason" (Pepper 1989). It is this autonomy of thinking, or critical reflexivity, that underpins transformation theory and challenges previously accepted assumptions, values, or beliefs. The challenge for conservation educators is to understand their target audiences: their values and beliefs and the socio-political and cultural dimensions (the human dimensions approach to conversation is a topic discussed throughout this book). One of the key ways of understanding target audiences is through the use of attitude surveys – a subject that is touched on later in this chapter and summarized in the last chapter of this book by Bath.

Who are the target audiences? Education programs in wildlife conservation tend to be aimed at three distinct groups, although this is not always explicit.

- Children,
- Adult groups advocating wolf conservation, and
- Adult groups opposed to wolf conservation.

The latter group poses the biggest challenge for wolf conservationists, educators, and managers because they often resist conservation and education initiatives. A key point is that those who have negative attitudes and behaviours toward wolves are not a homogenous group, but rather a complex mix of different social groups with different socio-political and cultural backgrounds.

Education for Children

Education on wolf issues for children follows the conventional route of focusing on integration with the formal education system, i.e., education carried out over a set period of time, in an institutional setting and working to a set curriculum. There are also many examples of informal and non-formal education initiatives outside of the school setting. Educating younger children is a formative process and is achieved through acculturation and socialization with parents, teachers, and mentors providing the framework for the knowledge, skills, and experience that children acquire. Within this context, values, beliefs, attitudes, and behaviours are accepted uncritically. The period for the formal education is usually from the age of 5 or 6 (in some countries, from age 7), and through to adolescence (Peters 1966; Jarvis 1998).

Education for Wolf Advocates

There are many groups essentially advocating wolf conservation, including biologists, veterinarians, conservationists, educators, biodiversity managers, policy-makers, government officials, researchers, artists, biocentrists, and ecocentrists. If these groups want to participate in and promote wolf-related education, they require a degree of knowledge and skill. For education to fulfil its true role in developing critically reflective and autonomous thinkers, wolf advocates also need to go through a process of learning in order to be able to plan, implement, and deliver effective Wolf Conservation Education Programs (WCEPs). It is important that wolf advocates understand the concepts, processes, and theories of education and learning, as well as identify and understand the problems to be addressed, the target audiences, and what motivates these groups and their attitudes and behaviours. Just as importantly, advocates need to understand their own values and beliefs and what motivates their own attitudes and behaviours.

Education for Adults Opposed to Wolf Conservation

Education for adults opposed to wolves and their conservation often is the primary goal of WCEPs, with the aim of changing negative attitudes and behaviours for the benefit of wolves. Numerous surveys show that those with the most negative attitudes tend to be hunters, farmers, poachers, livestock growers, rural dwellers, and some policy-makers (Kellert 1985a; Kellert et al. 1996; Bath 2000; Bath and Majic 2001; Williams et al. 2002; Andersone and Ozoliņš 2004b; see Bath, this volume). In many cases, the negative attitudes and behaviours are motivated by a vested economic interest in reducing the numbers of wolves. Often this results in an adversarial situation between the pro-wolf and anti-wolf groups. The numerous lawsuits in the United States and elsewhere are a testament to this (see Bangs et al. and Stone, this volume). In other countries where there is conflict between the wolf advocates and opponents, this has led to public demonstrations following the natural restoration of wolves. For example, in France and Norway, adversarial conflicts have attracted international media attention in recent years.

A combination of chronological, biological, and emotional and psychological maturity signifies the onset of adulthood (Peters 1966; Rogers 1996; Jarvis 1998), and it is at this stage of development that transformative learning and critical thinking is most likely to occur (Brookfield 1987; Mezirow 1991). On reaching adulthood, attitudes and behaviours can become an integral part of a person's social and cultural identity, and, as a person moves through adulthood, they can become deeply embedded and thus more difficult to change. This is exacerbated where strong and long-held traditional and cultural beliefs continue to support and provide a backdrop for certain attitudes and behaviours. Attitudes toward wolves in Bulgaria are good examples of where entrenched beliefs and perceptions of the wolf are conveyed by various groups, including the media (Tsingarska 2003, 2004). The greatest challenge facing wolf educators is to make sense of the highly complex factors and situations that exist in the conservation of a species that continues to provoke such polarized perceptions and attitudes.

THE RISKS OF WOLF EDUCATION

Entrenched Attitudes toward Wolves

If and when wolf conservation is considered a priority, the main aim of educators is to try and change negative attitudes and behaviours, implying that some level of transformation needs to take place, not only within individuals, but also within social groups, which will remove or reduce the threat to wolves. Before applying transformative education strategies, however, educators need to understand human attitudes and the behaviours they are trying to change. Fortunately, a number of attitude surveys have been conducted in America and Europe by social scientists and biologists (Kellert 1985a; Kellert et al. 1996; Bath 2000; Bath and Majic 2001; Andersone and Ozoliņš 2004b), and reports that synthesize the surveys have been produced (Williams et al. 2002; Bath, this volume). Some social groups retain negative attitudes and these groups tend to be the ones most resistant to education and conservation strategies (Bath, this volume).

Clearly, this presents educators with a major challenge that communication initiatives and awareness raising do not wholly address. Challenges are similar when dealing with groups or with adults with entrenched attitudes. The danger is that education initiatives are simply 'preaching to the converted,' and there is not enough time spent engaging in dialogue with others who have opposing views (Rebstock 2005).

Advocacy, Indoctrination and Propaganda

Educators must be critically aware of their own beliefs and values regarding wolves when educating learners who may have a different set of beliefs and values. It is also important that conservation educators understand distinctions between education, advocacy, indoctrination, and propaganda. Many working for wolves and their conservation consider themselves wolf advocates. There is a danger that advocacy can lead conservationists delivering education to lean more toward propaganda and indoctrination simply because they feel their belief is correct (Johnson and Mappin 2005). The use of the word 'indoctrination' as a form of educational harm is a twentieth-century phenomenon, which is still valid nowadays and perhaps applicable to wolf education programs. A simple definition would be: "The inculcation of a proposition or set of propositions in the pupil that are said to be certain when the teacher knows they are uncertain and with a lack of regard for any evidence to the contrary" (Snook 1972).

Where indoctrination does become harmful is when the pupil is discouraged or prevented from achieving or acting upon their own value judgment or being able to exercise criticality. Conservation educators do need to be aware of the potential dangers of indoctrinating their own values and beliefs into others, especially children and mindful about the true purpose of education, which is to encourage critical thinking and reflexivity in order that the pupils or learners can arrive at their own value judgments. The result of this process might be that beliefs and values remain opposite or at least different to those of the wolf educator.

There are many definitions of the term 'propaganda,' and not all of them carry negative connotations. Where propaganda does have negative associations, it is seen as an attempt to persuade through deception: "the attempt to shape the thoughts and feelings of others, in ways conforming to the aims of the communicator" (Marlin 2002). A wealth of information about wolves is available in a variety of media: leaflets, posters, books, articles, documentaries, and websites. The aim of raising awareness through such communication strategies can be part of an overall education program, but it is rarely "education" in and of itself, although the content can be educational. However, some information disseminated through these methods could be seen as propaganda when they present a one-sided argument, misinformation, or selective facts or data that are biased. This applies to information and communication from both wolf advocates and wolf opponents.

PERSPECTIVE TRANSFORMATION

Jack Mezirow (1991), one of the forerunners of transformation theory, describes 'perspective transformation' as "the process of becoming critically aware of how and why our assumptions have come to constrain the way we perceive, understand, and feel about our world." Perspective transformation usually occurs following a dilemma or series of dilemmas that challenge culturally acquired beliefs and assumptions. Taylor (1998) observes that trigger events may be life-shattering occurrences such as natural disasters, or they may be personal upheavals, troubling contradictions between meaning systems, external social events, or cumulative internal changes.

The famous incident of Aldo Leopold's crisis point (Leopold 1949) is well documented by Fox and Bekoff in this volume, but it is worth reinterpreting in this chapter, as it is a good example of perspective transformation. Leopold's direct experience with a dying wolf influenced his change in attitude and brought about the sense of guilt and shame indicated by Mezirow (1991, see above). It must be pointed out, however, that it was some years later that he reflected on this particular experience in his essay

Thinking Like a Mountain (Meine 1987), and such reflection prompted Leopold to challenge his own assumptions and beliefs. Leopold's change had an immense impact on wildlife management practices; similarly, educators may attempt to foster changes in wolf conservation through perspective transformation of program participants.

There is a lack of theory applied to practice in environmental or ecological education (O'Sullivan 1999; O'Sullivan et al. 2002), and one of the unknowns is the practical effects of education programs. In the quest to protect and conserve wolf populations, one of the primary aims of scientists, conservationists, educators, and wildlife managers is to change (or transform) negative attitudes and behaviours toward wolves. It should be noted, however, that simply changing attitudes does not necessarily bring about a change in behaviour. In order to affect behaviours, Rogers (1996) argues for an incremental process in which educators should first identify what attitudes are really preventing learning changes and not just what the student-learner says they are. This is something that has already taken place in a number of countries (see Kellert 1985a; Kellert et al. 1996; Bath 2000; Bath and Farmer 2000; Williams et al. 2002; Røskaft et al. 2003; Andersone and Ozoliņš 2004b). Some of Rogers' other points advocate "group" working, which in essence mean adopting practices that are not totally adversarial (Skogen 2003). There is anecdotal evidence from a number of wolf projects that the work they have carried out on a non-adversarial basis with ranchers and hunters is showing some practical success (also see Stone and Wydeven et al., this volume), but further research is required to evaluate this fully.

WOLF EDUCATION AS A CONSERVATION STRATEGY

Forums for Knowledge on Wolves

Since the early 1940s, there has been a growing body of scientific knowledge about wolves and their conservation. This is widely disseminated both within and outside the wolf conservation community. Wolf-related websites have proliferated on the internet, and there are a number of wolf magazines that are distributed throughout the world. Numerous film documentaries have been made about wolves, and wolves feature in many documentaries about other species. Education is increasingly coming to the fore, and, through the internet and conference papers, we are seeing more examples of education practice and delivery.

Today, the stakeholders involved in wolf conservation are numerous and include: wolf biologists, ecologists, researchers, conservationists, educators, livestock growers, farmers, hunters, local communities in both rural and urban areas, policy and decision makers, wildlife managers, and, last but not least, schoolchildren. In recent years in particular, many of these groups have come together at conferences and symposia to discuss and debate wolves and their conservation. Education has been a key feature of these discussions, but now we need to take a more practical approach and use conservation education to foster critical awareness and reflexivity, with the aim of transforming negative attitudes and behaviours for the benefit of wolves and the wider biotic community.

Theunderlying assumption of this chapter that education will lead to more positive attitudes toward wolves is supported by some evidence (Naughton-Treves et al. 2003; Fox and Bekoff, this volume). However, not all information that may be conveyed in education programs is positive for wolves. For example, gaining knowledge on wolf depredation on livestock might obviously lead to negative attitudes. The potential effects on people attitudes of these "inconvenient truths" deserves further analyses, which might also explain the lack of correlation between education level and attitudes toward wolvesthat Bath found in some countries (this volume).

Conservation Education as a Discipline

Despite there being a widespread consensus that education is an important conservation strategy, there is a dearth of literature about conservation education, and in particular about WCEPs. (Jacobson 1995) References to conservation education in the literature on education in general are also scarce (O'Sullivan 1999; O'Sullivan et al. 2002).

Conservation Education needs to be recognized as a discipline in its own right or at the very least as a sub-discipline of *Environmental Education* within the field of wolf conservation. This will encourage further research to be undertaken in these disciplines which will provide a body of knowledge for conservation educators to draw upon. Research also needs to be undertaken on current *education* practice within wolf conservation and also within practice relating to other aspects of conservation and other species to establish models of best practice. WCEPs also need to be grounded in the wider context of environmental education. The broader message of the environmental movement is consciousness raising and "seeking reform at the material base of society, concurrent with education change, otherwise any effects of the latter will be ephemeral" (Pepper 1989). The social and political landscape is shifting on a global scale toward environmental protection and sustainable resource use, which will provide a climate in which conservation and environmental education can flourish.

Current Trends

At present education and communication initiatives within wolf conservation are fragmented, and there is a lack of cohesion between the natural science and social science disciplines. Organizations engaged in wolf conservation vary, with some wildlife managers being attached to academic institutions or government departments, and others to NGOs (non-government organizations), both large and small. Some WCEPs are run by well-funded organizations that employ trained staff. Some are run by overstretched, under-resourced managers whose main discipline is science and not education. In addition, as a result of the burgeoning environmental movement, an increasing number of NGOs are run by people passionate about conservation, but who have no formal training or experience as teachers or educators.

There are signs that this is already starting to change, and we need to build on this, bringing together research and work from science, ethics, education, social policy and reform, and environmental law. The World Wolf Congress in Banff, Canada, in 2003 went some way to addressing the issue of bridging the gap between science and community, and the subsequent International Wolf Conference in Colorado Springs in 2005 put education high on the agenda.

Transformation theory is just one example among the many different education theories that we need to explore and start applying to wolf conservation problems. Many wolf projects throughout the world would welcome this type of research. From this, models of best practice can be developed and disseminated.

CONCLUSION

Although there are numerous examples of education practice and delivery, there is still much work to be done. The evidence is often anecdotal, and there is a lack of an underpinning education theory, or if there is a theoretical foundation, it is not explicit.

As wolf conservation continues to evolve, there are signs of cross-disciplinary and multi-disciplinary approaches with natural scientists and social scientists sharing the platform at conferences and symposia and acknowledging education as one of a number of disciplines to be employed for the conservation of wolves. However, there is still a long way to go before conservation education is afforded the recognition it needs in order to build knowledge bases that will inform and guide conservation education practice.

Research is needed on conservation education, and the wider theories of education need to be assimilated into this. In short, we need more *educationalists* in wolf conservation. As discussed, WCEPs are implemented and delivered by a wide range of practitioners, not all of whom are trained or experienced in education as a discipline. Research is also needed on the current WCEPs throughout the world, and an evaluation of education and communication initiatives. The complexities involved in conservation education are multifarious, but this should not deter educators, researchers, and social scientists from exploring theory, current best practice, and ways of bringing about multi-disciplinary cohesion.

2.4 Working with People to Achieve Wolf Conservation in Europe and North America

Alistair J. Bath

INTRODUCTION: INCORPORATING HUMAN DIMENSIONS IN WOLF MANAGEMENT

As explained in previous chapters by Fox and Bekoff and by Taylor, Aldo Leopold understood in the early 1940s that game management, particularly deer management, was not as much about managing the game (deer) per se, but more about managing the people (Flader 1974). At that time, Leopold began to understand that wolves and deer were not really being managed as such, but instead it was people that were being managed; hunters had to be encouraged to either selectively shoot more of certain ages and gender of animals or to protect the species by not shooting them at all. People, through their different wants, needs, available technology, culture, and values decide what should be considered a resource, how valuable it is, and, in the case of wolves, whether they should be protected, exterminated, or managed with a regular harvest. Wolves have been seen as symbols of wilderness in North America when wilderness was not valued as a resource and wolves thus had to be exterminated (Young and Goldman 1944; Mech 1970). As described by Stone in this volume, today, that same wilderness has become valued by segments of North American society, and, for many, wolves are now seen as positive and valuable natural resources of this new wilderness resource. In many parts of Europe, where wild places are much harder to find, wolves have always coexisted with people. Various studies were conducted on public attitudes toward the species in Europe, which indicated that some Europeans valued wolves as a natural resource, while others were uncertain or opposed wolves (Moore 1994; Bjerke et al. 1998; Skogen 2001; Ericsson and Heberlein 2003; Bisi et al. 2007; Nilsen et al. 2007). In a changing Europe (politically and economically), wolf numbers are increasing, and areas that may have forgotten how to coexist with wolves are now facing the challenges of living once again next to this large carnivore (Boitani and Ciucci, this volume). Whether the wolf becomes a conservation success in Europe and North America will be measured not simply by wolf numbers or decreasing livestock damages, but by a greater tolerance and willingness of all aspects of society to coexist and share a cultural landscape with a large carnivore.

While biophysical scientists (e.g., biologists, ecologists) can determine wolf habitat requirements and home range sizes for wolves, conduct food habit and scat analysis studies to provide insights on prey selection, and calculate biological carrying capacity for wolves, such sound biophysical scientific research does not ensure wolf conservation. Wolves can only coexist with humans if people are willing to share landscapes, tolerate livestock losses, and accept possible risks to human safety and property (e.g., pets being killed; Treves et al. 2002; Naughton-Treves et al. 2003). Rather than biological carrying capacity, for successful wolf conservation, there must be a wildlife (e.g., wolf) acceptance capacity (Decker and Purdy 1988). This public acceptance of wolves may be based on a whole host of factors such as perceptions of risk and tolerance of that risk, fear of wolves, experience with wolves, knowledge, age, gender, proximity to a wolf pack, location of residence (e.g., rural or urban), and membership within a certain interest group (e.g., environmentalists, farmers, foresters, hunters) and occupation. Thus, large carnivore management, especially wolf management, tends to be more socio-political in nature than biological (Bath 1998), therefore requiring an understanding of public attitudes toward the species, beliefs and knowledge about wolves, and attitudes toward various management approaches. Only with this human-dimension understanding of the wolf-management equation can effective decisions be made and successfully implemented.

Human dimensions in wolf-management research can answer a variety of questions. Indeed, there are many dimensions or perspectives in any natural resource management issue (McCool and Guthrie 2001) and wolf management is no different. In fact most dimensions or perspectives in any resource management issue tend to be human in nature rather than biophysical (Dietz et al. 2003), although traditionally we have not learned as much about the human-dimension issues as the biophysical issues when trying to implement conservation efforts. When a wildlife manager suggests the need for a human-dimensions study, in many ways it is like asking a biophysical scientist to do some biology; both are extremely broad. Therefore the nature of human dimensions needs to be examined and defined, especially within the context of wolf management.

Mitchell (1989) suggests that there are seven dimensions or perspectives of resource management and that these vary over space and time; he organizes these elements illustrating the complexities of managing any resource, and wolf management is no different. Most of these perspectives are human-oriented and broadly could be considered human-dimension issues. For wolves, these might include:

- Economic (e.g., costs and benefits and values of landscapes and wolves),
- Social and cultural (e.g., attitudes, knowledge levels, expectations and behaviour toward wolves),
- Political (e.g., the nature of political will or lack thereof regarding wolf-management decision-making processes, particularly important during the wolf reintroduction efforts in Yellowstone National Park),
- Legal (e.g., policies, guidelines, national and international laws and conventions. For example, the Bern Convention is particularly important in getting the countries that are currently negotiating membership to the European Union [EU Accession Countries] to participate in creating wolf-management plans),

- Institutional arrangements (e.g., mandates of different agencies and their interactions with each other. Often different levels of government have never thought of working together on a wolf-management plan. For example, in Switzerland, there may be differences in management preferences at the canton level creating challenges of managing wolves which travel over many jurisdictional boundaries that may have differing mandates and levels of cooperation with each other; these are institutional arrangement issues).
- Technological perspectives (e.g., complex versus simple technologies to solve challenges in different societies such as uses of poison, availability of guns, infrastructure, etc.).
- Finally, there is the biophysical perspective (e.g., ecological understanding of habitats, wild animal populations, and prey-predator relationships); understanding the biology of the wolf is also needed to successfully achieve wolf conservation.

Traditionally, in wolf resource management many managers considered the biophysical perspective as the most important, or the only perspective in the resource management decision-making process. Considering the biophysical perspective or biophysical feasibility for wolves in isolation of human factors may not provide an accurate representation of the complete situation and may not result in conservation. For example, road density is often considered a limiting factor for wolf restoration because roads are associated with higher probabilities of negative interactions between humans and wolves (Mech et al. 1988; Mech 1989; Mladenoff et al. 1995; Mladenoff et al. 1999). These negative interactions could include illegal killings, traffic mortality, disturbance of young, inappropriate feeding of wolves, and inappropriate behaviour of hikers around wolves. However, if the human-dimension research suggested a public willingness to close roads, a low likelihood of illegal killings due to positive attitudes toward wolves, high public knowledge of wolves and awareness of appropriate behaviour within areas where wolves exist, the importance of road density would lessen, and the carrying capacity of the area for wolves might increase.

Increasingly with wolf-management issues, managers are realizing that the many other human perspectives of resource management must be considered for successful understanding, development, and implementation of management plans. These human-dimension perspectives also vary over space (i.e., local, regional, national, and international) and time (i.e., past, present, or future). Thus, managing wolves is a challenging balancing act of all of these perspectives involving an understanding of how they interact with each other, over space and time, and amongst the various interest groups who wish to play an active role in defining wolf conservation.

Human dimensions in wolf-management studies could address many of these human perspectives. For example, the economic value of wolves could be examined for a certain region or community. In Canada, until the early 1990s, every five years an economic valuation study was completed that examined the importance of wildlife (later changed to the importance of nature) to Canadians (Filion et al. 1993). Such economic human-dimension studies offered information on the average yearly expenditures by participants in wildlife viewing, recreational fishing, hunting, and outdoor recreational activities by province, thus allowing managers to see the economic benefits of wildlife and habitat conservation to their respective provinces. Certainly the many visitors who heard wolves howl in Algonquin Provincial Park in Ontario, Canada, would be part of this documentation of the millions of dollars Canadians spend on wildlife-related activities. The resulting study (Federal-Provincial-Territorial Task Force on the Importance of Nature to Canadians 2000) used actual expenditures (travel cost method) to determine economic values. It is also possible to examine economic values through contingent valuation techniques where individuals are asked about their "willingness to pay" for a wildlife experience such as a wolf-howling evening or their "willingness to get paid" for not taking a wildlife experience. Contingent valuation techniques were used to assess the amount of compensation the oil company Exxon was required to pay for the spilling of oil in Prince William Sound, Alaska, in 1989. A WWF-UK report (Goodwin et al. 2000) focused on tourism and large carnivores in Europe suggested the importance of wolves and bears to a recreational experience and to the local economy of rural areas.

Economic valuation studies provide one human-dimension perspective of the wolf resource management equation.

Social perspectives can be examined through attitudinal research such as attitudes toward wolf restoration in Yellowstone National Park (Bath 1991) or attitudes toward wolves and their management in Savoie and Des Alpes Maritimes, France (Bath 2000). Attitudes can be examined toward species, toward the utilization of areas, and toward management options. Human-dimension studies focused on a social perspective can explore factors affecting attitudes, influences of beliefs on attitudes, and public support or opposition for ideas being considered in management plans. Trade-off issues can be explored through the examination of the social perspective of resource management. For example, how will various publics respond to potential job losses compared to the amount of land put under various restrictions to protect a certain species such as wolves? Is there a certain breaking point beyond which the public is not willing to make the trade-off and support a certain decision? Having such knowledge can help managers make better decisions when balancing jobs versus wolf conservation.

Political and legal perspectives may involve studies of national, regional, and local policies, legislation, and decision-making processes. Some of these issues are currently being addressed in the human dimensions in wolf-management issues in Spain (see Blanco and Cortés, this volume). Studies examining attitudes of various interest groups toward wolf restoration in Yellowstone National Park and the lobbying and cooperation between groups (Bath and Buchanan 1989) could be considered an example of an institutional arrangements study. The study of human dimensions in wolf management in Croatia (Bath and Majic 2001) also explored the relationships, mandates, and goals of various interest groups. Each and all resource-management perspectives can provide data to enable better understanding of the people component of the wolf-management equation.

While human dimensions as a research field is well established in North America, it is still relatively new in Europe (although it is expanding rapidly), and, in general, limited research has focused on understanding wolf–human interactions on either continent – which is the major focus of this volume. Given this and the many human-dimension perspectives that could be explored in a chapter on understanding and addressing the people component of wolf management, I chose to focus on illustrating examples of research on public attitudes toward wolves mainly in France (where wolves have recently returned), Croatia (where wolves have always existed and went from full protection to a limited hunting quota), Portugal (where wolves are completely protected), Poland (where wolves can be managed), and the UK (where no wolves exist). In addition, the Croatian wolf-management planning process is used to illustrate an example of human dimensions as an applied facilitated workshop approach to working with a diverse group of interests toward a national wolf-management plan.

Overall, the purpose of this chapter is to compare results from various human-dimension research studies in various parts of Europe and North America at the same time. More specifically the chapter addresses the following human-dimension objectives:

- Understand public attitudes toward wolves and how they vary across countries, within countries, amongst interest groups, and within the same interest group,
- Understand public attitudes toward possible management approaches, thus exploring how much public support and opposition exists with respect to fully protecting wolves and hunting wolves,
- Target educational programs on key beliefs affecting attitudes and behaviour, identify what has been learned so far about the key messages influencing attitudes toward wolves,
- Understand the various factors that could influence attitudes toward wolves and wolf management,
- Identify the nature of conflict in wolf-management issues, the first step toward conflict resolution,
- Illustrate how interest groups were brought together, for example, to work toward consensus on the Croatian wolf-management plan and the early process of wolf-management planning in Bulgaria.

From a human-dimensions research perspective, identifying in a representative and quantitative way public attitudes toward wolves and wolf-management options can offer valuable insights to managers and help them understand where support and opposition lies before, during, and after implementing a policy decision. What perhaps is more powerful, though, is using human-dimensions as a facilitated workshop approach, as only this can truly begin to resolve issues moving the public closer to coexistence with wolves. Examples of both are discussed in this chapter.

METHODS

For each European study, a quantitative questionnaire was designed, similar to an instrument developed earlier during the proposed discussions of wolf reintroduction in Yellowstone National Park to assess attitudes, beliefs, attitudes toward management approaches, personal experience with wolves, and socio-demographic characteristics (Bath 1991). Identical questions translated into the country's native language allow for direct comparisons across countries across the specific items. While a variety of data-collection implementation techniques are available to human-dimension researchers to administer such a quantitative questionnaire (Fowler 1988; Sheskin 1985), primarily personal interviews were used to gather the data. Residents within specific regions of countries were randomly selected proportional to population so as to be representative of a study zone that had been previously defined by a set of characteristics (e.g., rural characteristics, livestock damages, cultural characteristics, wolf densities). For certain interest groups like hunters and foresters in Croatia, questionnaires were mailed. In the United Kingdom and in Spain, questionnaires were self-administered to teenagers in schools during class time and collected at the end of the class. In Poland, questionnaires to farmers were distributed through students in rural schools. In all cases sample sizes and response rates were considered large enough to be representative of the group and/or study zone. Data were collected at approximately the same time in each country with both the first data collected in late 1999/2000 and in the case of Croatia and Poland the second set of data collected in 2003 and 2006–2007, respectively.

Sample sizes of the general public in all countries were greater than four hundred in order to be accurate within the study zone plus or minus five percentage points, nineteen times out of twenty, basically the standard accepted for human-dimensions research. General public residents in all countries were selected in rural areas and small villages, omitting large urban centres.

In Croatia, data were collected from residents from three zones all within wolf range, but defined by varying wolf densities. Residents of Gorski kotar (n = 402) live with the highest density of wolves, Lika residents (n = 401) coexist with medium densities of wolves, while Dalmatian residents (n = 406) had the lowest density of wolves, but the most damage to livestock caused by wolves compared to the other two regions. Smaller samples of hunters (n = 209), foresters (n = 190), shepherds (n = 19), and students (n = 339) were also administered the questionnaire across the three zones (Bath and Majic 2001). Data were collected from the same zones four years later to explore residents' attitude change toward wolves. In France, data were collected from rural residents representative of Savoie (n = 403) and Des Alpes Maritimes (n = 397) once again avoiding larger urban centres. Smaller samples of hunters from Savoie (n = 22), environmental group members from Savoie (n = 88) and Des Alpes Maritimes (n = 86), and teenage students from Des Alpes Maritimes (n = 95) were also administered the questionnaire (Bath 2000). In Portugal, data were collected from a total of 1,209 residents from the general public from three regions: Aveiro/Viseu (n = 402), Guarda (n = 406), and Castelo Branco (n = 401). In addition, 328 students were interviewed in six high schools across the study area. Smaller sample sizes of livestock owners (n = 111) and hunters (n = 105) were achieved with respondents from each zone (Espirito-Santo 2007). In Poland, data were collected initially at the end of 1999 from hunters (n = 580), foresters (n = 363), farmers (n = 356), and teenagers (n = 1211) in four regions of the country. In 2006/2007, the study was repeated amongst hunters (n = 323), foresters (n = 563), farmers (n = 329), and teenagers (n = 1534).

While the wolf has been extinct from the United Kingdom for well over two centuries, the myths and mythology surrounding the animal lives on, as demonstrated by some of the responses from students throughout the UK. Students from schools randomly selected from across the United Kingdom were selected from England (3,206 students from 124 schools), Scotland (888 students from 36 schools), Wales (915 students from 33 schools), and Northern Ireland (1,145 students from 46 schools). Data were collected through a self-administered questionnaire distributed to students while in the classroom and collected immediately after completion, thus ensuring a 100 per cent response rate. To allow for further analysis of geographical variations, England was divided into northern and southern regions, based on the sampling that occurred within ten sub-regions (Bath and Farmer 2000).

RESULTS AND DISCUSSION

Public Attitudes toward Wolves

Public attitudes toward wolves do differ across the studied countries, within the countries across study zones, and between and within interest groups across space. However, overall public attitudes toward wolves are positive whether examining, for example, hunter's attitudes toward wolves in Croatia or Poland, or teenager's attitudes toward wolves in rural areas of Spain. Perhaps one of the most interesting results, in contrast to North America, where attitudes toward wolves have been described as a "love 'em or hate 'em relationship" suggesting attitudes exist at either end of the attitudinal spectrum with little middle ground between them, is the large percentage of neutral responses documented in Croatian and Northern Ireland teenagers, and also in the Croatian general public. In fact, attitudes in Croatia are changing and residents in rural areas are becoming more neutral toward wolves over time (Fig. 2.4.1). As extremely positive and extremely negative views decrease, there may be better opportunities

Which of the following best describes your feelings toward wolves?

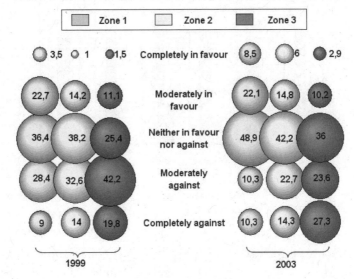

Which of the following best describes your feelings toward wolves?

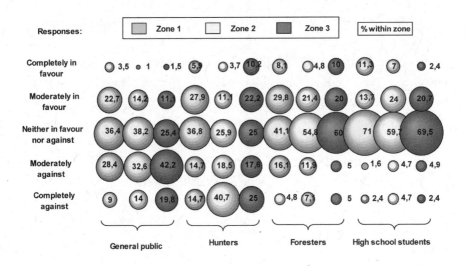

Figure 2.4.1. Croatian residents' feelings toward wolves.

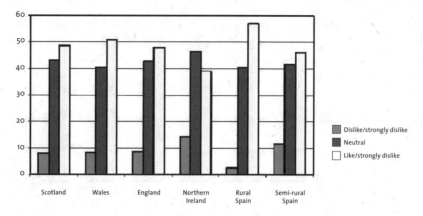

Figure 2.4.2. UK and Spanish teenagers' feelings toward wolves expressed as percentage of respondents.

to achieve coexistence between wolves and people. These neutral views are pronounced within the data collected from teenagers in particular. For example, approximately 70 per cent of Croatian students in Gorski kotar (zone 1) and Dalmatia (zone 3) chose "neither like nor dislike" when asked about their feelings toward wolves; 60 per cent of Lika (zone 2) respondents were also neutral.

Croatian attitudes of liking or disliking wolves varied considerably across the three zones of varying wolf densities. Attitudes also varied amongst interest groups, with foresters being more positive than some hunters. Perhaps even more interesting are the differing attitudes of hunters across the three zones in Croatia. Hunters in Gorski kotar (zone 1), where wolf densities are the highest, are much more positive than hunters in Lika (zone 2) and Dalmatia (zone 3). Foresters were more positive than Croatian teenagers, once again suggesting that experience with the large carnivore and its habitat may generate more positive attitudes.

More than 45 per cent of teenagers in Northern Ireland also expressed neutral responses, significantly higher than those in England, Scotland, and Wales (Fig. 2.4.2). In Spain, where there are more than two thousand wolves, Spanish teenagers in rural areas were more likely to express positive feelings toward wolves than semi-rural Spanish teenagers, and both were more positive than UK teenagers. Rural residents consistently tended to be more positive toward wolves than their urban or less rural counterparts, suggesting that those residents who have always coexisted with wolves have found ways to increase their public acceptance and tolerance of the large carnivore.

In Poland, foresters were the most positive interest group toward wolves, followed by hunters and teenagers, who were still positive. Polish farmers were the most negative toward the wolf. Teenagers, while positive, were in the middle of the spectrum, and not as it was expected (Bath and Farmer 2000; Bath and Majic 2001), at the most positive end. Once again these results suggest that in these European countries those respondents closest to wolves may in most circumstances hold more positive attitudes toward the animal than those with less experience with wolves. In contrast, attitudes in France were quite divided. In Des Alpes Maritimes, approximately 45 per cent liked or strongly liked wolves but more than 34 per cent disliked wolves in some way. In Savoie, 41 per cent of respondents liked or strongly liked wolves, whereas more than 35 per cent were neutral. The 'neutral group' constituted a candidate audience to target for value-persuasive messages to possibly influence attitudes (Fig. 2.4.3).

Public Attitudes toward Possible Wolf-Management Options

The following is an example of how human-dimensions research can offer managers insight into where public support and opposition exists for management options. Using data from two regions in France, one can see how the general public reacts to management options along a continuum from killing wolves by any means, hunting wolves year round, hunting wolves during a legal hunting season, and keeping wolves completely protected. The strongest opposition exists toward killing wolves by any means; in Savoie, most residents (55%) strongly disagreed with an additional 29 per cent also disagreeing. Residents from Des Alpes Maritimes were less opposed, with 44 per cent strongly disagreeing and an additional 33 per cent disagreeing to killing wolves by any means. Such opposition remains in response to hunting wolves year-round, although the strength of the

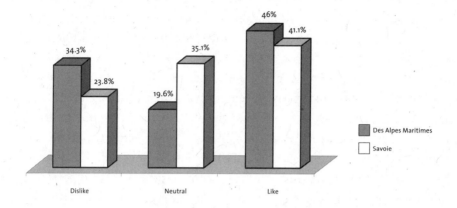

Figure 2.4.3. France general public's attitudes toward wolves.

opposition has changed. Only 26 per cent of Savoie residents strongly opposed year-round hunting but a further 48 per cent opposed this management option. Similar results exist from Des Alpes Maritimes residents (24% strongly opposed and 44% opposed). Most residents in both regions still opposed hunting wolves in a legal hunting season, although once again the percentages of strong opposition diminished to below 20 per cent in both regions. Approximately 33 per cent of residents in both areas indicated that they opposed a legal hunting season on wolves. It is interesting to note that most residents of Des Alpes Maritimes (51%) disagreed in some way to wolves remaining completely protected in their region. In contrast only 39 per cent of Savoie residents held this view, suggesting the need to be sensitive in management options to these regional differences. It is also interesting to note for France that it is the region of Des Alpes Maritimes where residents have had wolves a little longer; and perhaps this region's residents are now reaching their wolf acceptance capacity.

In Croatia, where there are more wolves than in France, the general public in all three zones supported hunting wolves in specific hunting seasons by an overwhelming 75 per cent across the regions. When asked whether wolves should be hunted year-round, residents with the highest densities of wolves in Gorski kotar were more strongly against this management option (69%) than those from Lika (57%) and Dalmatia (40%), where wolf numbers are lower. In fact, most residents from Dalmatia (52%) supported year-round hunting of wolves. From these data it could be hypothesized that as wolf densities increase or are perceived to increase by local residents, support for complete protection of wolves is reduced. However, those residents who have always coexisted with wolves might remain more likely to tolerate wolves and tend to not be as extreme in their viewpoints. Provided that general tendencies are uncertain, local studies should be conducted. Thus, managers could consider flexible management solutions to be sensitive to these regional differences within a country. In fact Croatia has taken such aspects into consideration by allowing a larger quota of wolves to be killed in Dalmatia compared to Gorski kotar.

In Portugal, residents with a positive attitude toward the value of wolves (57% of the general public) were in favour of total protection of the species and disagreed with any form of lethal control. In contrast, those residents who were negative toward wolves (43% of the general public) agreed with hunting wolves and controlling animals that killed livestock (Espirito-Santo 2007). Understanding attitudes toward the species and the value of the species to residents in this case allowed managers to predict support or opposition to lethal control measures. With such knowledge on somehow polarized opinions, managers could then map areas where conflicts would be greater on the landscape.

Strategies to Target Educational Programs

Research conducted by students under my supervision confirms that knowledge levels remain extremely low across European countries about basic facts of wolves, as it was shown also for North America (Bath 1991; Rodriguez et al. 2003), despite intensive educational efforts and massive amounts of outreach materials that are produced each year by various non-

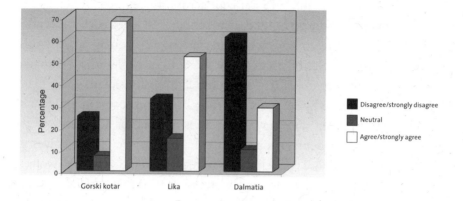

Figure 2.4.4. Understanding Croatian existence-values of wolves: "Whether or not I would get to see a wolf, it is important to me that they exist in my region."

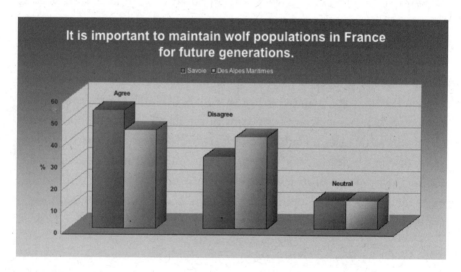

Figure 2.4.5. Understanding French future generation values of wolves.

governmental and governmental organizations (see Taylor, this volume). This may suggest that educational materials have rarely been designed after an initial assessment of beliefs about wolves has been done. Such an assessment would help the educators, ensuring that messages are not too complex or too simple, or on information that is not directly linked and thus is irrelevant to affecting attitudes. Factual messages that appear the most strongly linked to attitude focus on elements of fear about wolves such as the number of attacks and number of deaths caused by wolves on humans (even if extremely rare; see Linnell et al. 2002; McNay 2002), and the status of the population in terms of whether it is increasing, decreasing, or stable. Information on perceived numbers of wolves also seems important in relation to attitudes. Further results from the European human-dimension studies suggest that value-persuasive messages such as conserving wolves for future generations (or the broader ethical issues discussed by Fox and Bekoff in this volume) may be more important in influencing attitudes toward wolves than traditional factual-based messages.

In Croatia, in almost all regions and with most interest groups, strong support exists for allowing wolves to exist within the specific region. Most general public residents in Gorski kotar (69%) and Lika (52%) agreed that it was important that wolves exist within their region regardless of whether they were ever able to see a wolf or not (Fig. 2.4.4). In Dalmatia, attitudes were much less positive, suggesting the lack of an existence-value of wolves to Dalmatian residents. On the other hand, in France existence-values for wolves seemed imperative (Fig. 2.4.5).

Factors Influencing Attitudes toward Wolves

My students and I demonstrated that attitudes toward wolves and wolf-management options vary over space and within interest groups, and understanding factors affecting such attitudes can be challenging. Attitudes toward wolves are affected by fear, gender (females tend to be less positive toward wolves than males), experience with wolves, and sometimes knowledge about wolves, but depending upon the interest group these variables can have a small, large or even no effect on attitudes. For example, fear of

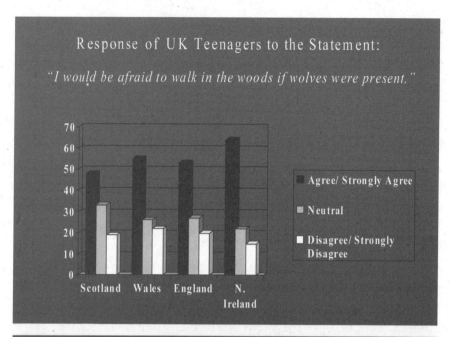

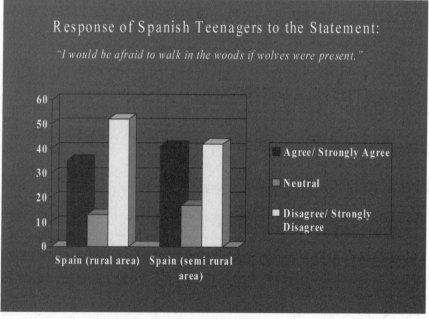

Figure 2.4.6. Understanding elements of fear, expressed as percentages. Responses of UK and Spanish teenagers to the statement: "I would be afraid to walk in the woods if wolves were present."

wolves does seem to influence Croatian hunters' attitudes toward wolves but has little to no impact on Croatian teenagers' attitudes. A farmer's direct experience with wolves tends to lead to negative attitudes toward wolves, yet environmentalists who see or hear a wolf tend to become even more positive toward the species. Knowledge, contrary to what might be expected (see Naughton-Treves et al. 2003), only sometimes affects attitudes but plays a bigger role as a predictor of fear. Older residents tend to be more negative toward wolves than younger residents, but this is probably more due to the era in which attitudes were formed, rather than attitudes changing over time. Finally, attitudes toward wolves are also influenced by the nature of residence whether considered rural or in an urban setting. Rural residents, contrary to what might be perceived, tend to be more positive toward wolves than less rural or even urban residents. These results contrasted with those of some North American studies, where attitudes where strongly correlated with education and tolerance for wolves was lower among local rural residents (see Williams et al. 2002, who reviewed more than thirty surveys).

Fear is one of the strongest predictors of attitude. UK teenagers and particularly those from Northern Ireland were significantly more afraid to hike in the woods if wolves were present than their rural Spanish teenager counterparts, who knew two thousand wolves or more existed in the country (Fig. 2.4.6). While only 35 per cent of rural teenagers in Spain claimed to be afraid to hike in the woods if wolves were present, teenagers from Scotland (48%), Wales (53%), England (53%), and especially Northern Ireland (65%) seemed more terrified. Rural teenagers in Spain were even less afraid than their semi-rural counterparts, of which 41 per cent indicated they would be afraid. Spanish teenagers also held more positive attitudes toward wolves than their UK counterparts. Northern Ireland teenagers were the least positive toward wolves of these teenage groups. In addition, Northern Ireland teenagers held the lowest knowledge scores about wolves of all groups, and knowledge was linked to attitude.

Nature of Conflict

The array of people and groups interested in wolves or affected by wolf presence may be in conflict for reasons other than wolves. Thus, surrogate conflicts may arise that are indicative of broader disputes (not directly wolf-related). For example, people coming from urban areas may be in conflict with rural residents, people relying on academic knowledge may experience tension with those relying on local knowledge, and people relying on "traditional principles" might not appreciate "modern values" or their promoters. Such surrogate or symbolic conflicts, which inevitably contribute to different attitudes toward wolves, are not discussed in this chapter. However, there are usually four types of more typical conflicts involved in any resource management issue, and wolf issues are no different. Understanding the nature of the conflict is the first step toward conflict resolution and then listening and learning, preparing a group to work toward solutions. Cognitive conflicts deal with a lack of knowledge or incorrect beliefs about the wolf. For example, many respondents often fear that the wolf may attack people and that wolves have killed people in the past, whereas, as explained above, such instances are extremely rare and sporadic. Others believe there are many wolves while others believe very few. If the conflict is really cognitive then educational programs targeted to the specific belief and delivered by a credible messenger through the appropriate medium should resolve the issue (see Taylor, this volume). While significant amounts of monies are spent to address what may be considered perceived cognitive conflicts in wolf-management issues, rarely is this the real conflict.

Conflicts could be over values. While a shepherd may wish to protect wolves, he/she may place a higher value on feeding his/her family especially if a wolf threatens his/her livestock. Understanding the hierarchy of values in wolf conservation can help address these concerns. A third type of conflict could concern costs and benefits. In Spain and Portugal, livestock owners were upset with the long length of time used to pay compensation damages, sometimes up to two years. The timeline for receiving compensation seemed remarkably longer than in North America (see

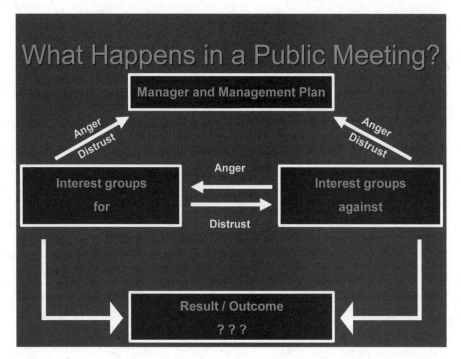

Figure 2.4.7. Typical scenario for a public meeting.

Stone, this volume). Other economic conflicts result over paying market price for a lamb in the spring when the worth of the lamb is less than if it had survived until the fall. Other economic issues arise from the environmentalist's perspective in that agriculture is already heavily subsidized, prompting the question by some environmentalists as to why there should be 100 per cent compensation when the government has already paid out a percentage of the value of the livestock in agricultural subsidies.

Research conducted in collaboration with my students highlights that the final type of conflict, which is known as 'behavioural conflict,' is the most common in natural resource management issues, These conflicts occur because of a lack of trust or credibility between individuals or agencies. Resolving conflicts about trust and credibility require listening to all concerns and getting groups working together in the same room. To achieve wolf conservation, it is this conflict that must be addressed first.

For example, hunters need to believe biologists and respect the views of environmentalists; environmentalists need to learn from the valuable information hunters can offer. To resolve these behavioural conflicts human dimensions needs to move beyond its research focus as demonstrated so far in this chapter to a much more applied approach. This human-dimensions facilitated workshop approach has been used in Croatia to develop its wolf-management plan.

Human Dimensions as a Facilitated Workshop Approach: The Croatian Wolf-Management Plan

Traditionally, managers who were usually a part of the government created a draft management plan based upon their own ideas, and then the government agency would typically present the "draft" plan to the various publics in a public meeting so as to be able to implement the plan quickly, proceeding to listen to public concerns only in a token way. At the public meeting there would be much mistrust between all groups and toward the government, thus culminating in no clear end result (Fig. 2.4.7). Usually it took the broader public only a few minutes to come to the conclusion that a nicely bound management plan with colour photos was not really a "DRAFT," but instead a finished document that really was not going to be changed. With little or no involvement from the various interest groups affected by or who could affect the decision, the plan typically was not accepted and rarely could be successfully implemented. The situation on the ground did not change significantly due to the lack of real public involvement, and hence conservation did not really occur. In fact, the first national wolf-management plan for Croatia basically took this approach.

After realizing that a Croatian Wolf Management Plan created with no real public involvement and advocating full protection of wolves was actually producing an increasing number of illegal killings of wolves, the Croatian State Institute for Nature Protection (Governmental Institution Centrally Responsible for Nature Protection, www.dzzp.hr/eng_title. htm), as well as scientists from academia, recognized that a new approach was needed. It is out of this need that the human-dimensions facilitated workshop approach emerged, resulting in a redistribution of power from decision-makers to various interest groups. This chapter analyzes the approach undertaken by the new Croatian Wolf Management Plan. However, similar approaches are advisable for other carnivores too and for other environmental plans in general, as it has been highlighted, for example, by Huber et al. (2008) for Croatian bears.

For a successful management planning process, the public must be involved early in the planning process and the management plan must be built from nothing, piece by piece, to a final product, ensuring consensus is gained at every step along the way. This means an active listening exercise. This higher level of public involvement is called 'joint planning' (Wistow and Brookes 1988; Margerum and Born 1995) and is implemented by bringing all the interest groups together to discuss issues based on principles, rather than positions. The human-dimensions facilitated workshop approach (also see Bath and Enck 2003) is a visual approach using cards of different colours and shapes that, once explained, clearly illustrated items that generated lots of discussion and items where there was immediate consensus (Fig. 2.4.8).

The wolf-management planning process in Croatia was inclusive, involving twenty-six organizations and approximately eighty different participants over the development of the plan. Names of participants as well as of organizations that were represented appear alphabetically at the beginning of the wolf-management plan indicating their support. Representatives covered a broad attitudinal spectrum involving organizations across various spatial scales. Represented organizations included county and national hunting associations, environmental organizations, national forestry associations, the departments of economic development at regional levels, university scientists, various national parks and protected areas across Croatia, the Livestock Breeders Association, the Croatian Livestock Selection Centre, the Ministries of Agriculture, Forestry and Water Management, the Ministry of Environmental Protection, Physical Planning and Infrastructure, and international representatives from the University of Slovenia and the Slovenian Department of Forestry. Efforts were made to involve international representatives also from another

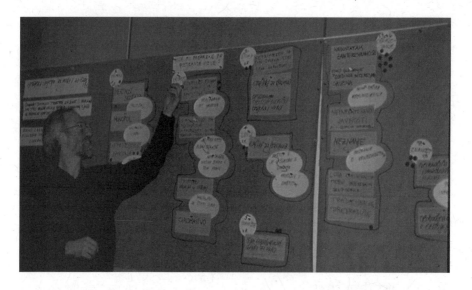

Figure 2.4.8. The author engaged in a human-dimensions facilitated workshop approach in Croatia.

neighbouring country, Bosnia and Herzegovina, but unfortunately they did not participate in the process. A likely contributing factor to this failure in collaboration was mutual distrust following the 1990s war between the Balkan countries, also including Croatia and Bosnia and Herzegovina. This experience highlights the importance of understanding history and politics while planning wolf management, as well as management of other resources.

The management plan was completely created by the participants in the process; no "draft" plan was created and presented first by some experts or promoting organizations. The group began with a blank document and discussed all aspects of the plan from the discussion rules and roles and responsibilities to the vision and values of the participants. The group also addressed biological and ecological aspects related to wolf management as well as the key issues facing wolf conservation, which were considered by the group as necessary objectives to address within the plan (e.g., wolf mortality, monitoring trends, implications of infrastructure, habitat requirements, livestock preventative measures, role of protected areas, and

Figure 2.4.9. The cover page of the Croatian Wolf Management Plan.

perceived social issues, etc.). Thus, many details of managing wolves in Croatia were discussed. There were eight human-dimensions facilitated workshops, with the final text of the management plan adopted at the ninth workshop. The overall goal throughout the process was to work "toward understanding and addressing the key issues in wolf management planning in Croatia" (Fig. 2.4.9). This statement also became the subtitle on the final document. A copy of the plan is available through the Large Carnivore Initiative for Europe website (www.lcie.org).

A similar process of working with various interest groups toward a wolf-management plan began in March 2008 in Bulgaria. Similar to how the Croatian wolf-management planning process started, the first workshop was used to define the roles and responsibilities of the participants and to identify whether all the interests affected by wolf presence in the area were actually represented in the room. The chief objective of the first workshop was to address behavioural conflicts among participants and to stimulate interest and a willingness to work together toward solutions. The group has agreed to meet on a regular basis requesting workshops designed to understand and address the key issues facing wolf-management planning in the country.

CONCLUSION

The wolf has coexisted with people in many parts of Europe and in some parts of North America for thousands of years (Mech 1970; Fritts et al. 2003). The fact that Europe and North America have recovering populations of wolves is evidence that wolves are resilient to some human impacts and possibly also an indictor of our willingness to coexist with this large carnivore (see Fox and Bekoff, this volume). As also described in this volume by Boitani and Ciucci, by Bangs et al., and by Wydeven et al., on both continents wolves continue to increase in numbers, and in most parts of Europe especially, the wolf is returning to a human-crafted and cultural landscape. As wolf numbers increase throughout Europe and wolf packs emerge, even close to urban centres like Rome, understanding the human dimensions of wolf management will be increasingly important. The challenge that exists for our global society is how much we are willing to share these increasingly busy landscapes. This will require managers to continue to integrate human dimensions into their decision-making processes, gathering the necessary scientific data to advise on social science questions (i.e., human dimensions as a research tool), and also to more actively engage the general public and various interest groups in listening exercises like those described in this chapter for Croatia and Bulgaria (i.e., human dimensions as a facilitated workshop approach). With increasing numbers of wolves and increasing numbers of people, demands on a limited land resource will require difficult decisions that will force us as a global society to think about our core values and our respect for a changing environment that may or may not include the same number of wolves or more.

In this book, Stone demonstrated how in the northwestern United States the issues of wolf conservation will continue to be defined by the public's willingness to tolerate damages, e.g. to livestock; similar considerations apply to wolves in other regions of North America and in Europe (Wydeven et al., Boitani and Ciucci, this volume). In general, our ability to share landscapes, share prey availability, share space, and truly strive for coexistence will determine the wolf's prospects. For example, fifty years in the future, we as a global society could have decreased livestock damages caused by wolves, improved livestock damage preventative measures, addressed compensation issues, and increased awareness of wolves; however, we still might have failed. If, fifty years in the future, we have actually created a more tolerant people willing to coexist with a large carnivore like the wolf, then perhaps we have succeeded. At the moment we focus mostly on minimizing impacts of the wolf and decreasing conflicts, but we need to truly shift the balance of this continuum of conflict-reduction to achieve coexistence. It is only then that we can say we have succeeded in wolf conservation.

LITERATURE CITED

Adaptive Management Oversight Committee (AMOC). 2005. Mexican wolf blue range reintroduction project 5-year review. Arizona Game and Fish Department, Phoenix, Arizona. Available from http://azgfd.gov/wolf (accessed October 2007).

Agocs, C. 2007. Conservation in action: making peace with coyote. Bay Nature. Berkeley, CA. Available from http://www.baynature.com/v07n01/v07n01_cia_coyote.html (accessed October 2007).

Aitken, G. 2004. *A new approach to conservation: the importance of the individual through wildlife rehabilitation.* Ashgate, Burlington, VT.

Allen, D. L. 1979. *Wolves of Minong: their vital role in a wild community.* Houghton Mifflin, Boston.

American Society of Mammoligists (ASM). 1999. Mammalian predator control in the United States (resolution passed June 20–24, 1999). University of Washington, Seattle.

Andersone, Ž., and J. Ozoliņš. 2004a. Food habits of wolves, *Canis lupus*, in Latvia. *Acta Theriologica* **49**:357–367.

Andersone, Ž., and J. Ozoliņš. 2004b. Public perception of large carnivores in Latvia. *Ursus* **15**:181–187.

Andersone, Ž., V. Lucchini, E. Randi, and J. Ozoliņš. 2002. Hybridisation between wolves and dogs in Latvia as documented using mitochondrial and microsatellite DNA markers. *Mammalian Biology* **67**:79–90.

Backes, D. A. 1997. *Wilderness within: the life of Sigurd Olson.* University of Minnesota Press, Minneapolis.

Bailey, R. G. 1995. Description of the ecoregions of the United States. 2nd edition. Miscellaneous Publication No. 1391. United States Department of Agriculture Forest Service, Washington, DC.

Baird, J. 2006. Rare wolf pays visit to Utah, dies in trap: discovery, second in Utah since '02, revives talk of recolonization. *The Salt Lake Tribune*, September 15, 2006. Available from http://www.sltrib.com/news/ci_4341765 (accessed September 2006).

Bangs, E. E., and S. H. Fritts. 1996. Reintroducing the gray wolf to central Idaho and Yellowstone National Park. *Wildlife Society Bulletin* **24**:402–412.

Bangs, E. E., and J. Shivik. 2001. Managing wolf conflict with livestock in the northwestern United States. *Carnivore Damage Prevention News* **3**:2–5.

Bangs, E. E., S. H. Fritts, J. A. Fontaine, D. W. Smith, K. M. Murphy, C. M. Mack, and C. C. Niemeyer. 1998. Status of the gray wolf restoration in Montana, Idaho and Wyoming. *Wildlife Society Bulletin* **26**:785–798.

Bangs, E., J. Fontaine, T. Meier, C. Niemeyer, M. Jimenez, D. Smith, C. Mack, V. Asher, L. Handegard, M. Collinge, R. Krischke, C. Sime, S. Nadeau, and D. Moody. 2004. Restoration and conflict management of the gray wolf in Montana, Idaho, and Wyoming. *Transactions of the North American Wildlife and Natural Resources Conference* **69**:89–105.

Bangs, E. E., J. A. Fontaine, M. D. Jimenez, T. J. Meier, E. H. Bradley, C. C. Niemeyer, D. W. Smith, C. M. Mack, V. Asher, and J. K. Oakleaf. 2005. Managing wolf-human conflict in the north-western United States. Pp. 340–356 in R. Woodroffe, S. Thirgood, and A. Rabinowitz, editors. *People and wildlife: conflict or coexistence?* Cambridge University Press, Cambridge.

Bangs, E., M. Jimenez, C. Niemeyer, J. Fontaine, M. Collinge, R. Krischke, L. Handegard, J. Shivik, C. Sime, S. Nadeau, C. Mack, D. Smith, V. Asher, and S. Stone. 2006a. Non-lethal and lethal tools to manage wolf/livestock conflict in the north-western United States. *Proceedings of the Vertebrate Pest Conference* **22**:7–16.

Bangs, E., M. Jimenez, C. Niemeyer, T. Meier, V. Asher, J. A. Fontaine, M. Collinge, L. Handegard, R. Krischke, D. Smith, and C. Mack. 2006b. Livestock guarding dogs and wolves in the Northern Rocky Mountains of the United States. *Carnivore Damage Prevention News* **8**:32–39.

Bath, A. J. 1991. Public attitudes in Wyoming, Montana, and Idaho toward wolf restoration in Yellowstone National Park. *Transactions of the 56th North American Wildlife and Natural Resources Conference* **56**:91–95.

Bath, A. J. 1998. The role of human dimensions in wildlife resource research in wildlife management. *Ursus* **10**:349–355.

Bath, A. J. 2000. Human dimensions in wolf management in Savoie and Des Alpes Maritimes, France. Large Carnivore Initiative for Europe. Available from http://www.lcie.org/Docs/HD/LCIE%20Bath%20Wolves%20in%20th e%20French%20Alps.pdf (accessed October 2007).

Bath, A. J. 2001. Human dimensions in wolf management in Savoie and Des Alpes Maritimes, France: Results targeted toward designing a more effective communication campaign and building better public awareness materials. Large Carnivore Initiative for Europe, IUCN Species Survival Commission.

Bath, A. J., and T. Buchanan. 1989. Attitudes of interest groups in Wyoming toward wolf restoration in Yellowstone National Park. *Wildlife Society Bulletin* **17**:519–525.

Bath, A. J., and J. W. Enck. 2003. Wildlife-human interactions in national parks in Canada and the USA. *Social Science Research Review* **4**:1–32.

Bath, A. J., and L. Farmer. 2000. Europe's carnivores: a survey of children's attitudes towards wolves, bears and otters. Large Carnivore Initiative for Europe (LCIE).

Bath, A. J., and A. Majic. 2001. Human dimensions in wolf management in Croatia: understanding attitudes and beliefs of residents in Gorski kotar, Lika and Dalmatia towards wolves and wolf management. Large Carnivore Initiative for Europe, IUCN Species Survival Commission. Available from http://www.lcie.org/Docs/HD/LCIE%20 Bath%20Croatia%20wo lf%20HD%201.pdf (accessed October 2007).

Beaufoy, G. 1998. The EU habitats directive in Spain: can it contribute effectively to the conservation of extensive agro-ecosystems? *Journal of Applied Ecology* **35**:974–978.

Bekoff, M. 2001. Human-carnivore interactions: adopting proactive strategies for complex problems. Pp. 179–195 in J. L. Gittleman, S. M. Funk, D. W. Macdonald, and R. K. Wayne, editors. *Carnivore conservation*. Cambridge University Press, London.

Bekoff, M. 2002. *Minding animals: awareness, emotions, and heart*. Oxford University Press, New York.

Bekoff, M. 2006a. *Animal passions and beastly virtues: reflections on redecorating nature*. Temple University Press, Philadelphia.

Bekoff, M. 2006b. Animal emotions and animal sentience and why they matter: blending "science sense" with common sense, compassion and heart. Pp. 27–40 in J. Turner and J. D'silva, editors. *Animals, ethics, and trade*. Earthscan Publishing, London.

Bekoff, M. 2007a. *The emotional lives of animals: a leading scientist explores animal joy, sorrow, and empathy and why they matter*. New World Library, Novato, CA.

Bekoff, M. 2007b. Aquatic animals, cognitive ethology, and ethics: questions about sentience and other troubling issues that lurk in turbid water. *Diseases of Aquatic Organisms* **75**:87–98.

Bekoff, M., and D. Jamieson. 1996. Ethics and the study of carnivores. Pp. 16–45 in J. L. Gittleman, editor. *Carnivore behavior, ecology, and evolution*. Cornell University Press, Ithaca, NY.

Berger, J. 1999. Anthropogenic extinction of top carnivores and interspecific animal behaviour: implications of the rapid decoupling of a web involving wolves, bears, moose and ravens. *Proceedings of the Royal Society of London, Series B* **266**:2261–2267.

Berger, K. M. 2006. Carnivore-livestock conflicts: effects of subsidized predator control and economic correlates on the sheep industry. *Conservation Biology* **20**:751–761.

Bibikov, D. I. 1982. Wolf ecology and management in the USSR. Pp. 120–133 in F. H. Harrington and P. C. Paquet, editors. *Wolves of the world: perspectives of behaviour, ecology, and conservation*. Noyes Publications, Park Ridge, NJ.

Bisi, J., S. Kurki, M. Svensberg, and T. Liukkonen. 2007. Human dimensions of wolf (*Canis lupus*) conflicts in Finland. *European Journal of Wildlife Research* **53**: 304–314.

Bjarvall A., and E. Isakson. 1982. Winter ecology of a pack of three wolves in Sweden. Pp. 146–157 in F. Harrington and P. Paquet, editors. Wolves of the World: Perspectives of Behavior, Ecology, and Conservation. Noyes, Park Ridge, NJ.

Bjerke, T., O. Reitan, and S. R. Kellert. 1998. Attitudes towards wolves in south-eastern Norway. *Society and Natural Resources* **11**: 169–178.

Blanco, J. C. 2001. El hábitat del lobo: la importancia de los aspectos ecológicos y socioeconómicos. Pp. 415–432 in J. Camprodon and E. Plana, editors. *Conservación de la biodiversidad y gestión forestal. Su aplicación en la fauna vertebrada.* Ed. Universidad de Barcelona, Barcelona.

Blanco, J. C. 2003. Wolf damage compensation in Spain. *Carnivore Damage Prevention News* **6**:7–9.

Blanco, J. C. 2004. Lobo – *Canis lupus.* In L. M. Carrascal and A. Salvador, editors. *Online encyclopedia of the Spanish vertebrates.* Museo Nacional de Ciencias Naturales, Madrid. Available from http://www.vertebradosibericos.org/ (accessed April 2007).

Blanco, J. C. 2005. La recuperación de un carnívoro adaptable en un ambiente cambiante. El caso del lobo en España. Pp. 221–250 in I. Jiménez and M. Delibes, editors. *Al borde de la extinción. Una visión integral de la recuperación de fauna amenazada en España.* EVREN, Valencia.

Blanco, J. C., and Y. Cortés. 2002. *Ecología, censos, percepción y evolución del lobo en España: Análisis de un conflicto.* Sociedad Española para la Conservación y Estudio de los Mamíferos (SECEM), Málaga.

Blanco, J. C., and Y. Cortés. 2007. Dispersal patterns, social structure and mortality of wolves living in agricultural habitats in Spain. *Journal of Zoology* **273**:114–124.

Blanco, J. C., L. Cuesta, and S. Reig. 1990. El Lobo en Espana: una vision global. Pp. 69–93 in J. C. Blanco, L. Cuesta and E. Reig, editors. *El Lobo (Canis lupus) en España: situation, problematica y apuntes sobre su ecologia.* Icona, Madrid, Spain.

Blanco, J. C., S. Reig, and L. Cuesta. 1992. Distribution, status, and conservation problems of the wolf *Canis lupus* in Spain. *Biological Conservation* **60**:73–80.

Blanco, J. C., Y. Cortés, and E. Virgos. 2005. Wolf response to two kinds of barriers in an agricultural habitat in Spain. *Canadian Journal of Zoology* **83**:312–323.

Boitani, L. 1982. Wolf management in intensively used areas of Italy. Pp. 158–172 in F. H. Harrington and P. C. Paquet, editors. *Wolves of the world: perspectives of behaviour, ecology, and conservation.* Noyes Publications, Park Ridge, NJ.

Boitani, L. 1986. Dalla parte del lupo. Mondadori Ass., Milano.

Boitani, L. 1992. Wolf research and conservation in Italy. *Biological Conservation* **61**:125–132.

Boitani, L. 1995. Ecological and cultural diversities in the evolution of wolf-human relationships. Pp. 3–11 in L. N. Carbyn, S. H. Fritts and D. R. Seip, editors. *Ecology and conservation of wolves in a changing world.* Canadian Circumpolar Institute, University of Alberta, Edmonton.

Boitani, L. 2000. Action plan for the conservation of wolves (*Canis lupus*) in Europe. *Nature and Environment Series, Convention on the Conservation of European Wildlife and Natural Habitat* **113**:1–81.

Boitani, L. 2003. Wolf conservation and recovery. Pp. 317–340 in L. D. Mech and L. Boitani, editors. *Wolves: behavior, ecology and conservation.* University of Chicago Press, Chicago.

Boitani, L., and P. Ciucci. 1993. Wolves in Italy: critical issues for their conservation. Pp. 75–90 in C. Promberger and W. Schröeder, editors. *Wolves in Europe: status and perspectives.* Munich Wildlife Society, Ettal, Germany.

Boitani, L., and P. Ciucci. 1998. The Italian way of saving wolves and shepherds: lessons to optimize conservation efforts. *Proceedings VII International Congress of Ecology.* INTECOL, Florence, Italy.

Boyd, D. K., and D. H. Pletscher. 1999. Characteristics of dispersal in a colonizing wolf population in the central Rocky Mountains. *Journal of Wildlife Management* **63**:1094-1108.

Braband, L. A., and K. D. Clark. 1992. Perspectives on wildlife nuisance control: results of a wildlife damage control firm's customer survey. *Proceedings of the 5th Eastern Wildlife Damage Control Conference* **5**:34–37.

Bradley, E. H. 2004. An evaluation of wolf-livestock conflicts and management in the north-western United States. University of Montana. Master's thesis.

Bradley, E. H., D. H. Pletscher, E. E. Bangs, K. E. Kunkel, D. W. Smith, C. M. Mack, T. J. Meier, J. A. Fontaine, C. C. Niemeyer, and M. D. Jimenez.

2005. Evaluating wolf translocation as a non-lethal method to reduce livestock conflicts in the north-western United States. *Conservation Biology* **19**:1498–1508.

Breitenmoser, U. 1998. Large predators in the Alps: the fall and rise of man's competitor. *Biological Conservation* **83**:279–289.

Breitenmoser, U., C. Angst, J-M. Landry, C. Breitenmoser-Wursten, J. D. C. Linnell, and J-M. Weber. 2005. Non-lethal techniques for reducing depredation. Pp. 49–71 in R. Woodroffe, S. Thirgood, and A. Rabinowitz, editors. *People and wildlife: conflict or coexistence?* Cambridge University Press, Cambridge.

Brenner, K. 2005. Coyotes get a reprieve: west Marin ranchers cut damage from predators the humane way. *Marin Independent Journal*, Nov. 13 issue, Novato, CA.

Brookfield, S. D. 1987. *Developing critical thinkers: challenging adults to explore alternative ways of thinking and acting.* Jossey-Bass (J. Wiley & Sons), San Francisco, CA.

Broom, D. M. 1999. The welfare of vertebrate pests in relation to their management. Pp. 309–29 in P. D. Cowan, and C. J. Feare, editors. *Advances in vertebrate pest management.* Filander Verlag, Furth, Germany.

Bruskotter, J. T., R. H. Schmidt, and T. L. Teel. 2007. Are attitudes toward wolves changing? A case study in Utah. *Biological Conservation* **139**: 211–218.

Bulte, E. H., and D. Rondeau. 2005. Why compensating wildlife damages may be bad for conservation. *Journal of Wildlife Management* **69**:14–19.

Capitani, C., I. Bertelli, P. Varuzza, M. Scandura, and M. Apollonio. 2004. A comparative analysis of wolf (*Canis lupus*) diet in three different Italian ecosystems. *Mammalian Biology* **69**:1–10.

Carbyn, L. N. 1982. Coyote population fluctuations and spatial distribution in relation to wolf territories in Riding Mountain National Park, Manitoba. *Canadian Field-Naturalist* **96**:176–183.

Carbyn, L. 1987. Gray wolf and red wolf. Pp. 359–376 in M. Novak, J. A. Baker, M. E. Obbard, and B. Malloch, editors. *Wild furbearer management and conservation in North America.* Ontario Ministry of Natural Resources, Toronto.

Carlsen, S. 2005. Marin County livestock protection program: presentation to the board of supervisors by Marin County agricultural commissioner's office. November 8, 2005. Available from http://www.co.marin.ca.us/depts/BS/Archive/Meetings_old.cfm?YYYY =2005 (accessed October 2007).

Carmichael, L. E., J. A. Nagy, N. C. Larter, and C. Strobeck. 2001. Prey specialization may influence patterns of gene flow of wolves of the Canadian Northwest. *Molecular Ecology* **10**:2787–2798.

Carroll, C., M. K. Phillips, N. H. Schumaker, and D. W. Smith. 2003. Impacts of landscape change on wolf restoration success: planning a reintroduction program based on static and dynamic spatial models. *Conservation Biology* **17**:536–548.

Carroll, C., M. K. Phillips, C. A. Lopez-Gonzales, and N. H. Schumaker. 2006. Defining recovery goals and strategies for endangered species using spatially- explicit population models: the wolf as a case study. *BioScience* **56**:25–37.

Casey, D., and T. W. Clark. 1996. *Tales of the wolf.* Homestead Publishing, Moose, WY.

Castroviejo, J., F. Palacios, J. Garzon, and L. Cuesta. 1975. Sobre la alimentazion de los Canidos ibericos. XII IUGB Congress, Lisboa, Portugal.

Celdran, M., and S. Moraud. 2006. Evaluation des dégâts et politique de protection: coûts et résultats à l'échelle de l'arc alpin. In Loup, élevage- S'ouvrir à la complexité. Séminaire technique. 15–16 June 2006, Aix-en-Provence.

Charudutt, M., P. Allen, T. McCarthy, M. D. Madhusudan, A. Bayatjargal, and H. T. Prins. 2003. The role of incentive programs in conserving the snow leopard. *Conservation Biology* **17**:1512–1520.

Ciucci, P., and L. Boitani. 1998a. Wolf and dog depredation on livestock in central Italy. *Wildlife Society Bulletin* **26**:504–514.

Ciucci, P., and L. Boitani. 1998b. Il Lupo: elementi di biologia, gestione , ricerca. Documenti Tecnici no. 23. Istituto Nazionale per la Fauna Selvatica, Università di Bologna, Italy.

Ciucci, P., and L. Boitani. 1999. Nine-year dynamics of a wolf pack in the Northern Apennines, Italy. *Mammalia* **63**:377–384.

Ciucci, P., and L. Boitani. 2005. Conflitto tra lupo e zootecnia in Italia: Metodi di studio, stato delle conoscenze, prospettive di ricerca e conservazione. *Biologia e Conservazione della Fauna* **115**:26–51.

Ciucci, P., L. Boitani, F. Francisci, and G. Andreoli. 1997. Home range, activity and movements of a wolf pack in central Italy. *Journal of Zoology, London* **243**:803–819.

Ciucci, P., V. Lucchini, L. Boitani, and E. Randi. 2003. Dew-claws in wolves as evidence of admixed ancestry with dogs. *Canadian Journal of Zoology* **81**:2077–2081.

Ciucci P., L. Boitani, and L. Maiorano. 2005. Long-distance wolf dispersal from Italy to France revamps the need for transboundary wolf management plans. Frontiers of Wolf Recovery. International Wolf Center, Colorado Springs, October 1–4, 2005.

Clark, T., M. Rutherford, and D. Casey. 2005. *Coexisting with large carnivores: lessons from Greater Yellowstone.* Island Press, Washington, DC.

Clevenger, A. P., and N. Waltho. 2005. Performance indices to identify attributes of highway crossing structures facilitating movement of large mammals. *Biological Conservation* **121**:453–464.

Corsi, F., E. Duprè, and L. Boitani. 1999. A large-scale model of wolf distribution in Italy for conservation planning. *Conservation Biology* **13**:150–159.

Cortés, Y. 2001. Ecología y conservación del lobo en medios agrícolas. PhD thesis. Universidad Complutense, Madrid.

Cozza, K., R. Fico, M. L. Battistini, and E. Rogers. 1996. The damage-conservation interface illustrated by predation on domestic livestock in central Italy. *Biological Conservation* **78**:329–336.

Crawford, M. 2006. DNA testing on possible wolf will take time. Burlington Free Press October 12, 2006. Available from http://www.burlingtonfreepress.com/apps/pbcs.dll/ article?AID=/20061012/NEWS02/610120307&SearchID=7326035391203 (accessed October 2006).

Cuesta, L., F. Barcena, F. Palacios, and S. Reig. 1991. The trophic ecology of the Iberian wolf (*Canis lupus signatus* Cabrera, 1907): A new analysis of stomach's data. *Mammalia* **55**:23–9-254.

Decker, D. J., and K. G. Purdy. 1988. Toward a concept of wildlife acceptance capacity in wildlife management. *Wildlife Society Bulletin* **16**:53–57.

Decker, D. J., T. B. Lauber, and W. F. Siemer. 2002. *Human-wildlife conflict management: a practitioners' guide.* Cornell University, Ithaca, NY.

Defenders of Wildlife. 2004. *Northern Rockies wolf compensation guidelines.* Defenders of Wildlife, Washington, DC.

Defenders of Wildlife. 2007. The Bailey Wildlife Foundation wolf compensation trust. Defenders of Wildlife, Washington, DC. Available from http://www.defenders.org/wolfcomp.html (accessed October 2007).

Dietz, T., E. Ostrom, and P. C. Stern. 2003. The struggle to govern the commons. *Science* **302**:1907–1912.

Echegaray, J., A. Illana, A. Hernando, F. Martínez de Lecea, J. Bayona, D. Paniagua, J. A. de la Torre, and C. Vilà. 2006. Estudio genético sobre la situación del lobo en el País Vasco. *Quercus* **245**:18–24.

Eggleston, J. E., S. S. Rixecker, and G. J. Hickling. 2003. The role of ethics in the management of New Zealand's wild mammals. *New Zealand Journal of Zoology* **30**:361–376.

Erb, J., and S. Benson. 2004. Distribution and abundance of wolves in Minnesota, 2003–04. Minnesota Department of Natural Resources Report. Minnesota Department of Natural Resources, Minneapolis.

Ericsson, G., and T. A. Heberlein. 2003. Attitudes of hunters, locals, and the general public in Sweden now that the wolves are back. *Biological Conservation* **111**: 149–159.

Espirito-Santo, C. 2007. Human dimensions in Iberian wolf management in Portugal: attitudes and beliefs of interest groups and the public toward a fragmented wolf population. Memorial University of Newfoundland. Master's thesis.

Espuno, N., B. Lequette, M.-L. Poulle, P. Migot, and J-D. Lebreton. 2004. Heterogeneous response to preventive sheep husbandry during wolf recolonization of the French Alps. *Wildlife Society Bulletin* **32**:1195–1208.

Estes, J. A. 1998. Concerns about the rehabilitation of oiled wildlife. *Conservation Biology* **12**:1156–1157.

European Commission. 2006. Nature and biodiversity barometer: sites of community importance. European Commission, Brussels. Available from http://ec.europa.eu/environment/nature/nature_conservation/useful_info/barometer/pdf/sci.pdf (accessed April 2007).

Fabbri, E., V. Lucchini, A. Santini, R. Caniglia, P. Taberlet, L. Fumagalli, J. M. Weber, F. Marucco, L. Boitani, and E. Randi. 2007. From the Apennines to the Alps: Colonization genetics of the naturally expanding Italian wolf (*Canis lupus*) population. *Molecular Ecology* **16**:1661–1671.

Federal-Provincial-Territorial Task Force on the Importance of Nature to Canadians. 2000. *The importance of nature to Canadians: the economic significance of nature-related activities*. Environment Canada, Ottawa.

Fernández, A., J. M. Fernández, and G. Palomero. 1990. El lobo an Cantabria. Pp. 33–44 in J. C. Blanco, L. Cuesta and E. Reig, editors. *El Lobo (Canis lupus) en España: situation, problematica y apuntes sobre su ecologia*. Icona, Madrid.

Filion, F. L., E. DuWors, P. Boxall, P. Bouchard, R. Reid, P. A. Gray, A. Bath, A. Jacquemot, and G. Legare. 1993. *The Importance of wildlife to Canadians: highlights of the 1991 Survey*. Canadian Wildlife Service. Ottawa.

Fischer, H. 1989. Restoring the wolf: Defenders launches a compensation fund. *Defenders* **64**:9–36.

Flader, S. L. 1974. *Thinking like a mountain*. University of Nebraska Press. Lincoln.

Fonseca, F. P. 1990. O lobo (*Canis lupus signatus* Cabrera, 1907) em Portugal: Problemática da sua conservação. PhD dissertation, University of Lisboa, Portugal.

Fowler, F. J. 1988. *Survey research methods: applied social research methods series*, vol. 1. 2nd ed. Sage, Newbury Park, CA.

Fox, C. H. 2001. Taxpayers say no to killing predators. *Animal Issues* **31**:27.

Fox, C. H. 2006a. Seeking justice. *Animal Issues* **37**:12–13.

Fox, C. H. 2006b. Coyotes and humans: can we coexist? Pp. 287–293 in R. M. Timm and J. M. O'Brien, editors. *Proceedings of the 22nd Vertebrate Pest Conference*. University of California, Davis, CA.

Fox, M. W. 1992. *The soul of the wolf*. Lyons & Burford, New York.

Fox, J. L., and R. S. Chundawat. 1995. Wolves in the transhimalayan region of India: the continued survival of a low-density population. Pp. 95–103 in L. N. Carbyn, S. H. Fritts, and D. R. Seip, editors. *Ecology and conservation of wolves in a changing world*. Canadian Circumpolar Institute, Occasional Publication No. 35, Edmonton, AB.

Fox, C. H., and C. M. Papouchis. 2005. *Coyotes in our midst: coexisting with an adaptable and resilient carnivore*. Animal Protection Institute, Sacramento, CA.

Fritts, S. H. 1982. Wolf depredation on livestock in Minnesota. Resource Publication No. 145. U.S. Fish and Wildlife Service, Washington, DC.

Fritts, S. H., and L. N. Carbyn. 1995. Population viability, nature reserves, and the outlook for gray wolf conservation in North America. *Restoration Ecology* 3:26–38.

Fritts, S. H., and L. D. Mech. 1981. Dynamics, movements, and feeding ecology of a newly-protected wolf population in northwestern Minnesota. *Wildlife Monograph* 80:1–79.

Fritts, S. H., W. J. Paul, L. D. Mech, and D. P. Scott. 1992. Trends and management of wolf-livestock conflicts in Minnesota. United States Fish and Wildlife Service Resource Publication No. 181. United States Fish and Wildlife Service, Washington, DC.

Fritts, S. H., E. E. Bangs, and J. F. Gore. 1994. The relationship of wolf recovery to habitat conservation and biodiversity in the north-western United States. *Landscape and Urban Planning* 28:23–32.

Fritts, S. H., E. E. Bangs, J. A. Fontaine, M. R. Johnson, M. K. Phillips, E. D. Koch, and J. R. Gunson. 1997. Planning and implementing a reintroduction of wolves to Yellowstone National Park and central Idaho. *Restoration Ecology* 5:7–27.

Fritts, S. H., R. O. Stephenson, R. D. Hayes, and L. Boitani. 2003. Wolves and Humans. Pp. 289–316 in L. D. Mech and L. Boitani, editors. *Wolves: behavior, ecology and conservation*. University of Chicago Press, Chicago.

Frommer, F. 2006. Wisconsin banned from killing gray wolves. Associated Press, August 11, 2006.

Fuller, T. K. 1989. Population dynamics of wolves in north-central Minnesota. *Wildlife Monographs* **105**:1–41.

Fuller, T. K. 1995. Guidelines for gray wolf management in the northern Great Lakes Region. International Wolf Center Technical Publication No. 271. International Wolf Center, Minnesota.

Fuller, T. K., W. E. Berg, G. L. Radde, M. S. Lenarz, and G. B. Joselyn. 1992. A history and current estimates of wolf distribution and numbers in Minnesota. *Wildlife Society Bulletin* **20**:42–55.

Fuller, T. K., L. D. Mech, and J. F. Cochrane. 2003. Wolf population dynamics. Pp. 161–191 in L. D. Mech and L. Boitani, editors. *Wolves: behavior, ecology, and conservation*. University of Chicago Press, Chicago.

Gehring, T. M., and B. A. Potter. 2005. Wolf habitat analysis in Michigan: an example of the need for proactive land management for a carnivore species. *Wildlife Society Bulletin* **33**:1237–1244.

Geist, V. 2006. The North American model of wildlife conservation: a means of creating wealth and protecting public health while generating biodiversity. Pp. 285–293 in D. M. Lavigne, editor. *Gaining ground: in pursuit of ecological sustainability*. International Fund for Animal Welfare, Guelph, Canada, and University of Limerick, Limerick, Ireland.

Gill, R. 1990. Monitoring the status of European and North American Cervids: The global environment monitoring system. GEMS Information Series No. 8, Nairobi, Kenya.

Girman, D. J., M. G. L. Mills, E. Geffen, and R. K. Wayne. 1997. A molecular genetic analysis of social structure, dispersal, and interpack relationships of the African wild dog (Lycaon pictus). *Behavioral Ecology and Sociobiology* **40**:187–198.

Glöde, D., R. Bergström, and F. Pettersson. 2004. Intäktsförluster på grund av älgbetning av tall Sverige ("Income losses due to moose browsing on Scots pine in Sweden"). Arbetsrapport Nr 570, Skogforsk, Uppsala (in Swedish).

Godinho, R., S. Lopes, and N. Ferrand. 2005. Análise genética das populaçoes portuguesas de lobo: estructuraçao en dois grupos principais, ausência de hibridaçao com o cao e implicaçoes para a consevaçao. Page 42 in

Abstracts of the 2nd Portuguese-Spanish Congress on the Iberian Wolf. 12–15 November 2005, Castelo-Branco, Portugal.

Goodwin, H., G. Johnston, and C. Warburton. 2000. WWF UK campaign for Europe's carnivores 8: tourism and carnivores: the challenge ahead. World Wildlife Fund – United Kingdom. Available from http://www.lcie.org/Docs/Education%20and%20process/WWF%20UK%20Goodwin%20Tourism%20and%20carnivores.pdf (accessed May 2008).

Haber, G. C. 1996. Biological, conservation, and ethical implications of exploiting and controlling wolves. *Conservation Biology* **10**:1068–1081.

Hadidian, J., C. Fox, and B. Lynn. 2006. The ethics of 'pest control' in humanized landscapes. Pp. 500–504 in R. M. Timm and J. M. O'Brien, editors. *Proceedings of the 22nd Vertebrate Pest Conference*. University of California, Davis.

Haight, R. G., L. E. Travis, K. Nimerfro, and L. D. Mech. 2002. Computer simulation of wolf removal strategies for animal damage control. *Wildlife Society Bulletin* **30**:1–9.

Harper, E. K., W. J. Paul, L. D. Mech, and S. Weisberg. 2008. Effectiveness of lethal, directed wolf-depredation control in Minnesota. *Journal of Wildlife Management* **72**:778–784.

Harrington, F. H., and L. D. Mech. 1982. An analysis of howling response parameters useful for wolf pack censusing. *Journal of Wildlife Management* **46**:686–693.

Heisey, D. M., and T. K. Fuller. 1985. Evaluation of survival and cause-specific mortality rates using telemetry data. *Journal of Wildlife Management* **49**:668–693.

Hendrickson, J., W. L. Robinson, and L. D. Mech. 1975. Status of the wolf in Michigan, 1973. *American Midland Naturalist* **94**:226–232.

Holt, R. D. 1977. Predation, apparent competition, and structure of prey communities. *Theoretical Population Biology* **12**:197–229.

Huber, D., J. Kusak, A. Majic-Skrbinsek, D. Majnaric, and M. Sindicic. 2008. A multidimensional approach to managing the European brown bear in Croatia. *Ursus* **19**: 22–32.

Huntzinger, B. A., J. A. Vucetich, T. D. Drummer, and R. O. Peterson. 2005. Wolf recovery in Michigan, 2002–2005 summary report. Michigan Technological University, Houghton, Michigan.

Ionescu, O. 1993. Current status and prospect for the wolf in Romania. Pp. 50–55 in C. Promberger and W. Schröder, editors. *Wolves in Europe: status and perspectives*. Munich Wildlife Society, Ettal, Germany.

Irwin, T. 1995. *Plato's ethics*. Oxford University Press, Oxford.

Jacobson, S. K. 1995. *Conserving wildlife: international education and communication approaches: methods and cases in conservation science*. Columbia University Press, New York.

Jarvis, P. 1998. Adult and continuing education: theory and practice. Routledge, London.

Jedrzejewska, B., W. Jedrzejewski, A. N. Bunevich, L. Miłkowski, and H. Okarma. 1996. Population dynamics of wolves *Canis lupus* in Białowieza Primeval Forest (Poland and Belarus) in relation to hunting by humans, 1847–1993. *Mammal Review* **26**:103–126.

Jedrzejewski, W., K. Schmidt, J. Theuerkauf, B. Jedrzejewska, N. Selva, K. Zub, and L. Szymura. 2002. Kill rates and predation by wolves on ungulate populations in Białowieza Primeval Forest (Poland). *Ecology* **83**:1341–1356

Jickling, B., and P. C. Paquet. 2005. Wolf stories: reflections on science, ethics, and epistemology. *Environmental Ethics* **27**:115–134.

Johnson, E., and M. Mappin. 2005. *Environmental education and advocacy: changing perspectives of ecology and education*. Cambridge University Press, London.

Karlsson, J., and M. Sjöström. 2007. Human attitudes towards wolf conservation, a matter of distance. *Biological Conservation* **137**:610–616.

Kellert, S. R. 1985a. Public perceptions of predators, particularly the wolf and the coyote. *Biological Conservation* **31**:167–189.

Kellert, S. R. 1985b. *The public and the timber wolf in Minnesota*. Yale University Press, New Haven, CT.

Kellert, S. R. 1996. *The value of life: biological diversity and human society*. Island Press, Washington, DC.

Kellert, S. R., M. Black, C. R. Rush, and A. J. Bath. 1996. Human culture and large carnivore conservation in North America. *Conservation Biology* **10**:977–990.

Kellert, S. R., J. N. Mehta, S. A. Ebbin, and L. L. Lichtenfeld. 2000. Community natural resource management: promise, rhetoric, and reality. *Society and Natural Resources* **13**:705–715.

Kirkwood, J. K., A. W. Sainsbury, and I. Bennett. 1994. The welfare of free-living wild animals: methods of assessment. *Animal Welfare* **3**:257–273.

Knickerbocker, B. 2006. Forest Service plans to ease limits on killing predators. *Christian Science Monitor*, June 16, 2006. Available from http://www.cs-monitor.com/2006/0616/p02s01-usgn.html (accessed October 2007).

Kohn, B., J. Frair, D. Unger, T. Gehring, D. Shelley, E. Anderson, and P. Keenlance. 1999. Impacts of a highway expansion project on wolves in Northwestern Wisconsin. Pp. 53–65 in G. Evink, D. Zeigler, and P. Garret, editors. *Proceedings of the Third International Conference on Wildlife Ecology and Transportation*. Florida Department of Transportation, Tallahassee, FL.

Kojola, I., H. Otso, T. Katri, H. Kalevi, H. Samuli, and R. Seppo. 2004. Predation on European wild forest reindeer (*Rangifer tarandus*) by wolves (*Canis lupus*) in Finland. *Journal of Zoology, London* **263**:229–235.

Kojola, I., J. Aspi, A. Hakala, S. Heikkinen, C. Ilmoni, and S. Ronkainen. 2006. Dispersal in an expanding wolf population in Finland. *Journal of Mammalogy* **87**:281–286.

Leopold, A. 1949. *A Sand County almanac, and sketches here and there*. Oxford University Press, New York.

Lesniewicz, K., and K. Perzanowski. 1989. The winter diet of wolves in Bieszczady Mountains. *Acta Theriologica* **34**:373–380.

Lessard, R. B. 2005. Conservation of woodland caribou (*Rangifer tarandus caribou*) in west-central Alberta: a simulation analysis of multi-species predator-prey systems. University of Alberta. Dissertation.

Liberg, O., H. Andrén, H.-C. Pedersen, H. Sand, D. Sejberg, P. Wabakken, M. Åkesson, and S. Bensch. 2005. Severe inbreeding depression in a wild wolf, *Canis lupus*, population. *Biology Letters* **1**:17–20.

Linnell, J., and H. Brøseth. 2003. Compensation for large carnivore depredation of domestic sheep 1994–2001. *Carnivore Damage Prevention News* 4:11–13.

Linnell, J.D.C., M. E. Smith, J. Odden, J. E. Swenson, and P. Kaczensky. 1996. Carnivores and sheep farming in Norway: strategies for the reduction of carnivore-livestock-conflicts: a review. *NINA Oppdragsmelding* **443**:1–116.

Linnell, J.D.C., R. Andersen, T. Kvam, H. Andrén., O. Liberg, J. Odden, and P. Moa. 2001a. Home range size and choice of management strategy for lynx in Scandinavia. *Environmental Management* 27:869–879.

Linnell, J.D.C., J. Swenson, and R. Andersen. 2001b. Predators and people: conservation of large carnivores is possible at high human densities if management policy is favourable. *Animal Conservation* 4:345–350.

Linnell, J.D.C., R. Andersen, L. Balciauskas, J. C. Blanco, L. Boitani, S. Brainerd, U. Breitenmoser, I. Kojola, O. Liberg, J. Loe, H. Okarma, H. C. Pedersen, C. Promberger, H. Sand, E. J. Solberg, H. Valdmann, and P. Wabakken. 2002. The fear of wolves: a review of wolf attacks on humans. *NINA Oppdragsmelding* **731**:1–65.

Linnell, J.D.C., H. Broseth, E. J. Solberg, and S. M. Brainerd. 2005a. The origins of the southern Scandinavian wolf *Canis lupus* population: potential for natural immigration in relation to dispersal distances, geography and Baltic ice. *Wildlife Biology* **11**: 383–391.

Linnell, J.D.C., C. Promberger, L. Boitani, J. E. Swenson, U. Breitenmoser, and R. Andersen. 2005b. The linkage between conservation strategies for large carnivores and biodiversity: the view from the "half-full" forests of Europe. Pp. 381–399 in J. C. Ray, K. H. Redford, R. S. Steneck, and J. Berger, editors. *Large carnivores and biodiversity conservation*. Island Press, Washington, D.C.

Linnell, J.D.C., E. B. Nilsen, U. S. Lande, I. Herfindal, J. Odden, K. Skogen, R. Andersen, and U. Breitenmoser. 2005c. Zoning as a means of mitigating conflicts with large carnivores: principles and reality. Pp. 162–175 in R. Woodroffe, S. Thirgood, and A. Rabinowitz, editors. *People and wildlife*. Cambridge University Press, Cambridge.

Linnell, J.D.C., V. Salvatori, and L. Boitani. 2007. *Guidelines for population level management plans for large carnivores*. LCIE and Istituto Ecologia Applicata, Rome.

Llaneza, L., and J. C. Blanco. 2002. *Diagnóstico de las poblaciones de lobo en Castilla y León*. Dirección General de Conservación de la Naturaleza, Valladolid.

Llaneza, L., and J. C. Blanco. 2005. Situación del lobo (*Canis lupus* L.) en Castilla y León en 2001: evolución de sus poblaciones. *Galemys* **17**:18–28.

Llaneza, L., V. Sazatornil, E. J. García, V. Palacios, and O. Hernández. 2005. Estudios recientes sobre la situación del lobo ibérico en Asturias. Page 48 in Abstracts of the 2nd Portuguese-Spanish Congress on the Iberian Wolf. 12–15 November 2005, Castelo-Branco, Portugal.

Lopez, B. 1978. *Of wolves and men*. Scribners, New York.

Macdonald, D. W., L. Boitani, and P. Barrasso. 1980. Foxes, wolves and conservation in the Abruzzo mountains. *Biogeographica* **18**:223–235.

Margerum R. D., and S. M. Born. 1995. Integrated environmental management: moving from theory to practice. *Journal of Environmental Planning and Management* **38**:371–392.

Marlin, R. 2002. Propaganda and the ethics of persuasion. Broadview Press, Peterborough, ON.

Masson, J. M., and S. McCarthy. 1995. *When elephants weep*. Delacorte, New York.

Mata, C., I. Hervás, J. Herranz, F. Suárez, and J. E. Malo. 2005. Complementary use by vertebrates of crossing structures along a fenced Spanish motorway. *Biological Conservation* **124**:397–405.

McCool, S. F., and K. Guthrie. 2001. Mapping the dimensions of successful public participation in messy natural resources management situations. *Society and Natural Resources* **14**:309–323.

McIntyre, R. 1995. *War against the wolf: America's campaign to exterminate the wolf*. Voyageur Press, Stillwater, MN.

McNay, M. E. 2002. A case history of wolf-human encounters in Alaska and Canada. Wildlife Technical Bulletin 13, Alaska Department of Fish and Game, Juneau, Alaska. Avaialble from http://www.wildlife.alaska.gov/pubs/techpubs/ research_pdfs/techb13_full.pdf (accessed May 2008).

Mech, L. D. 1970. *The wolf: ecology and behaviour of an endangered species*. Natural History Press, Garden City, New York.

Mech, L. D. 1989. Wolf population survival in an area of high road density. *American Midland Naturalist* **121**:387–389.

Mech, L. D. 1995. The challenge and opportunity of recovering wolf populations. *Conservation Biology* **9**:270–278.

Mech, L. D. 1998a. Estimated costs of maintaining a recovered wolf population in agricultural regions of Minnesota. *Wildlife Society Bulletin* **26**:817–822.

Mech, L. D. 1998b. *The arctic wolf: ten years with the pack*. Voyager Press, Stillwater, Minnesota.

Mech, L. D. 2000. *The wolves of Minnesota: howl in the heartland*. Voyageur Press, Stillwater, MN.

Mech, L. D. 2001. Managing Minnesota's recovered wolves. *Wildlife Society Bulletin* **29**:70–77.

Mech, L. D. 2006. Prediction failure of a wolf landscape model. *Wildlife Society Bulletin* **34**: 874–877.

Mech, L. D., and L. Boitani. 2003. Wolf social ecology. Pp. 1–34 in L. D. Mech and L. Boitani, editors. *Wolves: behavior, ecology, and conservation*. University of Chicago Press, Chicago.

Mech, L. D., S. H. Fritts, G. L. Radde, and W. J. Paul. 1988. Wolf distribution and road density in Minnesota. *Wildlife Society Bulletin* **16**:85–87.

Meine, C. 1987. Aldo Leopold's early years. Pp. 17–39 in J. B. Callicott, editor. *Companion to a Sand County almanac: interpretive and critical essays*. University of Wisconsin Press, Madison.

Meine, C. 1988. *Aldo Leopold: his life and works*. University of Wisconsin Press, Madison.

Meriggi, A., and S. Lovari. 1996. A review of wolf predation in southern Europe: does the wolf prefer wild prey to livestock? *Journal of Applied Ecology* **33**:1561–1571.

Merrill, S. B. 2000. Road density and gray wolf, *Canis lupus*, habitat suitability: an exception. *Canadian Field-Naturalist* **114**:312–313.

Merrill, S. B., and L. D. Mech. 2000. Details of extensive movements by Minnesota wolves (*Canis lupus*). *American Midland Naturalist* **144**:428–433.

Mezirow, J. 1991. *Transformative dimensions of adult learning*. Jossey-Bass, San Francisco, CA.

Michigan Department of Natural Resources (DNR). 1997. Michigan gray wolf recovery and management plan. Michigan Department of Natural Resources, Lansing, MI.

Mills, L. S. 1995. Edge effects and isolation: red-backed voles on forest remnants. *Conservation Biology* **9**:395–403.

Minnesota Department of Natural Resources (MNDNR). 2001. Minnesota wolf management plan. MNDNR, Wildlife Division, St. Paul, MN. Available from http://files.dnr.state.mn.us/natural_resources/animals/mammals/wolves/wolfplan2000.pdf (accessed October 2007).

Mitchell, B. 1989. *Geography and resource analysis*. 2nd ed. John Wiley and Sons. New York.

Mladenoff, D. J., T. A. Sickley, R. G. Haight, and A. P. Wydeven. 1995. A regional landscape analysis and prediction of favorable gray wolf habitat in the northern great lakes region. *Conservation Biology* **9**:279–294.

Mladenoff, D. J., R. G. Haight, T. A. Sickley, and A. P. Wydeven. 1997. Causes and implications of species restoration in altered ecosystems: a spatial landscape projection of wolf recovery. *BioScience* **47**:21–31.

Mladenoff, D. J., T. A. Sickley, and A. P. Wydeven. 1999. Predicting gray wolf landscape recolonization: logistic regression models vs. new field data. *Ecological Applications* **9**:37–44.

Mladenoff, D. J., A. Murray, K. Clayton, T. A. Sickley, and A. P. Wydeven. 2006. <L. D. Mech???> Critique of Our Work Lacks Scientific Validity. *Wildlife Society Bulletin* **34**:878–881.

Montag, J. 2003. Compensation and predator conservation: limitations of compensation. *Carnivore Damage Prevention News* **6**:2–6.

Moore, R. S. 1994. Metaphors of encroachment: hunting for wolves on a central Greek Mountain. *Anthropology Quarterly* **67**: 81–88.

Morell, V. 2008. Wolves at the Door of a More Dangerous World. *Science* 319: 890–892.

Musiani, M., and P. C. Paquet. 2004. The practices of wolf persecution, protection, and restoration in Canada and the United States. *BioScience* **54**:50–60.

Musiani, M., T. Muhly, C. C. Gates, C. Callaghan, M. E. Smith, and E. Tosoni. 2005. Seasonality and reoccurrence of depredation and wolf control in western North America. *Wildlife Society Bulletin* **33**:876–887.

National Agriculture Statistical Services (NASS). 2002. 2002 census of agriculture. United States Department of Agriculture, Washington, DC. Available from http://www.agcensus.usda.gov/Publications/2002/index.asp (accessed October 2007).

National Agricultural Statistics Service<CHECK NAME> (NASS). 2006. Cattle death losses 2005. Agricultural Statistics Board, U.S. Department of Agriculture, Washington, DC.

Naughton, L., A. Treves, R. Grossberg, and D. Wilcove. 2005. Summary report, 2004/2005 public opinion survey: wolf management in Wisconsin. University of Wisconsin, Madison. Available from http://www.geography.wisc.edu /livingwithwolves/public_reports.htm (accessed October 2007).

Naughton-Treves, L., R. Grossberg, and A. Treves. 2003. Paying for tolerance: rural citizens' attitudes toward wolf depredation and compensation. *Conservation Biology* **17**:1500–1511.

Nemtzov, S. C. 2003. A short-lived wolf depredation compensation program in Israel. *Carnivore Damage Prevention News* **6**:16–17.

Nie, M. A. 2003. *Beyond wolves: the politics of wolf recovery and management.* University of Minnesota Press, Minneapolis.

Nie, M. 2004. State wildlife governance and carnivore conservation. Pp. 197–218 in N. Fascione, A. Delach, and M. E. Smith, editors. *People and predators: from conflict to co-existence.* Island Press, Washington, DC.

Nilsen, E. B., E. J. Milner-Gulland, L. Schofield, A. Mysterud, N. C. Stenseth, and T. Coulson. 2007. Wolf reintroduction to Scotland: public attitudes and consequences for red deer management. *Proceedings of the Royal Society of London, Series B* **1612**: 995–1002.

Nowak, S., R. W. Mysłajek, and B. Jędrzejewska. 2005. Patterns of wolf, *Canis lupus*, predation on wild and domestic ungulates in the Western Carpathian Mountains (S. Poland). *Acta Theriologica* **50**:263–276.

Nyhus, P. J., S. A. Osofsky, P. Ferraro, F. Maden, and H. Fischer. 2005. Bearing the cost of human-wildlife conflict: the challenges of compensation schemes. Pp. 107–122 in R. Woodroffe, S. Thirgood, and A. Rabinowitz, editors. *People and wildlife*. Cambridge University Press, Cambridge.

Oakleaf, J. K., C. Mack, and D. L. Murray. 2003. Effects of wolves on livestock calf survival and movements in Central Idaho. *Journal of Wildlife Management* **67**:299–306.

Oakleaf, J. K., D. L. Murray, J. R. Oakleaf, E. E. Bangs, C. M. Mack, D. W. Smith, J. A. Fontaine, M. D. Jimenez, T. J. Meier, and C. C. Niemeyer. 2006. Habitat selection by recolonizing wolves in the northern Rocky Mountains of the United States. *Journal of Wildlife Management* **70**:554–563.

Okarma, H., W. Jędrzejewski, K. Schmidt, S. Śnieżko, A. N. Bunevich, and B. Jędrzejewska. 1998. Home ranges of wolves in Białowieża Primeval Forest, Poland, compared with other Eurasian populations. *Journal of Mammalogy* **79**:842–852.

O'Sullivan, E. 1999. *Transformative learning: education vision for the 21st century.* Zed Books, London.

O'Sullivan, E. V., A. Morrell, and M. A. O'Connor. 2002. *Expanding the boundaries of transformative learning: essays on theory and praxis.* Palgrave, New York.

Palacios, B. 1997. El lobo en el Parque Nacional de los Picos de Europa. Pp. 43–60 in B. Palacios and L. Llaneza, editors. *Primer Seminario sobre el lobo en los Picos de Europa.* SECEM- Grupo Lobo, Asturias.

Palmer, J. A. 1998. *Environmental education in the 21st Century – theory, practice, progress and promise.* Routledge, London.

Papageorgiou, N., C. Vlachos, A. Sfougaris, and E. Tsachalidis. 1994. Status and diet of wolves in Greece. *Acta Theriologica* **39**:411–416.

Paquet, P., and C. Callaghan. 1996. Effect of linear developments on winter movements of gray wolves in the Bow River Valley of Banff National Park, Alberta. Pp. 46–66 in G. Evink, D. Zeigler, P. Garret, and J. Berry, editors. *Transportation and wildlife: reducing wildlife mortality and improving wildlife passageways across transportation corridors.* Florida Department of Transportation, Tallahassee.

Parsons, D. R. 1998. "Green fire" returns to the southwest: reintroduction of the Mexican wolf. *Wildlife Society Bulletin* **26**:799–807.

Paul, W. J., and P. S. Gipson. 1994. Wolves. Pp. 123–129 in S. E. Hygnstrom, R. M. Timm, and G. E. Larson, editors. *Prevention and control of wildlife damage.* University of Nebraska Press, Lincoln.

Pepper, D. 1989. *The roots of modern environmentalism.* Routledge, New York.

Peters, R. S. 1966. *Ethics and education.* George Allen & Unwin, Oxford.

Peterson, R. O. 1977. Wolf ecology and prey relationships on Isle Royale. United States National Park Service Science Monograph Series 11. United States National Park Service, Washington, DC.

Peterson, R. O., and P. Ciucci. 2003. The wolf as a carnivore. Pp. 104–130 in L. D. Mech and L. Boitani, editors. *Wolves: behavior, ecology and conservation.* University of Chicago Press, Chicago.

Peterson, R. O., N. J. Thomas, J. M. Thurber, J. A. Vucetich, and T. A. Waite. 1998. Population limitation and the wolves of Isle Royale. *Journal of Mammalogy* **79**:487–841.

Pletscher, D. H., R. R. Ream, R. Demarchi, W. G. Brewster, and E. E. Bangs. 1991. Managing wolf and ungulate populations in an international eco-system. *Transactions of the North American Wildlife and Natural Resources Conference* **56**:539–549.

Pletscher, D. H., R. R. Ream, D. K. Boyd, D. M. Fairchild, and K. E. Kunkle. 1997. Population dynamics of a recolonizing wolf population. *Journal of Wildlife Management* **61**:459–465.

Pollock, K. H., S. R. Winterstein, C. M. Burich, and P. D. Curtis. 1989. Survival analysis in telemetry studies: the staggered entry design. *Journal of Wildlife Management* **53**:7–15.

Potvin, M. J., T. D. Drummer, J. A. Vucetich, D. E. Beyer, R. O. Peterson, and J. H. Hammill. 2005. Monitoring and habitat analysis for wolves in Upper Michigan. *Journal of Wildlife Management* **69**:1660–1669.

Poulle, M-L., B. Lequette, and T. Dahier. 1999. La recolonisation des Alpes par le loup de 1992 à 1998. *Bulletin Mensuel de la Office National de la Chasse* **242**:4–13.

Povilitis, A., D. R. Parsons, M. J. Robinson, and C. D. Becker. 2006. The bureaucratically imperiled Mexican wolf. *Conservation Biology* 20:942–945.

Promberger, C., and W. Schröeder. 1993. *Wolves in Europe: status and perspectives.* Munich Wildlife Society, Ettal, Germany.

Pullianen, E. 1993. The wolf in Finland. Pp. 14–20 in C. Promberger and W. Schröeder, editors. *Wolves in Europe: status and perspectives.* Munich Wildlife Society, Ettal, Germany.

Radeloff, V. R., R. B. Hammer, and S. I. Stewart. 2005. Rural and suburban sprawl in the U.S. Midwest from 1940 to 2000 and its relation to forest fragmentation. *Conservation Biology* **19**:793–805.

Randi, E., and V. Lucchini. 2002. Detecting rare introgression of domestic dog genes into wild wolf (*Canis lupus*) populations by Bayesian admixture analyses of microsatellite variation. *Conservation Genetics* 3:31–45.

Randi, E., F. Francisci, and V. Lucchini. 1995. Mithocondrial DNA restriction-fragment-length monomorphism in the Italian wolf (*Canis lupus*) population. *Journal of Zoological Systematics and Evolutionary Research* **33**:97–100.

Randi, E., V. Lucchini, M. F. Christensen, N. Mucci, S. M. Funk, G. Dolf, and V. Loeschke. 2000. Mithocondrial DNA variability in Italian and east European wolves: detecting the consequences of small population size and hybridization. *Conservation Biology* **14**:464–473.

Ream, R. R., and U. I. Mattson. 1982. Wolf status in the northern Rockies. Pp. 362–381 in F. H. Harrington and P. C. Paquet, editors. *Wolves of the world: perspectives of behavior ecology, and conservation.* Noyes Publications, Park Ridge, NJ.

Rebstock, G. A. 2005. We cannot afford to see people as opponents. *Conservation in Practice* **6**:45–46.

Reig, S., and W. Jedrzejewski. 1988. Winter and early spring food of some carnivores in the Bialowieza National Park, eastern Poland. *Acta Theriologica* **33**:57–65.

Reiter, D. K., M. W. Brunson, and R. H. Schmidt. 1999. Public attitudes toward wildlife damage management and policy. *Wildlife Society Bulletin* **27**:746–758.

Rigg, R. 2001. Livestock guarding dogs: their current use world wide. IUCN/SSC Canid Specialist Group Occasional Paper No 1. Available from http://www.canids.org/occasionalpapers/ (accessed October 2007).

Ripple, W. J., and R. L. Beschta. 2004. Wolves, elk, willows, and trophic cascades in the upper Gallatin range of southwestern Montana, USA. *Forest Ecology and Management* **200**:161–181.

Ripple, W. J., E. J. Larsen, R. A. Renkin, and D. W. Smith. 2001. Trophic cascades among wolves, elk, and aspen on Yellowstone National Park's northern range. *Conservation Biology* **102**:227–234.

Robbins, J. 2005. The look of success. *Conservation In Practice* **6**:October-December. Available from http://www.conbio.org/cip/article64wol.cfm (accessed October 2007).

Robinson, M. 2005. Predatory bureaucracy: the extermination of wolves and the transformation of the west. University of Colorado Press, Boulder.

Rodriguez, M., P. R. Krausman, W. B. Ballard, C. Villalobos, and W. W. Shaw. 2003. Attitudes of Mexican Citizens about Wolf Translocation in Mexico. *Wildlife Society Bulletin* **31**:971–979.

Rogers, A. 1996. *Teaching adults.* Open University Press, Buckingham, UK.

Rollin, B. E. 2006. *Science and ethics.* Cambridge University Press, London.

Røskaft, E., T. Bjerke, B. Kaltenborn, J. D. C. Linnell, and R. Andersen. 2003. Patterns of self-reported fear towards large carnivores among the Norwegian public. *Evolution and Human Behaviour* **24**:184–198.

Roy, L. D., and M. J. Dorrance. 1976. Methods of investigating predation of domestic livestock: a manual for investigating officers. Alberta Agriculture, Edmonton.

Salvatori V., and J. Linnell. 2005. Report on the conservation status and threats for wolf in Europe. Council of Europe (Strasbourg) Document No. T-PVS/Inf (2005)16. Council of Europe, Strasbourg, France.

Savelli Giannuzzi, B., F. Antonelli, and L. Boitani. 1998. Large Carnivore conservation and the agricultural subsidy system in Europe. Isituto di Ecologia Applicata, Rome.

Schmidt, R. H. 1989. Animal welfare and animal management. *Transactions of the North American Wildlife and Natural Resources Conference* **54**:468–475.

Schmidt, R. H., and T. P. Salmon. 1991. Social, political, legal, and ethical aspects of wildlife damage management. *Proceedings of the Great Plains Wildlife Damage Control Conference* **10**:169–170.

Schröder, W., and C. Promberger. 1993. European wolf conservation strategy. Pp. 2–7 in C. Promberger and W. Schröeder, editors. *Wolves in Europe: status and perspectives*. Munich Wildlife Society, Ettal, Germany.

Schweitzer, A. 1924. Memoirs of childhood and youth. Allen and Unwin, London.

Schwerdtner, K., and B. Gruberb. 2007. A conceptual framework for damage compensation schemes. *Biological Conservation* **134**:354–360.

Sebastián, J. 1997. Los aprovechamientos ganaderos en el Parque Nacional de los Picos de Europa. Pp. 63–78 in B. Palacios and L. Llaneza, editors. *Primer seminario sobre el lobo en los Picos de Europa*. SECEM- Grupo Lobo, Asturias.

Seielstad, M. T., E. Minch, and L. L. Cavalli-Sforza. 1998. Genetic evidence for a higher female migration rate in humans. *Nature Genetics* **20**:278–280.

Sheskin, I. M. 1985. Survey research for geographers: resource publications in geography. Association of American Geographers, Washington, DC.

Sillero-Zubiri, C., and M. K. Laurenson. 2001. Interactions between carnivores and local communities: conflict or co-existence? Pp. 283–312 in J. L. Gittleman, S. M. Funk, D. W. Macdonald, and R. K. Wayne, editors. *Carnivore conservation*. Cambridge University Press, London.

Skogen, K. 2001. Who's afraid of the big, bad wolf? Young peoples respones to the conflicts over large carnivores in eastern Norway. *Rural Sociology* **66**: 203–226.

Skogen, K. 2003. Adapting adaptive management to a cultural understanding of land use conflicts. *Society and Natural Resources* **16**: 435–450.

Smith, D. W., and G. Ferguson. 2005. *Decade of the wolf: returning the wild to Yellowstone*. The Lyons Press, Augusta, GA.

Smith, D. W., R. O. Peterson, and D. B. Houston. 2003. Yellowstone after wolves. *BioScience* **53**:330–340.

Smith, D. W., D. R. Stahler, D. S. Guernsey, and E. E. Bangs. 2006. Wolf restoration in Yellowstone National Park. Pp. 242–253 in D. R. McCullough,

K. Kaji, and. M. Yamanaka, editors. *Wildlife in Shiretoko and Yellowstone National Park: lessons in wildlife conservation from two world heritage sites.* Shiretoko Nature Foundation, Japan.

Snook, I. A. 1972. *Indoctrination and education.* Routledge & Kegan Paul, London.

Soulé, M. E. 1985. What is conservation biology? *BioScience* **35**:27–34.

Soulé, M. E. 2002. History's lesson: build another Noah's Ark. High Country News 24. May 13, 2002. Paonia, Colorado. Available from http://www. hcn.org/servlets/ hcn.Article?article_id=11219 (accessed October 2007).

Soulé, M. E., and J.W. Terborgh. 1999. *Continental Conservation: Scientific foundations of regional reserve networks.* Island Press, Washington, DC.

Soulé, M. E., J. A. Estes, J. Berger, and C. M. Del Rio. 2003. Ecological effectiveness: conservation goals for interactive species. *Conservation Biology* **17**:1238–1250.

Soulé, M., J. Estes, B. Miller, and D. Honnold. 2005. Strongly interacting species: conservation policy, management, and ethics. *BioScience* **55**:168–176.

Spanish Statistics Institute. 2007. Censo ganadero. Available from: http://www. ine.es/inebase/cgi/axi?AXIS_PATH=/inebase/temas/t01/a097/a1998/ 10/&FILE_AXIS=a40011.px&CGI_DEFAULT=/inebase/temas/cgi. opt&COMANDO=SELECCION&CGI_URL=/inebase/cgi/ (accessed April 2007).

Stenlund, M. H. 1955. A field study of the timber wolf (*Canis lupus*) on the Superior National Forest, Minnesota. Technical Bulletin No. 4. Minnesota Conservation Department, Minneapolis.

Stronen, A. V., R. K Brook., P. C. Paquet, and S. Mclachlan. 2007. Farmer attitudes toward wolves: Implications for the role of predators in managing disease. *Biological Conservation* **135**:1–10.

Swenson, J. E., and H. Andrén. 2005. A tale of two countries: large carnivore depredations and compensation schemes in Sweden and Norway. Pp. 323–339 in R. Woodroffe, S. Thirgood, and A. Rabinowitz, editors. *People and wildlife: conflict or co-existence?* Cambridge University Press, Cambridge.

Talegón, J. 2002. Los daños del lobo en Zamora. Pp. 121–123 in L. Llaneza and J. C. Blanco, editors. *Diagnóstico de las poblaciones de lobo en Castilla y León.* Dirección General de Conservación de la Naturaleza, Valladolid.

Taylor, E. W. 1998. The theory and practice of transformative learning: a critical review. Information Series No. 374. ERIC Clearinghouse on Adult, Career, and Vocational Education, Columbus, OH.

Teel, T. L., A. A. Dayer, M. J. Manfredo, and A. D. Bright. 2002. Regional results from the research project entitled: "wildlife values in the west." Project Report No. 58. Colorado State University, Fort Collins, CO.

Terborgh, J., J. A. Estes, P. C. Paquet, K. Ralls, D. Boyd-Heger, B. Miller, and R. Noss. 1999. The role of top carnivores in regulating terrestrial ecosystems. Pp. 60–103 in M. E. Soulé and J. Terborgh, editors. *Continental conservation: scientific foundations of regional reserve networks.* Island Press, Washington, DC.

Terborgh, J., L. Lopez, P. Nuñez, M. Rao, G. Shahabuddin, G. Orihuela, M. Riveros, R. Ascanio, G. H. Adler, T. D. Lambert, and L. Balbas. 2001. Ecological meltdown in predator-free forest fragments. *Science* **294**:1923–1926.

Teruelo, S., and J. A. Valverde. 1992. *Los lobos de Morla.* Circulo de Bibliofilia Venatoria, Madrid.

Thiel, R. P. 1985. Relationship between road densities and wolf habitat suitability in Wisconsin. *American Midland Naturalist* **113**:404–407.

Thiel, R. P. 1993. *The timber wolf in Wisconsin: the death and life of a majestic predator.* University of Wisconsin Press, Madison.

Thiel, R. P., and J. H. Hammill. 1988. Wolf specimen records in Upper Michigan. *Jack-Pine Warbler* **66**:149–153.

Treves, A. R., and L. Naughton-Treves. 2005. Evaluating lethal control in the management of human-wildlife conflict. Pp. 86–106 in R. Woodroffe, S. Thirgood, and A. Rabinowitz, editors. *People and wildlife: conflict or coexistence?* Cambridge University Press, London.

Treves, A., R. R. Jurewicz, L. Naughton-Treves, R. A. Rose, R. C. Willging, and A. P. Wydeven. 2002. Wolf depredation on domestic animals in Wisconsin, 1976–2000. *Wildlife Society Bulletin* **30**:231–241.

Treves, A., L. Naughton-Treves, E. K. Harper, D. J. Mladenoff, R. A. Rose, T. A. Sickley, and A. P. Wydeven. 2004. Predicting human-carnivore conflict: a spatial model derived from 25 years of data on wolf predation on livestock. *Conservation Biology* **18**:114–125.

Tsingarska, E. 1997. Bulgaria: *revival of traditional method for livestock protection. European Wolf Newsletter No. 5. European Subgroup of the IUCN Wolf Specialist Group.* Available from *http://www.wolfinfo.org/EWN/ewn5_e.htm (accessed October 2007).*

Tsingarska, E. 2003. Wolf analysis and education about large carnivores – annual report 2003. Balkani Wildlife Society, Sofia.

Tsingarska, E. 2004. Wolf study and conservation program – annual report 2004. Balkani Wildlife Society, Sofia.

United States Department of Agriculture-Wildlife Services (USDA–WS). 2003. Mission and philosophy of the WS Program. Wildlife Services Directive 1.201. United States Department of Agriculture, Washington, DC.

United States Fish and Wildlife Service (USFWS). 1980. Northern Rocky Mountain wolf recovery plan. USFWS, Denver, CO.

United States Fish and Wildlife Service (USFWS). 1987. Northern Rocky Mountain wolf recovery plan. USFWS, Denver, CO.

United States Fish and Wildlife Service (USFWS). 1988. Interim wolf control plan: northern Rocky Mountains of Montana and Wyoming. USFWS, Denver, CO.

United States Fish and Wildlife Service (USFWS). 1992. Recovery plan for the eastern timber wolf. U.S. Fish and Wildlife Service, Twin Cities, MN.

United States Fish and Wildlife Service (USFWS). 1994. The reintroduction of gray wolves to Yellowstone National Park and central Idaho: final environmental impact statement. USFWS, Denver, CO.

United States Fish and Wildlife Service (USFWS). 1999. Interim wolf control plan for north-western Montana and the panhandle of northern Idaho (excluding the experimental population area). USFWS, Denver, CO.

United States Fish and Wildlife Service (USFWS). 2004. Gray wolves in the northern Rocky Mountains: status of gray wolf recovery, week of 1/16–1/23,

2004. USFWS, Helena, MT. Available from http://westerngraywolf.fws. gov/WeeklyRpt04/wk01232004.htm (accessed October 2007).

United States Fish and Wildlife Service (USFWS). 2005a. Regulation for nonessential experimental populations of the western distinct population segment of the gray wolf: final rule. *Federal Register* **70**:1286–1311.

United States Fish and Wildlife Service (USFWS). 2005b. Mexican wolf recovery program: January 1 – December 31, 2004. Progress Report #7. USFWS, Albuquerque, NM.

United States Fish and Wildlife Service (USFWS). 2006a. Gray wolf recovery weekly progress reports 1995–2006. USFWS, Helena, MT. Available from http://www.fws.gov/mountain-prairie/species/mammals/wolf/ (accessed October 2007).

United States Fish and Wildlife Service (USFWS). 2006b. Endangered and threatened wildlife and plants: gray wolf: advance notice of proposed rulemaking. *Federal Register* **71**:6634–6660.

United States Fish and Wildlife Service (USFWS). 2006c. Mexican wolf recovery program: January 1 – December 31, 2005. Progress Report #8. USFWS, Albuquerque, NM.

United States Fish and Wildlife Service (USFWS). 2006d. Proposed western Great Lakes gray wolf distinct population segment: summary of the proposal to delist the gray wolf western Great Lakes distinct population segment, March 16, 2006. USFWS, Fort Snelling, MN. Available from http:// www.fws.gov/midwest/WOLF/archives/ 2006pr_dl/2006pr_dlsum.htm (accessed October 2007).

United States Fish and Wildlife Service (USFWS), Nez Perce Tribe, National Park Service, Montana Fish, Wildlife and Parks, Idaho Fish and Game, and United States Department of Agriculture-Wildlife Services (USDA-WS). 2005. Rocky Mountain wolf recovery 2004 annual report. USFWS, Helena, MT.

United States Fish and Wildlife Service (USFWS), Nez Perce Tribe, National Park Service, and United States Department of Agriculture Wildlife Services. 2006. Rocky Mountain wolf recovery interagency annual reports 1989–2005. USFWS, Helena, MT.

United States Fish and Wildlife Service (USFWS), Nez Perce Tribe, National Park Service, Montana Fish, Wildlife & Parks, Idaho Fish and Game, and United States Department of Agriculture Wildlife Services. 2007. Rocky Mountain wolf recovery 2005 and 2006 interagency annual report. USFWS, Helena, MT.

Valière, N., L. Fumagalli, L. Gielly, C. Miquel, B. Lequette, M-L. Poulle, J-M. Weber, R. Arlettaz, and P. Taberlet. 2003. Long-distance wolf recolonization of France and Switzerland inferred from non-invasive genetic sampling over a period of 10 years. *Animal Conservation* **61**:83–92.

Valverde, J. A. 1971. El lobo español. *Montes* **159**:229–241.

Van Camp, J., and R. Gluckie. 1979. A record long-distance move by a wolf (*Canis lupus*). *Journal of Mammalogy* **60**:236.

Verardi, A., V. Lucchini, and E. Randi. 2006. Detecting introgressive hybridization between free-ranging domestic dogs and wild wolves (*Canis lupus*) by admixture linkage disequilibrium analysis. *Molecular Ecology* **15**:2845–2855.

Vilà, C., U. Vincente, and J. Castroviejo. 1995. Observation on the daily activity patterns in the Iberian wolf. Pp. 335–340 in L. N. Carbyn, S. H. Fritts and D. R. Seip, editors. *Ecology and conservation of wolves in a changing world.* Canadian Circumpolar Institute, University of Alberta, Edmonton.

Vilà, C., A-K. Sundqvist, Ø. Flagstad, J. Seddon, S. Björnerfeldt, I. Kojola, A. Casulli, H. Sand, P. Wabakken, and H. Ellegren. 2003a. Rescue of a serverely bottlenecked wolf (*Canis lupus*) population by a single immigrant. *Proceedings of the Royal Society of London, Series B* **270**:91–97.

Vilà, C., C. Walker, A-K. Sundqvist, Ø. Flagstad, Ž. Andersone, A. Casulli, I. Kojola, H. Valdmann, J. Halverson, and H. Ellegren. 2003b. Combined use of maternal, paternal and bi-parental genetic markers for the identification of wolf–dog hybrids. *Heredity* **90**:17–24.

Wabakken, P., H. Sand, O. Liberg, and A. Bjärvall. 2001. The recovery, distribution, and population dynamics of wolves on the Scandinavian peninsula, 1978–1998. *Canadian Journal of Zoology* **79**:710–725.

Wabakken, P., H. Sand, I. Kojola, B. Zimmermann, J. M. Arnemo, C. Pedersen, and O. Liberg. 2007. Multistage, long-range natal dispersal by a Global

Positioning System–collared Scandinavian wolf. *Journal of Wildlife Management* **71**:1631–1634.

Weaver, J. 1978. The wolves of Yellowstone. Natural Resources report No. 14. United States National Parks Service, Washington, DC.

Williams, C. K., G. Ericsson, and T. A. Heberlein. 2002. A quantitative summary of attitudes toward wolves and their reintroduction (1972–2000). *Wildlife Society Bulletin* **30**:575–584.

Wistow, G., and T. Brookes. 1988. *Joint planning and joint management.* International Specialized Book Service Inc., Portland, OR.

Woodroffe, R., and J. R. Ginsberg. 1998. Edge effects and the extinction of populations inside protected areas. *Science* **280**:2126–2128.

Woodroffe, R., S. Thirgood, and A. Rabinowitz. 2005. *People and wildlife: coexistence or conflict?* Cambridge University Press, Cambridge.

Wydeven, A. P., and J. E. Wiedenhoeft. 2005. Status of the timber wolf in Wisconsin: performance report, 1 July 2004 – 31 June 2005. Endangered Resources Report #132. Wisconsin Department of Natural Resources, Madison.

Wydeven, A. P., R. N. Schultz, and R. P. Thiel. 1995. Gray wolf *(Canis lupus)* population monitoring in Wisconsin 1979–1991. Pp. 147–156 in L. N. Carbyn, S. H. Fritts, and D. P. Seip, editors. *Ecology and conservation of wolves in a changing world.* Canadian Circumpolar Institute, Occasional Publication No. 35, Edmonton, AB.

Wydeven, A. P., R. N. Schultz, and R. A. Megown. 1996. Guidelines for carnivore track surveys during winter in Wisconsin. Endangered Resources Report No. 112. Wisconsin Department of Natural Resources, Madison.

Wydeven, A. P., D. J. Mladenoff, T. A. Sickley, B. E. Kohn, R. P. Thiel, and J. L. Hansen. 2001. Road density as a factor in habitat selection by wolves and other carnivores in the Great Lakes Region. *Endangered Species UPDATE* **18**:110–114.

Wyoming Game and Fish Department (WGFD). 2003. Draft Wyoming gray wolf management plan. WGFD, Cheyenne, WY. Available from http://www.sublette.com/examiner/v2n34/draftwolfplan.pdf (accessed October 2007).

Young, S. P. and E. A. Goldman. 1944. *The wolves of North America*. American Wildlife Institute, Washington, D. C.

Zabel, A., and K. Holm-Müller. 2008. Conservation performance payments for carnivore conservation in Sweden. *Conservation Biology* **22**:247–251.

Zamora, R., and S. F. Ortuño. 2003. La economía de la *dehesa* y el desarrollo rural: la Sierra Morena sevillana. *Observatorio Medioambiental* **6**:253–275.

Zimen, E., and L. Boitani. 1975. Number and distribution of Wolves in Italy. *Zeitschrift für Saugetierkunde* **40**:102–112.

Zimen, E., and L. Boitani. 1979. Status of the wolf in Europe and the possibilities of conservation and reintroduction. Pp. 43–83 in E. Klinghammer, editor. *The behavior and conservation of wolves*. Garland Press, New York.

Colour Photos

Young pups at a den in the arctic tundra of the Northwest Territories, Canada. When adult, these wolves will be nearly white. ©Frame

A few European Wolves are recolonizing the Alps, coming from Italy. In this rare photo, a wolf has typically short summer fur. ©Dettling

A New Era for Wolves and People

Young pup near a den in the forests of Yellowstone National Park, U.S.A. When adult, this wolf will be grey. Wolves there are grey or black (most commonly) or also white. ©Weselmann

Pups playing (to the right) or 'playing serious' (to the left) in Yellowstone National Park, U.S.A.. Such playing is important to test social interactions among pack members. ©Weselmann

This photo was taken in Banff National Park, Canada and portrays a caring mom (to the right) and a gently submissive pup. In protected areas, wolves are less fearful of people and also frequent roads during the day. ©Dettling

This wolf from Canada is an adult female that is greying little by little – note the white hairs. ©Dettling

Many wolves in North America, like this one from Minnesota, U.S.A., are black, but develop white hairs with adulthood and aging. Wolves may observe people from a distance, then generally move away. ©Olson

Canadian female wolf a bit wary of the photographer (photo taken from a distance with tele-lens).
©Dettling

If undisturbed by people (for example, in Canadian Parks), wolves like travelling in open areas, where they can spot prey from a greater distance than in dense forest. ©Dettling

During the long Canadian winters, wolves may spend time sniffing under the snow in search of food, such as little rodents or leftovers from a carrion. ©Dettling

Wolf at ease in the snow of Yellowstone National Park, U.S.A. Wolves may negotiate deep snow better than their prey. ©Weselmann

Adult wolf, also from Yellowstone National Park, U.S.A. staring at the photographer with great confidence and perhaps some curiosity. ©Weselmann

Typical colour pattern for a grey wolf from the forested areas of North America. Other wolves may be black or, rarely, white. Depending on the background colours, some wolves may be barely visible to prey species. ©Olson

Typical colour pattern for any wolf from the arctic and sub-arctic tundra regions of America and Eurasia.
©Musiani

White, black, and grey wolves may occur in the same pack. The photo is from Jasper National Park, Canada, and shows a near white and a black wolf, with white hairs that are signs of maturity and aging. ©Olson

Wolves using body language in Banff National Park, Canada, to beg for food (wolf to the left). Such language is also symbolic, and begging for food, for example, is a sign of submission and trust. ©Dettling

A New Era for Wolves and People

Wolves often interact with bears, such as this grizzly in Banff National Park, Canada. Such interactions typically occur around carrion where the two species compete for food. ©Dettling

A pack of Yellowstone wolves in which some individuals sleep in the snow, while other wolves wrestle and thus establish hierarchies. Wolves live throughout the Northern Hemisphere and do not seem bothered by cold. ©Weselmann

Frozen rivers and lakes are important travel routes for wolves in the winter, as in these cold regions of Canada. While moving there, they also search for prey, such as beaver. ©Dettling

Also in the summer, wolves may travel around bodies of water where they can spot prey from greater distances than in forested areas. Visitors to Jasper National Park, Canada, have sometimes spotted wolves there. ©Olson

In general, canids such as wolves do not mind water. ©Dettling

Wolves that are white or pale are better concealed in the winter snow than in the forest during the summer.
©Olson

During the summer (or in early autumn as in the photo), white wolves are easily visible in the tundra, whereas they are camouflaged in the snow of the winter. White wolves may be efficient predators of caribou throughout the long winters in the Northwest Territories and Nunavut, Canada. ©Cluff

Wolves in a pack typically hunt together and then consume their kill together. Photo from Yellowstone National Park, U.S.A. ©Weselmann

Wolves seem to prefer elk in North America or red deer in Eurasia, but may kill any species of ungulates available. In this photo from Wyoming, U.S.A., two wolves consume an adult male elk. ©Olson

Consuming a kill often takes days. Wolves may gorge on the spot or carry parts to eat elsewhere alone and with other pack members. Photo from Yellowstone National Park, U.S.A. ©Weselmann

Wolves eat large mammalian herbivores whose carcasses provide food also to other scavengers like these ravens in Yellowstone National Park, U.S.A. ©Weselmann

Wolves' tolerance for other species at kill sites is not high and they may chase away scavengers such as this magpie in Wyoming, U.S.A. ©Weselmann

Wolf trapping and hunting is allowed in various countries, including Canada. People may sell wolf pelts to be used as clothes or simply as a hunting trophy. ©Paquet

Wolves often use areas around human features such as roads. In areas such as Yellowstone National Park, U.S.A., some people are good at spotting wolves while others do not notice them at all. ©Dettling

In areas such as Yellowstone National Park, U.S.A., wolves are learning not to fear people. Wolves and other species (such as bison) may therefore interact around roads. ©Dettling

Researchers study wolves to understand their role in ecosystems. In the photo, a Canadian crew is using a helicopter to capture wolves with nets. Some wolves may elude such efforts – note the net on the ground, bottom-left of photo. ©Musiani

Researchers find that wolves are eclectic predators capable of killing various species. However, wolves' dentition is most adapted to killing large mammals. In this photo, note the contrast between pelt colour and the dark background of the arctic tundra during the summer. ©Cluff

A New Era for Wolves and People

Index

C

California sea otters, 127
Canada, 8, 103, 129
  economic valuation studies on wildlife,
      177
  Trans-Canada highway (Banff), 52
  wolf dispersal from, 95, 129
  wolf population, 69, 95
  wolf protection, 95
  wolves translocated from, 128
Canada lynx, 137
canid diseases, 135
canine parvovirus, 79–80, 87
Cantabrian Mountains, 45, 48–50, 63
C.A.P. *See* European Common
      Agricultural Policy (C.A.P.)
caribou migration patterns, 54
Carpathian wolf population range, 21
carrying capacities (livestock)
  C.A.P.'s effect on, 33
carrying capacities for wolves, 92, 174, 176
Castile, 45, 48, 50
  hunting reserve, 49
  wolf management (culls), 43
Catalonia, 17
cattle, 58, 106, 144, 146–47
  grazing (NRM), 98
  grazing (unprotected), 59 (*See also*
      livestock husbandry)
children, education for, 162, 165. *See also*
      teenagers
Ciucci, P., 3–6, 10, 52, 87
Clayton, Idaho, 153
coexistence, 1–3, 8, 30, 126, 180, 184, 199
  appropriate behaviour in areas with
      wolves, 176
  human dimensions facilitated
      workshops and, 11, 26, 173–74
  practical models of, 134–36
  reducing conflict, 153
  by reducing economic damage, 36–37
collaborative process (need for), 120, 157
collective wolf management, 10. *See also*
      participatory wildlife management
Colorado, 100, 137, 141

compensation for predator presence, 135
compensation programs, 3, 8–9, 16, 23–24,
      31–32, 50, 65–66, 133, 141–58
  cost-share indemnification programs,
      135–36
  elimination of, 39
  funding (government funding), 49, 62,
      142–43
  funding (owner contributions), 152
  funding (private programs), 101, 144
  incentive for non-lethal methods, 135,
      150
  increasing farmers' tolerance to wolves,
      31
  insurance, 49
  investigation of claims, 146, 150, 152
  politically popular, 102
  Spain, 44
  tolerance and, 148–49
Compound 1080, 133
conflict, 192. *See also* wolf-human conflict
  about trust and credibility, 193
  cognitive conflicts, 192
  compensation to reduce conflicts,
      142–45
  economic conflicts, 192–93
  livestock conflicts, 24, 26, 31–32, 109
  non-lethal, proactive conflict
      management, 152–56
  social conflicts caused by wolves, 43
  between wolf advocates and opponents,
      92, 163
conservation biology, 138
  ethical axioms, 124
  individual *vs.* species issue, 127–28
  not value-free, 124
conservation campaigns, 16. *See also*
      animal advocacy and conservation
      organizations
conservation education as a discipline, 169
conservationists (stakeholders), 168
contingent valuation techniques, 177
Cortés, Yolanda, 3–4, 87
coyotes, 142, 151
Croatia, 178–79

European Commission, 6, 35–36
European Common Agricultural Policy
(C.A.P.), 32. *See also* subsidies
negative impacts on environment, 38
wolf conservation goals and, 33
European protected areas, 29–30, 37
European Union's Habitat Directive. *See*
Habitat Directive
experience with wolves, 185
as predictor of attitude, 189, 191

F

farmers, 9, 31–32, 163, 168
attitude toward wolves, 185
compensation (*See* compensation
programs)
fear, 33, 119–20, 128, 174
as predictor of attitude, 189, 191
federal delisting of wolves, 82, 90–91,
118–19, 130. *See also* Endangered
Species Act; status
Federal-Provincial-Territorial Task Force
on the Importance of Nature to
Canadians (2000), 177
Fenno-Russian wolf populations, 65
Finland, 23
wolf dispersal from, 21–22, 65
fladry, 152–54
forest cover, 16, 24, 42, 48, 50, 55, 60,
63–65, 70, 91. *See also* names of
specific forests
as predictor of wolf occupancy, 80–81
public, 69, 85, 92, 98
Russian, 21
second growth, 72
Temperate Steppe Forest, 104, 111
foresters, 174, 180–81, 185
Fox, Camilla H., xv, 8, 10, 173
France, 17, 28, 179
attitudinal research, 178
compensation costs, 24
conflict between wolf advocates and
opponents, 163
human attitudes toward wolves, 33,
163, 185–86, 189

human dimensions study, 181
man-made barriers (highways), 52
wolf populations, 22, 64
Franco-Italian wolves, 43, 64
colonized Pyrenees, 45, 54
fraudulent claims. *See* compensation

G

Galicia, 45, 49
gender as predictor of attitude, 189
genetic diversity, 4, 22, 27, 41, 64–66
genetic surveys, 52
Germany, 21–22, 26–27
Glacier National Park, 98
goats, 59, 106, 144–47
Goldman, Edward, 10
gray wolf. *See* wolves
grazing. *See* livestock husbandry
Great Lakes Region, 4. *See also* Michigan;
Minnesota; Wisconsin
population estimates and growth rates,
70, 76–79
population monitoring, 86
public ownership of land in, 72
Sarcoptic mange, 79
ungulate populations, 70, 87
white-tailed deer population, 87
wolf bounties, 70
wolf recovery, 118
Greater Yellowstone area (GYA), 98
landowner control of wolves, 108
suitable wolf habitat, 100
Greece, 16, 18, 23
"group" working, 167
guard dogs, 106, 135–36, 145–47, 152, 154
guarding animals, 101

H

habitat, 4, 24, 46, 112, 174
adequate prey and lack of human
persecution, 75
agricultural habitats, 46–47, 53, 60
alpine, 53

livestock guard dogs. *See* guard dogs
livestock husbandry methods, 28, 38, 42,
    47, 60, 62, 65, 112, 151
    alternate grazing, 147, 153
    dehasas (Spain), 48
    human surveillance, 147
    improving, 126, 130, 133, 135, 147,
        150, 155 (*See also* preventive
        husbandry methods)
    predator/livestock coexistence
        strategies, 136
    unprotected grazing, 59, 62, 98, 110
livestock management, 56, 58–59
livestock producers, 10, 97, 163, 168
    economic incentives, 32–33
    non-lethal preventative measures, 147,
        150
Livestock Producers Advisory Council, 157
livestock production, 95
llamas, 136, 144–47
local communities (stakeholders), 168

M

Macedonia, former Yugoslavian republic
    of, 18, 23
Mackenzie River, 54
Maine, 129
Marin County, California
    non-lethal cost-share program, 135
Mata, C., 52
Mech, L.D., 88–89
meta-population approach to wolf
    conservation, 6, 35, 37
Mexican wolf population, 41
Mexican wolf reintroduction program,
    125–26, 134
Michigan, 69–70, 72, 74, 90, 118
    depredation management, 76
    habitat protection, 85
    legal protection (wolves), 71
    lethal controls of depredating wolves,
        82, 123
    natural recovery of wolves, 129
    suitable habitat, 88
    wolf monitoring and management, 91

wolf population decline (1997), 79
wolf population estimates, 79
wolf population growth, 76–77, 86–87
wolf recolonization, 86
wolves listed as threatened, 71
Midwest Wolf Stewards, 91
minimum viable population (MVP), 26, 82
Minnesota, 29, 69–70, 72, 90, 118
    compensation costs, 24, 62
    lethal control (depredation
        management), 76, 81
    natural recovery of wolves, 129
    population surveys, 86
    public hunting and trapping seasons, 85
    suitable habitat, 88
    wolf bounty, 70–71
    wolf depredation management, 72, 76,
        81, 91
    wolf population, 79, 81, 86
    wolf population growth (recovery),
        76–77, 129
    wolves listed as threatened, 71
Minnesota state management plan, 130
Mitchell, B., 175
Mizirow, Jack, 166
Mladenoff, D.J., 80–81, 88, 90
Montana, 98, 150
    causes for wolf mortality, 121
    control plan for wolves in, 107
    landowner control of wolves, 108
    naturally recolonizing wolves, 141
    range riders, 154
    state Fish and Game agencies, 108
    state-managed wolf compensation
        programs, 157
    suitable wolf habitat, 98, 100, 104
    wolf dispersal from Canada, 95
    wolf eradication, 95
    wolf population growth, 97
    wolf recovery, 103
moose, 16, 70, 72
Mott, William, 144
multidisciplinary wolf management, 9, 170
Murie, Adolph, *The Wolves of Mount
    McKinley*, 10
Musiani, Marco, xiii

lambing sheds, 136
livestock carcass removal, 147–48, 155
Spain, 66
by wolf opponents, 155, 157
prey density, 80, 87
prey population management (Europe), 24
prey populations, 29, 48, 98
Europe, 16
Great Lakes Region, 72
"probable" losses, 145–46
problem wolves, 107–11, 133, 142
Producer Subsidy Equivalent (PSE), 32
propaganda, 165–66
'propaganda' by wolf experts, 119
protected areas. *See also* names of national
   forests; state and national parks
   Minnesota and Ontario, 72
   Natura 2000 network of protected
      areas, 37, 43
protected status, 70–71. *See also*
   Endangered Species Act
public harvest, 82, 85, 90, 97
   increased tolerance for wolves, 113
   major debate in Great Lakes states, 92
public opinion, 4. *See also* human attitudes
   on possible management approaches,
      179, 185–87
   shift from persecution to restoration, 95
   shift to humanistic/moralistic approach,
      132
public opinion management, 16, 28
pup survival, 75, 80, 87
Pyrenees, 17, 28, 41, 43, 45, 52–54, 64
   livestock husbandry practices, 65

R

radio collars, 42, 49, 74, 100–101, 103
radio-telemetry monitoring, 25, 63, 74, 104
raising awareness, 166
ranchers, 123, 126, 129
   compensation programs, 9, 101, 143–44
   education and outreach for, 135–36, 167
      (*See also* livestock producers)
   on Livestock Producers Advisory
      Committee, 157

non-lethal deterrents, 153–55
   responsibility for losses, 130
   range riders, 147, 152, 154
recovery goals for wolf populations, 5
reindeer depredation, 143
reintroduced wolves
   "experimental, non-essential" status,
      129
relocation of wolves, 81, 109, 128
researchers (stakeholders), 168
River Duero, 43–45, 55, 60
River Ebro, 64
River Tajo corridor, 64
road density, 29, 75, 87–88, 98, 176
   as predictor for wolf distribution, 80
roads, 55
   wolf dispersal and, 51–53
Rogers, E., 167
Romania, 16, 21, 32
   lethal control of wolves, 143
   wolf habitat, 24
   wolf protection, 23
Russia, 21–22

S

Salamanca province, 46, 60
Salmon Challis National Forest, 153
Sarcoptic mange, 79–80
Sawtooth National Forest, 153–54
Scandinavia, 21–22
   wolf habitat, 24
   wolf populations, 26, 65
Scandinavian reindeer husbandry, 65
schoolchildren (stakeholders), 168
sheep, 56, 58, 65, 98, 106, 143–44, 146
   turbo-fladry night corrals, 153
sheep farmers, 32
shepherding, 136
shepherds, 33, 38, 56, 58, 62–63, 135, 143,
   147
   conflicts with wolves, 24
   livestock compensation programs, 23
Shimeld, Susan, xvii
Sierra Morena, 17, 43–45, 49